BEYOND BUSINESS

BEYOND BUSINESS

JOHN BROWNE

with Philippa Anderson

Weidenfeld & Nicolson

LONDON

First published in Great Britain in 2010
by Weidenfeld & Nicolson

3 5 7 9 10 8 6 4

A CIP catalogue record for this book
is available from the British Library.

ISBN-13 978 0 297 85915 4
ISBN TPB 978 0 297 85916 1

Typeset by Input Data Services Ltd,
Bridgwater, Somerset

Printed and bound in the UK by
CPI Mackays, Chatham ME5 8TD

The Orion Publishing Group's policy is to use papers
that are natural, renewable and recyclable products and
made from wood grown in sustainable forests. The logging
and manufacturing processes are expected to conform to
the environmental regulations of the country of origin.

Weidenfeld & Nicolson

The Orion Publishing Group Ltd
Orion House
5 Upper Saint Martin's Lane,
London, WC2H 9EA

An Hachette UK Company

www.orionbooks.co.uk

To my mother

CONTENTS

INTRODUCTION

I had started to write this book while I was CEO of BP, but I never got very far with it. After I left the company I resolved to return to the task. The book I have now written is very different from the one I had originally planned.

This book is organised around places in which I have worked and lived. I have chosen to do so because the people in a place make a memory and allow my story to be told. In each place, dates and times are not strictly sequential so that I can tell my tale with what I know now, rather than along the straight arrow of time; a timeline is included for reference.

It is a memoir and not an autobiography; I do not cover everything about my life and times. What I have written about are some of the most exciting, happy and miserable events of my 61 years. I have never kept a diary so have had to rely on my recollections but I have made every effort to check facts wherever possible and to provide sufficient context around these events.

At the end of this volume are some important acknowledgements. Without the friendship, loyalty and support of generations of those who worked in BP, many of these stories would not have happened. I would like to thank them all before I begin my tale.

NEW YORK

Compass

The problem was how to poach the fish. Cookery classes had made it seem so easy. Now I had eight people coming to dinner and no idea where to start.

The fish in question was a large striped bass bought at the Jefferson Market on 6th Avenue early that morning. Balducci's had been my next stop for other exciting ingredients. I had even found time to browse the neat rows of novels in the bookstore, and then wander back through Washington Square.

This leisurely shopping on the sunny sidewalks of Greenwich Village was a most agreeable way to pass the time. After all, I had hardly any work to do at BP because we could not get approval to build the pipeline from Prudhoe Bay to Valdez, the Trans Alaska Pipeline. When I had first arrived in Anchorage in 1969, everything had looked set to start. But construction had never even begun. There had been a host of issues to do with land rights and the environment.

Within months of moving down to New York, in mid 1971, the workload had begun to slacken. It was no use trying to work with our partners without a purpose; it just provoked tensions. Things got so tight that we used writing paper on both sides and pencils down to the eraser. First there were efficiencies, then no travel, and then hardly any work.

Now it was June 1973. I was 25 and making good use of the time on my hands.

I started to enjoy life. Cooking was just one new enjoyable pastime. I also discovered the joy of good conversation, opera and contemporary art. SoHo (south of Houston Street), at first glance, seemed to be a deserted place where litter blew down dusty streets. But galleries had begun to open on the ground floors of empty warehouses and artists' lofts were starting to occupy the cavernous top floors. I liked nothing better than to wander around and discover what was new. Huge canvases showed off the fresh, different work of artists such as Chuck Close and Richard Estes. I had my own camera, a Nikon SLR, and time to explore the area, taking photographs and enlarging them in the small darkroom I had created in my Greenwich Village apartment.

The apartment had come about through a chance encounter because of a leaking shower. When I first moved to New York, my accommodation was dreadful: a dismal tiny studio in the building on the corner of 47th Street and 2nd Avenue. I was unsure of how to orient myself in this big city and I had few friends. However, as luck would have it, the problems with the shower led to my meeting the tenant of the studio below. François Delas worked for the French state telephone company and, as we were both dissatisfied with our accommodation, we agreed that if we combined our rental we could afford to share a larger half-decent apartment.

Greenwich Village was the obvious choice. It was then the centre of the city's young universe and at the heart of its vibrant music scene with the Bitter End Café; Bob Dylan was one of the Village's more notable residents. We found the ideal three-bedroom apartment but neither of us realised that we were taking on a prohibited sublet from the famous folk singer Richie Havens. Our legal problems ended us in the small claims court. But once this was resolved, Waverley Place became home for more than three years.

The apartment occupied the parlour floor of a classic New York Brownstone. It had a large through room with high ceilings, white walls except for one which was rough exposed brick, a sturdy fireplace and stripped wooden floor. The only thing that spoilt the ambience was the heavily barred windows. My parents came to New York and my mother gave me advice on decor. Her additions included bright yellow curtains, a fluffy carpet and a rubber plant, all very fashionable in the 1970s.

With my interest in art, I started to collect prints by David Hockney who had become popular in the US. These prints were added to the walls, along with some of François' amateur paintings. Soon we were entertaining because we had the best apartment of our growing set of friends. My cookery course with the celebrity chef of the time, James Beard, enabled me to master the intricacies of court-bouillon, béarnaise sauce and hollandaise sauce. This was not just to fill my time but to satisfy my competitive need to demonstrate that the English could cook just as well as the French.

Ambition was far from my thoughts. But this carefree existence ended in October 1973 with a momentous world event. The OPEC nations imposed an embargo on oil exports to the US following the start of the Yom Kippur War. Suddenly, rationality trumped emotion. The US needed its own domestic supply of oil.

Any remaining opposition to the Trans Alaska Pipeline was brushed aside. The pipes and equipment had waited on the frozen banks of the Yukon River for almost five years. Now they were needed and we were racing to get the pipeline built.

I was back in the thick of it, working long hours on computer simulations of subsurface oil flows and on engineering challenges. There was little or no time for anything outside of work.

Drama and events

Little did I realise then that my "adventure in oil" – for it was certainly more than a career – would follow a similar pattern.[1] My life's adventure would not only be touched by momentous events on the world stage but would also be shaped by political intrigue, and by rivalry between nations and companies, to access and control the most valuable world resource at the end of the 20th century: oil.

But I would not be a passive observer. I would become one of the characters on the stage. And, in my own way, I too would touch and shape events. I was in the oil business at a particular time when advances in science, economic factors, strong political leaders and engineering would create new opportunities and bring about significant change.

In 1966, I signed up as a university apprentice with an oil company, part-owned by the British government. Just as I left university in 1969, the Apollo 11 programme landed man on the moon. One of its greatest legacies was the opportunity to see the world in context as a fragile oasis of life in a vast universe. For many, including me, this was the dawn of a sense of responsibility for the planet and its occupants. And that sense grew and grew and was the backdrop to my time at BP.

The oil crisis of the 1970s, which put an end to my leisurely time in New York, started a deep recession. After decades of stability, everything changed in the oil industry. And that change continued as the world went on to experience something very different: the extraordinary power of the market economy. "Flattening of the world" started. Thomas Friedman, in his classic *The World is Flat*, explains how the flattening process began to happen at incredible speed and indirectly or directly touch "a lot more people on the planet at once". The transition to the new era had enormous potential for disruption as it was not an "orderly transfer of power from the old winners to the new winners".[2]

During the 40 years I spent in the oil industry, history has ebbed and flowed in tune with our understanding of energy; nations have risen and fallen in line with its availability. And relationships between nations have shifted dramatically.

When I started my career, Harold Wilson was the British Prime Minister and Richard Nixon was President of the US. In time they would be followed by international leaders determined to change the order of things. Prime Minister Margaret Thatcher pursued her agenda of privatisation and that included BP. This finally released the company from its governmental state of mind. It could become more commercial and competitive. Mrs Thatcher and President Reagan helped to bring President Gorbachev in from the cold. The Berlin Wall came down and the global stage changed. Many doors opened and we seized the opportunities. And at the same time rapidly changing technology, including the advent of the microprocessor, made huge differences to the way BP could explore and produce oil.

When I became CEO of BP in 1995, oil was plentiful and cheap and margins were low. The price of oil was $17 a barrel and would fluctuate from $9 a barrel to $67 a barrel just in the 12 years of my tenure as CEO. I had to learn to balance optimism with pessimism, recognising that political change would create many different opportunities and risks. In 1995, the rise of Brazil, Russia, India and China was regarded as neither significant nor sustainable. The ubiquitous power of the internet had not yet been felt. But the important influence of the NGOs was starting to become much more apparent. I would be at the helm of BP during a period when across the globe in almost every industry, in every aspect of life, it would seem as if "the patterns of the past" were being scrambled.[3]

In 1995, there was an air of malaise surrounding the oil industry. It was seen as dirty, old-fashioned, short on ethics, driven solely by profit, and not a place where people were proud of what they did. BP had been through a crisis, cutting its dividend for the first time, but had recovered.

It was an average, middleweight company. I knew that the company had to change and grow or it would not survive.

I went on to transform BP into Britain's leading business and a global giant. BP became the world's second largest non-state oil company by market capitalisation. From the end of 1995 to the end of 2006, the company's market capitalisation increased almost five-fold; total share-holder returns were 130 per cent greater than those from the FTSE-All Share index; dividends trebled; earnings per share rose seven-fold; production almost trebled; and oil and gas reserves almost doubled. In 12 years, the company would achieve a long list of firsts, breaking new ground in new countries, including Russia and China. BP became a force to be reckoned with.

There had been a yearning desire for leadership in BP; much as in politics and business today. The company needed purpose and values. But leadership involves far more than any one individual. It requires trusted people to support and challenge, teams to bring the purpose alive, an internal structure for delivery, and lasting alliances with reliable partners.

I learnt these and many other things from great people who took the time to coach me. I learnt from successes. But mostly I learnt from the painful experience of setbacks. I joined BP because I liked solving problems. I thought those problems would be about rocks and costs. From that simple view I developed an understanding of what it takes to solve the very different and complex problems I encountered as I progressed through the company.

This, then, is my story of how I learnt about leadership in a tough industry. It is about the insights I gained as I transformed a company, challenged a sector, and prompted political and business leaders to change. My adventures included going toe-to-toe with tyrants, despots and elected leaders while bringing them around to my way of thinking in order to develop and maintain great business opportunities. They involved keeping a firm eye on day-to-day detail while not losing a clear view of the economic and political context within which the company operated. And they encompassed engineering feats which in many ways rival those of going to the moon. It is very much about how the world of business really works.

I have had to choose whom and what to leave out of this story. I cannot include every destination, for I have travelled the world. But certain places on my travels were markers on my journey. And it is to those places that I will take you, from my first taste of oil in Iran to my search for new sources of energy in Brazil.

My story is also one of failure and human frailty. In the end, despite all the tough judgements I had made in business, I allowed emotion to trump the rational on a personal matter.

The story of my life had been inextricably entwined with the story of BP. After more than 40 years that deep connection was abruptly severed as my secret, private life collided with my public, business life at frightening speed in full view of the world.

But the seeds of art, culture and music, sown in that hot summer of 1973 in Greenwich Village, New York, have flourished into lifelong interests; they continue.

And the fish for the dinner party? That turned out just fine.

1

IRAN

First oil

26 May 1958: An oil well was on fire. For a boy of ten it was a great excitement. I was among the expatriate children invited to the Fields Golf Club at Masjid-i-Suleiman to hear the heroic firefighter, Myron Kinley, recount tales of his dangerous exploits.

Kinley had flown thousands of miles from Houston to cap the massive blowout of the Ahvaz No. 6 well. He had attempted to tackle the fiery blaze several times but had failed and he was now to entertain us while waiting for a change in the wind.

Kinley seemed to have stepped out of a boy's comic. In my young mind he could easily match Dan Dare's endeavours in the weekly *Eagle*, or those of characters in the adventure books I had been eagerly devouring over the previous few years. He had a stunning track record of taming 400 oil well blowouts, and the scars and a crippled right leg to prove it.

Kinley told us he had never been beaten, though it had taken him "six months once to lick a fire that had been burning for two years in Romania". All eyes were on him as he explained what had happened at Ahvaz No. 6 well. With a concoction of pipes, water, balloons and a bicycle pump, he simulated the pressure build-up. Then he showed us how the massive blowout had happened – with a huge bang.

By this time, the fire had been raging uncontrollably for more than a month. And even the "indispensable man of the oil industry",[1] with his uncanny mix of skill and luck, had been unable to tame the monster. I had been with my father to Haft Kel where the charred derrick and tangle of pipes remained as testimony to the fearsome power of a previous blowout.

But the Ahvaz No. 6 blowout was live and ablaze. It began on the morning of 19 April 1958. Within seconds a gigantic cloud of fire

Iran: where I first discovered oil

seemed to set the sky alight. At night we could see the red and orange glow from the hill where we lived, which was more than 50 miles away. Nearer to the site, the noise and stench from the unrelenting inferno were overwhelming.

Kinley arrived on the fifth day of the fire. His reputation at the time was second to none. Firefighters Red Adair and Boots & Coots would follow in his footsteps. It took him many days just to clear the tangle of red-hot debris before he could start to tackle the blaze. With help from the Iranian crew, Kinley toiled in temperatures as high as 120° C.

Many of the crew had worked with him seven years earlier on the

Rig 20 fire at Naft Safid; then, one of the biggest, most spectacular, fires in the history of oil. People still talked about the long tangle of steel pipe that shot 2,000 feet into the sky, like a writhing snake, with one of Kinley's explosive charges.

At Ahvaz 6, a constant spray of water on to flameproof vehicles was required. The crew had to use hand signals as the screaming fire was so deafening. It would take five explosions and 47 days to blow the fire out completely and a further 18 days to cap the well. There was talk that every day the uncontrollable fire had cost a million dollars.

After his Ahvaz 6 exertions, 60-year-old Kinley decided it was time he gave up fighting oil well fires. Returning to the US, he tackled a further two fires before he retired for good.[2]

But I was only just beginning with oil. I had been a few months in Iran with my parents and everything about the industry and this exotic country enthralled me.

Lazy days

My father was working at Masjid-i-Suleiman, which everyone called MIS. I have memories of a hot and idyllic life. This revolved around the swimming club, open-air cinema – *Ben Hur* being one of the favourite films – ice-cold Coca-Cola, horse riding and Caesar, our German Shepherd. Bicycle trips with friends were a feature of many lazy days.

I liked to play golf with my father at the club. The fairways were simply cleared rock sand (*sabkah*) and the "greens" were oiled sand, which formed a surface as smooth as freshly rolled grass. For a boy who loved nothing better than Meccano (a toy construction kit popular in the 1930s to 1950s), aeroplanes and trains, my great excitement was when my father took me to see the oil fields. Every time we ventured out we discovered something new and different – an abandoned oil derrick, a working drilling rig, or a producing well with a separator. I would imagine what they were doing. At the well head I listened to the sound of oil gurgling below. Very often there was a pervasive smell of oil or sulphur.

Visits to the local bazaar with my mother were an assault on every sense, with sights, sounds and smells of which a young boy in the UK could only dream. Iran was a land of colour. Exquisite red and ochre carpets in the bazaar, bright blue skies, amber deserts, and the intense turquoise blue of the Karoun River as it flowed through the gorge at Lali. In the first few days of spring, the desert would show a short-lived, vague shimmer of green shoots, and small red tulips and bright yellow narcissi would appear beside the road before being overcome by the increasing heat.

Our first home was a single storey, stone-built house, with a manicured, heavily watered Bermuda grass lawn, in an expatriate compound on the hillside at Naf Tak. Later, in my teenage years, we moved to Scotts Crescent. These grander houses were prefabs brought over from the US. They had all the mod cons of the 1960s, from fitted kitchen to smart bathroom. Three servants lived behind our house: a cook, a girl who did all the laundry and a male *ferash* who seemed to be employed to clean the stone floor continually.

Apart from events at the Fields Golf Club, the swimming pool and the adjacent open-air cinema, people made their own entertainment; smartly dressed couples came to our house in the evening to play bridge. Mixed drinks were very much the fashion and caviar was plentiful, though guests would probably have preferred hard-to-come-by cheese on toast. It was a time when people had more style than money, but compared to how I remembered life in England, this seemed to me to be luxury.

Roots

I had, in fact, only lived in England for very brief periods by this time.

My father, also John Browne, had been an officer in the British Army. He met and married my mother, Paula, in Germany shortly after the Second World War. I was born in Hamburg in February 1948 and was their only child.

Germany and briefly Therfield, near Royston in England, had been my homes until my father was posted to Singapore in 1952. It is one of my earliest memories as we travelled there by troopship; it seemed such an adventure. I discovered many things in this new and exotic place – large jars of sweets, for one thing, which were rationed in England for a long time after the war.

We lived in a "black and white" colonial house, relying on the natural circulation of air, rather than air conditioning, to combat the intense heat and humidity. The Tanglin School, which I attended, finished at midday as it was far too hot to concentrate in the afternoon. Then, the best place to go was the air-conditioned cinema or the Gillman swimming pool.

My memories of that time now comprise snake charmers and fortune tellers, whom my mother particularly liked, although I do not think she relied on their words. There were ice-cream cakes for birthdays which were cut with my father's ceremonial sword. There was Amah who looked after me since my parents were often out. Soldiers guarded our house and took me to school in a truck during the troubles with Malaya; my father's predecessor had been shot dead. Monkeys were in the garden and, given any chance, would snatch food from the kitchen or dining table. And there were plenty of friends with whom to play what would now be regarded as politically incorrect war games. It was a period in which the last vestiges of the British Empire were disappearing.

Before the outbreak of the war, my mother had trained in hat design and she opened her own hat shop: The Hat Box, at 18 Battery Road. With her friend, Winifred Winter, she cleverly used her millinery skills and her eye for colour and shape to meet the fashion demands of expatriate wives. She had an extraordinary attention to detail and loved to contrast rather than to co-ordinate exotic and vibrant colours. Vivid feathers and ribbons, delicate hand-made flowers, tiny sparkling sequins and luminous beads were added to different hat shapes brought over from Freemans of London.

The Singapore newspaper, reporting on the opening of The Hat Box in late 1952, described my mother as a "vivacious brunette". An army officer's wife would have been expected to be involved in coffee mornings, charitable ventures, or entertaining people to tea, rather than to show any sign of enterprise – but, then, my mother did not fit in with the norm.

In June 1953, my mother's hats were much in evidence at Singapore parties for Queen Elizabeth II's Coronation day. I just about remember the red, white and blue smoke from the warplanes in the Coronation fly-past as my father was on the parade ground with his troops.

We returned to live in the UK when my father's commission ended in 1955, as the number of people in the military were reduced following the end of the Second World War and the final demise of the British Empire. Originally from Norfolk, my father wanted to return to East Anglia but needed to be near London. Cambridge was the obvious choice as it was a good place from which to commute.

We first rented 71 Chesterton Road from a university professor and I started at the local primary school, St Luke's. After a few months, we moved to number 88, which my parents bought. Next door to our family doctor, the rambling, plain, red-brick Victorian house had a large garden with a shed and places to explore.

I liked the house, especially the garden, but our return to the UK was probably quite a shock for my mother. She had been living the good life of a fashionable designer in Singapore. The first rented house in Chesterton Road was very ordinary and the second was certainly not grand.[3] My father had to set about finding a job − which he did with Iranian Oil Services, a company providing employees to a consortium of oil companies in Iran. And my mother soon realised that she too would have to work. We had lodgers who helped to pay the bills and she set up another hat business at home: Paula Browne, Continental Milliner.

All this was not only a great contrast to Singapore, but also very different from her life in Hungary before the Second World War. I was eight years old before I began to understand all this.

December 1956: I arrived home from school one day to find our house crammed with visitors. They were all speaking in a foreign language. The top two floors were given over to the lodgers but these new visitors were in our part of the house, on the ground and first floors. They were in the front parlour, overlooking the road, and in the dining room, which overlooked the back garden. I eventually found my mother, with yet more visitors, in the kitchen at the back of the house. She was in her element. She had set about cooking a large pan of delicious-smelling goulash for the guests and she too was chatting in the foreign language, which I recognised as Hungarian, but could not understand.

We often had visitors but never so many. Over the next few months we had numerous Hungarians coming and going. Some moved in as lodgers upstairs. One woman who stayed was an opera singer. I found her with my mother in the front parlour one day and was invited in to listen to her sing.

She was a very large lady. When seated at the upright piano, she began to pull some extraordinary facial expressions. Even before she began to sing I was struggling to contain myself. And then she opened her mouth. Her voice was overpowering and seemed to completely fill the room. I had never heard anything like it. I burst out laughing.

The singer ignored me. She must have been totally self-absorbed. But my mother cautioned me silently with a small shake of her head. Later, when we were alone, I was reprimanded by my mother for being rude. She explained to me that I had to be polite to our guests because they were "émigrés". I had never heard the word before. She told me they had escaped from Hungary where there had been a revolution.[4]

I knew my mother came from somewhere different but this was the first time I actually saw her as foreign. I am sometimes reminded of this little incident when I go to the opera, a pastime I now love.

I assumed then that our guests were all my mother's friends. Years later, I discovered she had never met them before. My mother was merely a member of a network of people in the UK who agreed to accommodate the flood of Hungarian refugees. Some stayed in the UK but many went across to the US and Canada.[5] The arrival of the Hungarian émigrés at our Cambridge house must have caused my mother some excitement and triggered in her a series of mixed emotions.

My mother's family was from Transylvania[6] and were solid bourgeois stock of good standing in the local community. Her father had owned land and traded cattle. Even so, her mother, who was Jewish and from Vienna, was thought to have married below her status. The fact that my mother's background was Jewish never struck me as unusual. Nor did it seem unusual that my mother had later been accepted as Catholic. All this was part of me and did not seem to be anything other than normal, even when I attended daily services at an Anglican school.

My mother did not leave Hungary; she was taken by the Nazis. Almost all her family perished during the Second World War. My mother survived over a year in a concentration camp, Auschwitz. As a child I could never have understood what this meant to her, and she hardly talked about what happened until shortly before she died.

In fact when she was alive, very few people knew of her background. It was not relevant. She would say to me she had three lives: the time before the war, the time with my father, and then the time with me after my father's death. The war was not a life. I am in no doubt that her experiences created the deep-seated beliefs which shaped me significantly.

My education, for example, was important to her. Time and again she said: "Your education is vital. No one can take that away from you." Her ordeal made her believe that everything else could disappear overnight. If you were left with nothing but still had your brains, education and drive, at least you could start again.[7]

Educated in Vienna, she spoke five languages – English, Romanian, Hungarian, German and French. With these skills and her own drive she had rebuilt her life after the Second World War. After liberation, she went to work as an interpreter for the British Army in Itzehoe in Germany. With no family and her homeland now part of the Soviet bloc behind the Iron Curtain, she had nowhere else to go.

That was when she had met my father; he was the army administrator for the area. Getting married was not easy. My mother was a stateless person with no records and my father had a difficult time getting approval to marry her.

The cataclysmic events of the war defined both my parents. My mother lost everything and was thrust into a new life. My father also gained a new life. The difference was he escaped from his working class past. His father had been a painter journeyman and his mother a nursing sister at Norwich hospital.

Their backgrounds – and, perhaps, their characters – were the source of some tension in later years. My mother in many ways was more competent, ambitious and outgoing than my father. She was better educated and better at organising and managing their financial affairs.

This family history was the source of my mother's aspirations for me. My mother wanted me to have everything she had lost because of the war and to have more than my father ever had.

What my father thought of all our Hungarian visitors I never knew. He was busy commuting to London for his new job with Iranian Oil Services. In early 1957 this took him out to Iran, to be employed by BP, formerly the Anglo-Iranian Oil Company. Initially he had to go unaccompanied and so my mother and I stayed behind in Cambridge for almost 12 months. My memories of that time are happy: school, which I enjoyed, a constant stream of visitors to the house, and the dining-room table strewn with long, beautiful vivid blue and green feathers for my mother's hat making.

She seemed to be able to turn her hand to anything. When she married she had never been inside a kitchen but she took control and soon became an accomplished cook. She passed her appreciation of good cooking and good food on to me.

During this time in Cambridge, we would go together to a small

Polish delicatessen, opposite St John's College. When we opened the door the exotic and pungent smells came wafting out. We bought Liptauer cheese, bottled cucumbers, sauerkraut, paprika and spicy sausages, as a substitute for what my mother thought of as bland English food.

We left Cambridge at the end of 1957 to join my father in Iran. I attended the American School in MIS for a year with other expatriate children but that idyllic life soon came to an abrupt end. I had to return to England. I was sent to boarding school.

Boarding school

15 January 1959: I was put on an aeroplane in Abadan to go by way of Beirut and Rome to London. The journey took over 15 hours. My destination was a prep school, a private school for boys of between 8 and 13 years of age: the junior school of The King's School Ely. My father said boarding school would "make me a man"; my mother thought sending one's children away to school "barbaric".

I was uncertain. Within days of arrival I had made up my mind. I hated it. It was freezing cold, particularly arriving from the desert heat of Iran. The accommodation in old cathedral buildings was extremely basic; this was no luxury. Our common room was a Norman undercroft, a dark, dank crypt-like place with one anthracite burner tucked in a corner.

The food was dreadful, mainly offal which I have never been able to eat since. Learning was by rote and discipline was corporal. Physical punishment was deemed acceptable in British prep schools in those days.

Bullying was part of the game. This was *Lord of the Flies* for real.[8] You had to be tough and develop survival instincts. I was small in stature and chubby (I had a thyroid problem which was not diagnosed until my early twenties) but learnt fast. You did not get picked on if people liked you, or if you were good at something – in my case, swimming and theatre. And, of course, I could talk about Iran and about oil, which none of the other boys could.

We had two *exeat* weekends a term, when you were let out, but as my parents were overseas I had to stay with friends. I missed my parents and they missed me. Years later my mother said that sending me away to school was one of the biggest regrets of her life.

I stayed at the junior school until I was 13 and then went on to the senior school of the same establishment. This turned out to be much better. Perhaps I had become used to things, but it seemed less austere and the school staff more enlightened. Many years later I would become a governor of the school. I am now its Patron.

Summer holidays

The one redeeming feature of being sent to school in England was the flights back and forth to Iran on the latest aeroplanes such as the Comet 4 and the Lockheed Electra. Then, air travel was an unusual experience. The flights were all first class; people dressed fashionably in "travel clothes"; cabin attendants were "air hostesses", usually young and middle class. The service included free packs of cigarettes in tins of 25 with brands such as State Express 555 and Piccadilly Black & White. The objective of a young boy was to get his hands on one of these packs. I never succeeded. My mother, however, smoked and kept the tins to store sequins and beads for her hats.

Stepping out of the aeroplane on my return to Abadan felt like walking into an oven; temperatures were often above 50° C in summer. Abadan, a big city on the southern coast of Iran, was the site of the large refinery and export terminal to which a pipeline had been built in 1913. By the 1940s it had become the biggest refinery in the world.

I travelled on from Abadan to MIS on a de Havilland Dove, a 1950s small short-haul airliner, which flew turbulently over the desert. And of course I would be looking out for my mother waiting anxiously for me at the small airport at MIS.

I returned to Iran for the summers in my teenage years and felt I was back where I belonged. However, one summer a bad fall from a horse resulted in damage to my back, which curtailed my sporting activities. I needed something else to do so I began to read about Iran's deep and violent history and its cultural heritage. Thousands of years of civilisation had given Iran a story as interesting as that of China.

I explored historical sites including Persepolis, Shiraz and Isfahan. In those days, tourism was rare but there were no restrictions on sightseeing. My trip to Isfahan, with my mother and school friends who came out from the UK, sparked an interest which would later win me a scholarship to Cambridge. We walked freely around grand palaces and mosques, many of which were created by Shah Abbas in the 16th century. We marvelled at the impressive Naqsh-e Jahan Square, which was large enough for a polo match. The Chehel Sotoun Palace, the so-called "Palace of Forty Columns", particularly appealed to me; it has only twenty columns but appears to have forty because of the reflection in its formal pool.

My sense that my parents were very different from my friends' parents continued to develop in Iran. It was not only that my mother dressed stylishly, enjoyed different foods, and continued to make her hats, but she also mixed far more with Iranians than the other expatriate wives did. She also spoke her version of English with a distinctive Hungarian accent. I was sure that she did this deliberately. People may have thought her unusual but excused her as she was "continental".

I too was encouraged to mix. When I was at the American school, all my friends had been white Caucasian expatriate children but I developed a diverse group of local friends during those long summer holidays.

My father treated the Iranians with great respect. He insisted that I had to be very polite to the servants, Bahktiari from South Iran, even if my friends were not. In many ways the organisation and functioning of expatriates in Iran still resembled colonial societies, with a prevalent superior mindset and no integration into local communities.[9]

Certainly the male white British bias had been made explicit in the Anglo-Iranian Oil Company's staff manual.[10] This directed that recruitment should be restricted to British subjects and those of European origin or descent, except in foreign countries where there was a legal or concessional obligation to employ local nationals. It was also not the company's policy at that time "to employ women on work which is normally regarded as men's work" and female staff who married were expected to resign and "no exceptions to this rule can be contemplated".

As my mother treated everyone the same, I did not think it was an issue if someone was of a different colour, could not speak English or dressed differently. It was an unconventional attitude then, but it sowed a seed which grew, during my business career, into a firm conviction of the merits of diversity.

Another seed sown in Iran was the fascination with the mystery and adventure of oil. I was taken by the allure of drilling – seeing something of value come out of the ground – and by the derring-do of men like Kinley. But I could have had no idea how entwined my own life would be with oil, and with BP, over the next half a century. I read books such as *Adventure in Oil*, by Henry Longhurst, and was impressed by the book's foreword by Winston Churchill which talked of "the pioneering of the vast oil industry of the Middle East [as] a story of vigour and adventure in the best traditions of the merchant venturers of Britain".[11]

This book told the tale of what had happened in Iran half a century before my arrival.[12] That story set the context for future events, not just in my life, or in the oil industry, but on the world stage.

Lucky oil strike

26 May 1908: Exactly 50 years before Myron Kinley's demonstration of an oil well blowout at the Fields Golf Club in MIS, and very close to the same spot, British engineer George Reynolds first discovered oil. That discovery was the origin of today's BP.

At the start of the 20th century, William Knox D'Arcy staked much of his fortune on finding oil in what was then Persia (now Iran), confident that the limestone Zagros mountains were exactly the sort of terrain where oil was formed and trapped in the anticlines. William Knox D'Arcy is often described as an "adventurer" though he never visited Persia. He was actually a speculator.

The region had long been known for its natural seeps of oil. Legends and stories abound of fire temples where "fire was miraculously lit" and "fire burns without fuel". As a young boy in MIS, I climbed over what was romantically known as the ruins of an ancient Zoroastrian[13] fire temple, called "the Mosque of Solomon".[14]

At the start of the 20th century, Persia was commercially and politically important to Britain. For many years the country had been caught between Victorian Britain and Tsarist Russia in the struggle for empire, known as the Great Game.[15] In the latter part of the 19th century, Russia had been rapidly expanding in Central Asia in search of a warm-water port. Britain, worried about the threat to India, saw Persia as a safeguard against Russian advances. Persia was variously depicted as a kitten being toyed with by a bear (Russia) and a lion (Britain) in a *Punch* cartoon, or as merely one of: "the pieces on a chessboard upon which is being played out a game for the domination of the world".[16]

With political cunning, which would advance Britain's interests in the region, D'Arcy's agent negotiated a very favourable 60-year deal with Shah Muzaffar al-Din to explore oil in a vast piece of terrain – five times the size of the UK – in the country's provinces on the southern part of the Persian Gulf.[17] The Shah's motive was money as he was in financial difficulty at the time.

Despite D'Arcy's confidence, years of fruitless search saw much of his fortune dwindle. George Reynolds, D'Arcy's hired explorer, and his crew toiled in arduous conditions but to no avail. By 1908, D'Arcy sold some of his shares in the venture to a Glasgow consortium, The Burmah Oil Company. But the company lost patience with both D'Arcy and the venture. Burmah Oil sent a telegram to Reynolds, who by this time was exploring near MIS, telling him to expect an important letter. The letter was to tell Reynolds to abandon the project.

While the letter was on its way, Reynolds was working on his last well, his final attempt. Incredibly, he struck oil. My father often took me to the site where that happened. By the 1950s it was in the MIS bazaar and marked with a plaque: MIS No. 1 well.

The Anglo-Persian Oil Company (APOC) was incorporated in April 1909. By 1914, the company became part-owned by the British government. The company's second chairman, Charles Greenway,[18] was in search of more investment for the company and Winston Churchill, then First Lord of the Admiralty, was seeking to secure a source of oil for the Royal Navy.[19] So the UK government bought half the company.

Persia, renamed Iran in 1935, was the company's sole source of supply (apart from a small oil field in Iraq) until 1934 and the predominant source of supply until 1951.[20] However, the original deal struck by D'Arcy, whereby the country received only a fraction of the revenue for its own oil, rankled with many. Despite various attempts to renegotiate the deal and a revised concession being drawn up in 1933, the matter finally came to a head.

In December 1951, Iran's newly elected Prime Minister, Mohammad Mossadeq, proclaimed that the oil industry was nationalised. The company (by then AIOC – the Anglo-Iranian Oil Company) was forced to leave the country.

An embargo on Iranian oil ensued. Britain froze Iran's assets and amassed a huge threatening naval force in the Persian Gulf. Fearing that Mossadeq might appeal to his Soviet communist neighbours for support, in 1953 the American CIA and British Secret Intelligence Service masterminded a covert plot.

An Iranian coup d'état followed, Mossadeq was deposed and the pro-Western Shah Mohammad Reza Pahlavi returned. He would reign until the Iranian revolution in 1979.

And so under the new regime oil began to flow again. A politically expedient international consortium was created, Iranian Oil Participants, of which AIOC was the largest shareholder.[21] Shortly after this, AIOC took the name of its original marketing subsidiary, British Petroleum (BP). The National Iranian Oil Company (NIOC) was also formed. There was a fairer 50/50 agreement between NIOC and the consortium. It was the same as other agreements then coming into force in the Middle East.

Expatriates from the UK, US and the Netherlands came back into the country. One of them was my father.

When the consortium companies returned to Iran in 1954 it was on a more equitable basis. This was not just about the share of the profits but also about people. Iranians were to be given significant jobs and education. Skills were to be transferred. This started with "non basic functions",[22] such as office management and estates, and progressed into technical areas. It was an indication of the way things would change around the world.

The legacy from this era is profound and far-reaching. The way in which companies and governments were seen to have exploited natural resources, particularly oil, started a pattern of instability, mistrust, and disagreement within and between countries. The world began to be concerned about the security of oil and gas and became suspicious of the motives of international oil companies, one of which I would eventually lead.

Education

But such big issues were far from my young thoughts. My father's job in Iran finished when I was 16 as his job was taken by an Iranian. I left Iran with a head full of ideas about exotic cultures and the oil industry. My parents went back to live in Cambridge, at a modern house they had bought in Stansgate Avenue, and I continued at boarding school.

My last two years at The King's School Ely were tough on my father's finances. When we were in Iran, half my fees were paid by his employer.

Now he was self-employed, working as a consultant in office design and planning, and he had to fund my education entirely.

I decided that I did not want my father to have to fund me through university, too. I was offered a place at St John's College, Cambridge to read Natural Sciences and I had two ideas. The first was to apply for one of the rare Trevelyan scholarships. Science students had to write on the arts, and art students had to write on the sciences. In Iran I had become very interested in photography and had begun to develop my own photographs. I had hundreds of images from my trip to Isfahan with my mother. So I went to the school library, public libraries and the Victoria and Albert Museum in London to find out more about Shah Abbas and Safavid architecture. I then wrote a rather flowery thesis, illustrated with my own photographs, on Isfahan. The result won me the lucrative Trevelyan scholarship which gave me £500 a year.

Meanwhile, I put my second idea into practice. I would apply to companies for a university apprenticeship. This would give me a stipend, pay my fees and provide work experience during the long summer vacations. I chose two companies: BP and the UK Atomic Energy Authority. I succeeded at both on the basis of my good school results. I chose BP. They paid my tuition fees and paid me £400 a year.

With this and the scholarship, I was very comfortable with £900 a year, a lot of money for any student in those days.

One of the first things we all learnt when we arrived at Cambridge was to pretend we were not working. Everything had to be done with apparent ease. It was not regarded as appropriate to be seen to work. You always had to appear to have time for people and conversation.

The reality was of course different. We had to study to pass our exams. So we all dissembled expertly. I would excuse myself from a long session of philosophy by saying I had to go and write a letter home; you could never let on that you were actually studying.

Years later I understood the logic behind this behaviour. It is a good lesson for today when students and business people make everyone aware of their efforts. If you always appear to be busy, people will think of you as unapproachable. There is no point in having an "open door" to your office unless you really are available to others, no matter how hard you are working.

I was at Cambridge when I first discovered computers. The computer laboratory at Cambridge had developed "Titan", one of the world's most advanced computing machines of the day. It was available for limited periods for students' use. I enjoyed writing programs – application software was practically unheard of in those days – to solve complex problems. This would stand me in good stead in the years to come.

The teaching method at Cambridge could best be described as providing opportunity, which you could either take or leave. If you took the opportunity, you met extraordinary people, legends in your subject. As a young man, I had thought that if people were famous they were probably dead. I realised that was not the case when I met Paul Dirac, one of the world's greatest physicists. Teaching involved imbuing you with an economy or austerity of thought. Building things from first principles, not having to remember vast amounts of data, and finding less than obvious relationships between facts were all things that were prized.

I had fun at Cambridge but never let my hair down. I was an active member of the Boat Club; I coxed eights. I went to parties but never drank excessively. From a very early age I was thought of as being very grown-up and this continued during my student years. I was not so serious that I could not enjoy a good laugh but I never fooled around. I had a drilled sense of behaviour, probably because I was guarded about my sexuality.

It was a few weeks before I graduated from Cambridge when I was made to understand vividly that business was not held in high regard.

June 1969: I had made a comment about considering a career in business, which prompted a reaction from one of my great and distinguished professors, Brian Pippard. While walking along King's Parade with a group of friends, I saw him coming towards us. He turned to his colleague and said: "This is Browne. He is going to be a captain of industry. Isn't that amusing?"

His jibe was both at me and business. I was one of the few who had achieved a First in Physics that year. Good students, if they were fascinated by the challenge of science and pursuit of knowledge, were expected to stay on to do a research degree and became academics.

A well-regarded alternative for those not attracted to academic life, or not quite good enough to make the grade, was to take the Civil Service examinations and enter government service. Banking was fine, so long as your family was actually in banking. Law was perfectly acceptable, as was medicine. Compared to these choices, finance – called a "job in the

City" in those days – was regarded as an inferior occupation. But it was still superior to a career in business. There was an unspoken but firm prejudice in the Cambridge environment that business was a waste of potential for high-fliers. It was considered vulgar.

I had toyed with the idea of research and was offered a position on a pioneering project at Madingley Rise.[23] This was to work with British geophysicists Drummond Matthews and Fred Vine on their continuing research into sea floor spreading, which went on to inform plate tectonics theory.

But, as far as my father was concerned, research was not real work. His view was that, while I thought I could be a terrific academic, I would probably get bored. He knew I loved solving problems and believed I could put my skills to best use in business. Besides, he reminded me, I had a very good offer from BP.

"At least try working in business. Don't just reject the opportunity," he said. Part of the attraction was that BP had told me I would go to the US. It would be my ticket to America.

We agreed I would work with BP for a year, in effect a sabbatical. He knew me better than I knew myself. Once immersed in oil, I was hooked. It would become the driving passion in my life. I would be with the company until 2007.

2

ALASKA

Opportunity

14 November 1969: I was not expecting a welcoming party, but I had hoped that at least someone from the office would be waiting to greet me. Arriving in a bitterly cold, dark Anchorage, on the once-a-week flight over the North Pole, it seemed I was on my own. Now I had to find a taxi to my accommodation: the Voyager Hotel.

The meagre building, lacking any architectural merit, was marooned in the centre of a lot, surrounded by snow and frozen mud. It was uninviting to say the least. I was too junior to warrant the smarter Captain Cook Hotel next door. And even if I had been more senior, there were no rooms. Anchorage was booming. More and more people were arriving every month, and beds were hard to come by.

Inside, the hotel cheered me even less. The noisy, smoke-filled bar was crammed with burly, beer-swilling men, with "working" women loitering at the entrance. Too tired to take it all in, I made my way upstairs to a pokey room.

Twenty-one and starting my first job the next day with BP, this was not quite how I had imagined big America.

My induction to the company, a few months before, had involved learning about oil exploration on a short course at the Great Fosters Hotel in Surrey, England. The luxurious 16th-century accommodation was a pleasant shock for a new graduate. But it was not all comfort, we also went to Kimmeridge and spent time on England's Jurassic coast, understanding rock formations and examining fossils.

Then my "posting orders" came through. BP, then part-owned by the British government, and seen by many as an arm of the Foreign Office, was still highly bureaucratic and posting orders meant exactly that. There was no say in the matter. I had been told earlier that I would

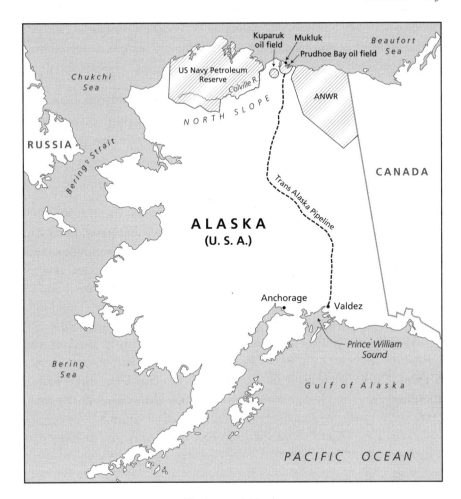

Oil changed Alaska

be going to the US. But Alaska? Was this America? I had hardly even heard of it.

Research made me slightly more enthusiastic. Although closer to the North Pole than to Washington,[1] Alaska had become the US's 49th state in 1959, just ten years earlier. The land was bought from Russia in 1867, for a price of less than two cents per acre, at the time regarded as an expensive folly.[2]

A significant oil field had just been discovered. This would be an opportunity to be involved in real oil exploration. I was given a BP clothing allowance to ensure I had the appropriate kit for the extreme climate. So, after much careful shopping, I thought I was well prepared.

But nothing could have prepared me for Anchorage. It was a wild place, not lawless, but certainly not sedate. And I soon discovered my hotel was indicative of the society. The Alaskan oil boom had attracted hordes of single, opportunist, get-rich, young men. There was not enough accommodation and bread often ran out by mid morning; you had to be up early to queue. Nightly binge drinking in sawdust-floored bars would often end in brawls in the street. I certainly began to learn more about life.

The streets were piled with snow in winter and when break-up came, as temperatures rose in the spring, they were a sea of mud. Only five years earlier, the town had been 80 miles from the epicentre of the Big One, the worst earthquake ever recorded in North America. One street had slipped downhill. Empty lots and missing buildings still bore witness to the damage.

Oil had brought adventure to Anchorage. And I stepped straight into this Klondike-spirit.

Pioneering spirit

Oil companies had been looking at Alaska for many years. As in Iran, there were stories of local people finding oil seeps. These were mainly on the treeless tundra of the North Slope, but with total darkness and temperatures of minus 50° C for three months of the year, exploration had been technically challenging.

In 1959, when areas became available for exploration, BP bought leases in the northern Brooks foothills close to the US Navy's 35,000-square-mile petroleum reserve.[3] BP geologists recognised similarities here with geological formations, so-called anticlines, which had been the tell-tale sign of large oil-bearing structures in the Middle East.

In this respect, BP was far-sighted. BP executives recognised they could not rely on stability in the Middle East – where they were accessing reserves in Kuwait, Iraq, Iran, Qatar, and Libya – and merely wait for a crisis and then react. They did not abandon the Middle East but implemented a parallel strategy to find a diversified set of new sources. As events turned out, the company would otherwise have been finished.

BP went out far and wide, including to Trinidad, Papua New Guinea and Nigeria. They even started exploring in the British North Sea. In

Alaska, there were many years of fruitless exploration in challenging conditions. But there was enough potential to persuade BP to continue. In particular, wider seismic surveys identified two promising prospects: a huge anticline near Colville River and a smaller faulted anticline at Prudhoe Bay.

In December 1964, BP acquired 318,000 acres around the Colville prospect. They had yet to drill there when eight months later, in July 1965, the Prudhoe Bay leases were auctioned. Other companies had begun to explore and had the benefit of seismic surveys, too. BP was outbid on the acreage immediately above the apparent crest of the anticline. That was purchased by a joint venture between Atlantic Rich-field Company (ARCO) and Humble Oil & Refining. BP, however, was successful in its bid for the land around the rim of the structure and thought this a good prospect as the oil-bearing section in similar fields in Iran had proven to be thicker and more prolific around the rim than at the crest.

The Colville prospect turned out to be dry but this did not deter the company from acquiring more leases, again around the flanks of the Prudhoe Bay field, in January 1967. But by early 1968, after nearly a decade of exploration, eight failed wells, and more than $30 million of sunk costs, BP decided to pull out of Alaska. The drilling rig was packed, ready to be shipped out when the Colville River would be ice-free in late spring.

Then, in March 1968, ARCO and Humble Oil struck oil with their last-chance well at the centre of the Prudhoe Bay structure. This was followed by a second successful well seven miles away. It was the first indication of a huge oil-bearing structure.

So just like Burmah Oil's instructions to George Reynolds in Persia some 60 years earlier, BP was about to walk away when a world-changing discovery was made. I soon realised that there were two important decisions about exploration: knowing *where* to start and knowing *when* to stop.

The stakes changed immediately. There was a frenzy of activity. BP decided not to withdraw from Alaska, encouraged by an approach from ARCO to purchase its Prudhoe Bay leases. They scrambled to get a new rig through the Bering Strait before the winter freeze. Within 12 months, in March 1969, BP hit oil in large quantities at its Put River No. 1 well. It had taken 10 years.

The company issued "only a tight lipped statement, giving no indication of the estimated quantity"[4] ahead of another competitive sale of
leases in Prudhoe Bay. Initial estimates for the Prudhoe Bay field were
around 10 billion barrels, comparable to giant fields in the Middle East.[5]
It was the largest ever oil field found in North America. BP's focus on
the flanks of the structure turned out to be a very shrewd move. They
were right; around 60 per cent of the oil was concentrated there.

The find in Prudhoe Bay was massive and valuable. Its development
as a producing field would turn out to be an enormous technical
challenge.

The North Slope was soon transformed, with a jetty on the shores of
Prudhoe Bay, gravel roads and a landing strip for aircraft. New businesses
were set up to provide supplies, ranging from cement to steel piping.
Base camps began to be built and the oil companies rushed to bring in
drilling rigs, vehicles and equipment. The race was on to develop the
discoveries, get the oil to market and find more oil.

By the time I arrived in November 1969, the small BP office in
Fireweed Lane, Anchorage – above a shop and next door to Dr Blood's
dental surgery – was a constant hive of activity. I joined as a trainee
petroleum engineer, the most junior of some 20 staff.

I had no fixed ideas and was not hidebound by previous experience
so I absorbed all I was told by others who had served their apprenticeships
elsewhere. John Saint, my ultimate boss, brought experience from
Trinidad. And Chuck McMaster, who had previously worked for Shell
in California, became a brilliant mentor. With little else to do, I learnt
about petroleum engineering, well testing, wire line operations – and
how to eat donuts 12 hours a day while waiting for something to do at
a drilling location.

Prudhoe Bay is 650 miles north of Anchorage. We would fly up in a
small plane to the newly built air strip at Dead Horse. On one of my
first trips, I went with BP's local manager, Geoffrey Larminie. A red-
headed Irish geologist, he smoked a pipe and was larger-than-life. He
arrived dressed for an English shooting party in plus fours and tweed
coat. Because of this remarkable costume, no one forgot who he was
and why he was there.

I discovered that the North Slope was vast, beautiful and very special –
more so than I could ever have imagined. In the bitterly cold winter
there are furious winds, snowdrifts and constant darkness; the sun never

makes it over the horizon. With spring comes light and you are almost blinded by endless glistening white – sometimes crystal blue – snow and ice.

In summer the sun never sets. The gentle warmth brings the thaw, creating lakes and rivers which attract flocks of birds. The top few inches of soil are then a boggy wilderness, dotted with a carpet of green shoots and tiny, fragile flowers, while the ground below remains permanently frozen. This is the permafrost, the permanently frozen subsoil, typical in the treeless tundra of the Arctic regions.

I worked on the BP exploration wells. It was part of learning on the job, doing what any petroleum engineer had to do. I was eager and enthusiastic and, because I kept asking questions, people were intrigued and keen to help me. There is no better way to learn. And what was exciting was that we had to find new answers to new questions.

How much oil was there? How do you drill a well through 2,000 feet of ice without melting the permafrost? How would the oil flow in the freezing temperatures? How could we build structures on ice? How could we move the rigs with no roads without damaging the tundra?

At one stage, Basil Butler, later to be chief executive of E&P (the exploration and production division), came out from the UK to find out if the oil, which was very hot, could be produced without melting the surrounding permafrost. If the permafrost had melted, there would have been some very big lakes. Complex insulation was developed but turned out to be unnecessary. It was the first time I met Basil and our paths crossed many times in the coming years. He was a very determined but extraordinarily polite man.

As the months went by, I moved from working on drilling rigs to working on other problems. These had to be solved in co-operation with other companies. That co-operation quickly became competition. Every company was looking at how to develop the field, how much it would cost, what it would produce and, importantly, what share of the costs and revenue it would get. The field was owned by a patchwork of surface lease owners and we had to agree on how much oil and gas each company owned and how we would operate the field as one entity. So owners worked together on some problems and in competition on others. Meetings were frequent, tough and involved endless negotiations.

From these meetings, I soon began to feel that our technology was lagging behind that of the American companies, particularly ARCO and Humble. I knew BP had to get up the curve quickly and to solve problems ahead of others. I was experiencing something very different from my peers back home in the government-protected BP. Working in America, and collaborating and competing with great American companies, taught me what competition really meant.

It is a truism that necessity is the mother of invention. To solve some of the more complex problems, we needed to invent tools and technology. Because of the work I had done at Cambridge, I knew we needed access to a computer. We needed a big one. And to start with, it had to be in Anchorage. So I found someone called Millett Keller.

Ingenuity

Millett had a Masters degree from Stanford and had opened something called a "computer bureau" in downtown Anchorage. He had an IBM 1130[6] and we swiftly became firm friends. During the day Millett was running Cobol programs for clients, creating statements for the local bank. In the evening, he would let me run the off-shift with programs I had written in Fortran.[7] BP had very few resources in Alaska. Here I found we could access the capability we required by buying it in at a low cost when it was not being used by someone else.

Millett became intrigued by what BP was trying to do; he would often work with me until late into the night. Among other things, we worked on computer-based mapping of the oil reservoirs. Together we stretched that poor machine to breaking point. Some of the original models and formulae created during that early phase would be in use for many years. They broke new ground, but today much of what we did seems commonplace. It is the same with any problem: when it is finally solved people wonder what the big deal was. As with the internet, which seems so obvious today.

I was in my element. This was more than a job; I was allowed to create things. I was using science and engineering to invent new ways to solve real problems. And I knew that what we were doing was not an academic exercise. The commercial stakes were massive. In such a competitive environment, innovation and speed were essential.

After six months of work in Anchorage, Millett and I decided that the poor IBM machine could cope no longer. He recommended we travel to California to find a machine with much larger processing power.

So we set off and went to Control Data Corporation (CDC) in Palo Alto. We just turned up and signed the most basic contract. They had a very large computer, a CDC 6600,[8] which we were allowed to hire at night. It filled a very large room with disk drives, tape drives, central processing units, card readers, flashing lights and so forth. It was attended by serious-looking men in white coats. It made you feel that you were in the presence of something very powerful, yet it was probably no more powerful than an office desktop today. I wrote the programs which were loaded on to the machine with punched cards. It took a long time to run a program and the machine was not sufficiently reliable to stay running for the 12 hours needed for a complete run. Starting and re-starting the program was a way of life. And each time we had to finish before the day shift started.

I also discovered an early example of computer visualisation using a cathode-ray tube and a light pen, a primitive version of today's touch screen and mouse. We eagerly adopted this technology which allowed us to do on a computer what had previously been done laboriously by hand. Here was a demonstration of the power of technology and a payback for my time at Cambridge. I realised I could do something that few others could do. Technology allowed me to glimpse into the future.

Paradigm shift

I was able to move out of the Anchorage Hotel and take over a tiny studio apartment when the local BP public relations manager left, but my salary was not enough to cover the rent of $400 a month. Once I had plucked up the courage to admit my plight, the matter was swiftly resolved. I got BP to pay me more. Later I shared a house on Tudor Way, then out of town but now very much downtown Anchorage, with three others from BP.

Because we were a small team, everyone had to get on with whatever there was to do. So after about a year, I started travelling to meet with BP's commercial partners in San Francisco, Seattle, Los Angeles and New York. I became more deeply involved in commercial negotiations and could see what was happening with the product of my technical work. I was a very junior team member but nonetheless welcome. The US was more open and less hierarchical than the UK at the time.

We were partnering with many different companies and I soon recognised that you need to abandon any preconceptions to collaborate effectively on a new venture. John Saint's experience in Trinidad meant he was a good person to work with and learn from because he approached projects with an open mind. And his broader way of thinking probably saved the BP operation in Alaska.

People came with narrow ideas based on their previous experience, typically from the Middle East where they had been trained. Production technology there was simple; huge reservoirs of oil meant very few wells needed to be drilled. Saint had worked on more difficult smaller oil fields in Trinidad. He looked at things differently from those who had worked in Kuwait, Iran or Iraq.

For many, however, the idea that a well in Alaska might produce a smaller amount of oil than a well in Iran required a big shift in thinking. In Alaska we started with wells spaced at 640 acres and went down to 80 acres in some places later. Old hands from Iran would say: "That's too many wells, that can't be viable." Many still wanted to focus only on wells, and hence oil fields, which were likely to be big producers. People would come up with the same argument time and again: "In Iran unless a well could produce 20,000 to 30,000 barrels a day we would have poured cement in and moved on."

An oil field that had been discovered and was thought to be too small to develop was Kuparuk. One of the things I realised as soon as I arrived in Anchorage was that we were in Alaska not just to develop Prudhoe Bay but also to find more good prospects. And I thought Kuparuk was one of these. Some, however, believed the Kuparuk field should be sold. In fact, my boss at the time appeared to want to sell it in exchange for a coal operation in Australia. Colleagues and I sensed that it could be valuable, and we developed the business plan which persuaded BP to keep the leases. Kuparuk turned out to be second only in size to Prudhoe Bay in the US.

People had to adjust their views on many things. Early Alaskan oil field development was "wild west" and this extended from extreme behaviour in Anchorage to strange activities in the field. From time to time, I saw people fishing using the dynamite employed in geophysics. They were just exploding the fish out of the water. I saw others writing obscene words in the permafrost, like some sort of polar graffiti, with a caterpillar tractor.[9]

At the time we thought little of it; standards were yet to improve. Oil field methods were more sophisticated than those employed by early explorers in the US in the 19th century but they were still primitive compared to best practice today.

We would test wells by burning the oil. We had a big pipe and would just let the oil flow out into a pit and then light it and measure the drop in pressure along the pipe to estimate the flow rate. It was extremely destructive and, if there was sand in the pit, the intense heat would turn it into glass. Far more sophisticated methods are used today.

Limited regulation around industrial processes and health and safety, and a sense that we were opening up a frontier, gave us the feeling that we could write the rules. We made many mistakes at the operational level. Sometimes we were insensitive and did not recognise that what we were doing was wrong. Arrogance prevailed.

Slowly, BP and the other oil companies began to recognise that they could not throw their weight around, as they had in the past. The world had changed by the end of the 1960s. We could no longer ignore the bigger picture. Success for the company meant that we had to adjust and consider wider concerns.

And two particular issues meant we could not just charge ahead: the indigenous Alaskan population and the natural environment.

Global oil, local people, local environment

In addition to the technical challenge of getting the oil out of the ground, we had to work out how to get it to market. The best option from a cost and safety perspective was a pipeline. But the shortest route for the pipeline was still 800 miles across Alaska, over three mountain ranges, across numerous rivers and through some of the most inhospitable terrain on earth to the ice-free port of Valdez, about a hundred miles to the east of Anchorage.

In June 1969, just before I arrived in Alaska, BP and the other oil companies, through the Trans Alaska Pipeline System (TAPS), had applied for a right-of-way permit to build the pipeline; the original plan was to bury the pipeline the whole way. Engineering issues absorbed everyone. How could the pipeline be made to withstand earthquakes? How could the pipeline cope with a temperature range of over a hundred degrees centigrade? It would be an enormous technical challenge but everyone believed it could be done.

There was a sense of political urgency. Concerns about finding alternative supplies to those from the volatile Middle East were intensifying. There was foreboding about security of oil supplies. OPEC had begun to flex its muscles and to talk of the use of the "oil weapon" (denying oil supplies to Israel's allies) in the Arab–Israeli conflict. Oil restrictions during the Suez Crisis in the previous decade had demonstrated only too well the vulnerability which came from dependence on Middle East oil.

And there was a sense of commercial urgency, too. Many oil companies had made significant investment in Alaskan exploration and needed to get oil out of the ground and to market to start repaying their debts.

But political and social issues were being overlooked. The oil companies had not appreciated how oil would change the lives of indigenous people in Alaska and how it would impact the environment of this last great North American wilderness.

The pipeline permit was refused by the Department of the Interior.

The oil companies, BP included, were shocked. Their focus had been on speed and state-of-the-art engineering. They had simply not foreseen the possibility that their plan might be rejected. And because the reasons for the rejection were so complex, they would take almost five years to resolve. This was something I would remember in years to come.

The Alaskan Federation of Natives demanded compensation before agreeing to grant a right of way. A coalition of environmental groups, including the Environmental Defense Fund, whom I would meet later in my career, wanted assurances that the fragile tundra and environment would not be damaged irreversibly.

The first hurdle was cleared in December 1971 when Congress approved the Alaska Native Claims Settlement Act, granting Alaska's indigenous population rights over 44 million acres, and nearly $1 billion in settlement of their hereditary claims; about half the money was to come from the federal treasury and the rest from oil revenue-sharing.

Environmentalists' concerns were not resolved that swiftly. In order to address environmental unease, BP and its partners agreed to elevate the pipeline, so the hot oil would not melt the permafrost, and to provide ramps to allow caribou and other wildlife to cross the elevated pipeline easily. Inside the company, there was grudging acceptance of these conditions, with many staff joking about caribou being more important than people. The tone was not right.

A long protracted legal battle followed. In February 1973 the US Court of Appeals blocked the issuing of permits for construction. Meanwhile I was kicking my heels in New York with little to do as these battles played out. I never quite understood why I had been asked to go to New York in the first place. New York is more than 3,000 miles from Alaska but I had been told that I needed to move there "to be based nearer to London".

In July 1973, Mike Gravel, the US Senator from Alaska, introduced an amendment bill to the National Environmental Policy Act, to protect the pipeline from any further court challenges and thus speed up its construction. When the bill came in front of the Senate, the vote was a tie, broken only by Vice President Spiro Agnew's casting vote. This key vote enabled the approval of the actual bill to start the pipeline construction.

Any remaining opposition to the pipeline faded when OPEC embargoed oil shipments to the US. The pipeline was then vital to ensure an uninterrupted supply of oil for US consumers. The Trans Alaska Pipeline Authorization Act became law on 16 November 1973 on the back of securing diverse domestic energy supplies. That quest for diversity would come back 30 years later as the world again worried about conflict in the Middle East.

Oil nationalisation

The OPEC embargo heralded a big change in the energy industry. Oil from OPEC countries accounted for around 65 per cent of the world's oil supply at the start of the 1970s. This gave OPEC significant power. BP had already had problems in Iran in the 1950s. And during the 1960s, international oil companies and producing countries had come to blows over a number of issues, including how to set the price of oil and what royalties should be paid. At the start of the decade five oil-producing countries – Iran, Iraq, Kuwait, Saudi Arabia and Venezuela – had come together to form the Organization of Petroleum Exporting Countries, more commonly known by the acronym OPEC,[10] initially to assert more authority on the international oil companies in terms of price. But OPEC's start belied its future political power.

The big international oil companies, which included BP, were known as the "majors" or the "Seven Sisters".[11] Outside of this group there were players, often US independents such as Occidental in Libya or Getty in Saudi Arabia, who were willing to offer more than the international oil companies to get a deal with the oil-producing nations. And growing demand started to increase the market power of the exporting nations.

The trigger for change came from Libya in 1970. Following Qadhafi's seizure of power in 1969, he forced first one oil company and then another to accept a higher price for oil and a higher tax rate on its production.

The rejection of contracts which oil-producing countries saw as unfair treaties, reflecting the asymmetry of power at the time of signature, was a sign of an underlying shift to the resource-holding country. On 16 October 1973 OPEC demonstrated its true clout by imposing a unilateral price increase of 70 per cent. This was followed by the total embargo of shipments of oil to the US on 20 October 1973. In New York, the shock was palpable.

Daniel Yergin, in his definitive history of the oil industry, *The Prize*, states: "The embargo signalled a new era for world oil … Petroleum had become the province of presidents and premiers, of foreign and finance and energy ministers, of congressmen and parliamentarians, of regulators and 'czars', of activists and pundits."[12]

Once the countries had found and exercised their muscle, the next step was a broad wave of oil nationalisation which swept through the industry and changed its shape irreversibly. By 1976 at least 18 countries had nationalised their oil-producing operations.

The OPEC countries had changed the rules and the international oil companies, such as BP, were now forced to change, too. Not only did these companies have to pack their bags, go home and start to search for oil elsewhere but they had to look at the very basis of their business.

For 60 years the oil business had been based on the remnants of colonial power and the muscle of the oil companies in a hierarchy that put the oil-producing nations at the bottom. It would be some time before countries that had nationalised their oil would invite the oil companies back. But when they did, it would be on a completely different and reciprocal basis and, in some countries, I would be involved.

But because BP had followed its dual strategy and had started to look elsewhere it already had two big new projects, the North Sea and Alaska, and these became known as its "two pipelines". After the long wait, construction of one of these pipelines, the Alaska pipeline, began in March 1975. The project took more than three years to complete and at its height employed more than 21,000 people.[13] As soon as it was finished, the renamed Alyeska Pipeline[14] began transporting crude oil and ramped up to a rate of 1.2 million barrels a day by the end of 1978.

I continued to work on the Prudhoe Bay project and, in 1974, was asked to move again. This time it was to San Francisco, "to be based nearer to Alaska". I never did understand the logic. After New York, San Francisco seemed provincial, but at least I would still be in the US. Here I chose to live in Cow Hollow, an area well known for its bars and restaurants. The downstairs of a two-up-two-down pre-earthquake house, in Filbert Street, parallel to the vibrant Union Street, became home. I would go back to see it in 2009; it had not changed.

I got to know some extraordinary people, including a couple who had recently opened a shop on Union Street to sell fine Californian wines. In 1974 that was an unusual venture since there was a strong belief that "fine" could not be applied to "Californian" when it came to wine. I would hang around their shop on Saturdays keeping them company when there were no customers; that happened frequently. I learnt a great deal from them, not just about Californian wine but about how to appreciate wine in general. And that gave me the confidence and passion to start my wine collection.

I had long since given up the idea of returning to the UK to do research. Maybe my father was right. It was not just that I was challenged by the science and engineering problems of oil, but I was getting more than my fair share of support and coaching from some great people in California. All jobs are made by the people you work with; it is about 90 per cent people and 10 per cent job content.

One of the more enlightened people at the time in San Francisco was a senior manager, Mike Savage. Years later he set up his own petroleum company and then became the General Director of San Francisco Opera. In the early 1970s he could see the way the business world was changing. Mike took a strong stance in favour of the indigenous Alaskan people and their heritage rights; he thought we should involve them in our work whenever possible. As part of the Alyeska Pipeline right of way, we made a commitment to recruit, train and promote them.

In time we gave contracts for catering, cleaning, and drilling to companies set up by indigenous Alaskans, so that their interests aligned with ours. Mike foresaw the need to involve local communities. He knew it was better to be one step ahead of regulation.

Risk and return

BP had accumulated massive debts so it was important to get Prudhoe Bay on stream as quickly as possible.

The hold-up in the approval of the pipeline certainly changed the economics of that part of the Prudhoe Bay project. Originally the pipeline was to cost $900 million, but by the time it was completed it had cost $8 billion and became the largest privately financed construction project ever attempted.[15]

By 1974 the price of oil had also increased dramatically. The oil embargo by OPEC resulted in oil prices quadrupling between September 1973 and January 1974.[16] If the price of oil had not gone up, would Prudhoe Bay have been economic? It is true that the increased oil price made the whole project viable. But as the price of oil went up so did the project's costs because of inflation. That is exactly what happened 30 years later in the middle of the 2000s – oil prices rose, costs went up.

Certainly the oil price rose enough to get the project going. I had worked on the economics and our original oil price assumption was $9 a barrel nominal delivered to Los Angeles. Our net revenue in Alaska was much lower because transportation costs were significant. There was barely enough to recover the capital cost of constructing the pipeline and the oil-production facilities.

It all appeared very marginal. And, on top of that, there were so many expensive changes to standards and designs. But in the end, over a 30-year period, good returns were earned as oil prices, operations and costs all kept improving.

All projects are a fine balance between risk and return. Sometimes the risks work out adversely and as a result nothing comes of the activity. That was the big lesson from an exploration prospect called Mukluk.

In 1983, off the coast in the shallow waters of the Beaufort Sea, around 25 miles north-west of Prudhoe Bay, Mukluk was identified as the next big opportunity. There was a fever-pitch mood. Forecasters were predicting continuing oil price rises. The prospect was said to be "no risk" with estimated reserves of around two billion barrels of oil. Companies were clamouring to buy leases.

BP was very successful at the auction; in fact I felt we had bought too many leases. I was working in London at the time and – having always been wary of the "no risk" label – I suggested to my most senior boss that BP sell some leases before drilling started. There was such hype about the prospect that we were able to sell them at a premium.

The prospect turned out to be dry. The view was that somehow the structure had breached and the oil had passed through to the other North Slope fields. In total more than $1.5 billion was spent on exploration leases in the area and more than $100 million on drilling. It will go down as one of the most expensive dry holes ever.

The bonanza of Prudhoe Bay and rising oil prices had seemed to promise unbroken success. The failure of Mukluk was a sharp reminder. In 1986, the oil price dropped dramatically and exploration would be turned down for a long time.

But then a disaster occurred which would change many things in Alaska, and indeed around the world.

The *Exxon Valdez* catastrophe

24 March 1989: It was five o'clock in the morning and I was fast asleep in the warmth of base camp on the North Slope when our general manager, George Nelson, woke me with the news. "We've got a message. There's some oil seeping around Valdez. It's from a tanker and they say it's Exxon's. But no one seems to be doing anything."

I knew straight away that something terrible had happened. My immediate response was: "Get someone to do something."

I was in Alaska to say farewell as I was leaving my job as the head of US E&P. I was to return to England to run BP's worldwide E&P. We were flying back to Anchorage that day and diverted the plane over Valdez. It was a chilling sight. A tanker, the *Exxon Valdez*, had run aground on Bligh Reef. Oil was flowing out from a gaping hole in its side to form a massive shadowy slick.[17] Dark oil stretched as far as the eye could see and the usual white ice floating in the dark sea was already tainted black. It seemed as if very little was happening. By then I had expected that response boats would be in the water trying to contain the spill within booms.

The sea in the Prince William Sound, off the coast of Alaska, was home to precious wildlife: seabirds, fish, sea otters and seals. Whales would be returning from the warm water in the south soon. Many people relied on fishing for their livelihoods. I could only hope that the wind buffeting our plane would keep the oil away from the rocky coves along the coastline.

I knew the repercussions for the industry would be huge. It was the start of a new chapter.

The oil companies were immediately put on the back foot. If this could happen to the environment around Valdez, what else might they do? *Exxon Valdez* damaged not just a fragile environment but also the flimsy trust in oil companies. Environmental NGOs would have a field day.

It was no use saying to NGOs that BP was better than its competitors. The industry was now measured by its weakest member, the one with the worst reputation. That oil company was now Exxon.

Regulation was increased. That was not a bad thing as it made people act responsibly. However, the bureaucratic, legal interpretation of regulations in a highly litigious society was costly and time consuming. We had to ensure there were no deviations and that our operation was perfect in terms of the law. This changed the way we did business in Alaska; we had to focus on compliance.

A lot of activity in offshore areas was closed down. And it made the opening of the Arctic National Wildlife Refuge (ANWR) in Alaska nigh on impossible.

Nearly 9 million acres of land had been set aside as ANWR in 1960, and a further 9 million acres added in 1980. A separate area of 1.5 million acres was called the coastal plain and BP wanted to drill in a small part of it. We genuinely believed that this would not materially affect the ecology or wildlife.

We were able to demonstrate that to explore we would hardly have to cross the main section of ANWR and we could use leading-edge technology, such as extended-reach drilling to develop any oil find with only a very small amount of equipment on the surface. However, no amount of argument would support our case. We soon realised that this was not about reason. This was about emotion. We were an oil company and we were portrayed as wanting to damage a beautiful place with blowing grass, wild flowers and an abundance of wildlife for the sake of short-term profits. We simply could not be trusted.

Those opposed to drilling in ANWR supported their case by saying there was so little oil that recovery efforts would not be worthwhile. It is true that, some years before, BP had drilled a well near ANWR which turned out to be virtually dry. But we had also drilled in the Refuge before it was closed.[18] Results were unclear and were never made public, but our view at the time, based on the only seismic data collected in the area by a petroleum-industry consortium in 1985, was that ANWR might possibly produce more than a million barrels of oil a day.

Opinion was polarised. On one side were those who said ANWR would be good for the economy, provide thousands of jobs and could produce enough oil to replace US oil imports from the Middle East, without harming the environment or the wildlife. And on the other side were those who wanted to protect ANWR from any drilling because of its environmental and ecological value.

ANWR became the *cause célèbre* of the 1980s. The discussions continue today. The debate around ANWR has become so emotive that I do not believe it will ever be opened up for oil drilling.

The bigger picture

For me, Alaska was a place where people were keen to help me learn. What I learnt stayed with me and informed me as a leader. I was of a generation that believed that technology would solve great problems. Computers were rare and frightening to some. To me they were a door to the future.

The design and delivery of the Prudhoe Bay development was a feat as great as the Apollo programme and it has proved to be enduring since, 30 years on, the field is still producing and the pipeline is still transporting. But what I learnt went beyond technology. It encompassed lessons about local communities, about the environment, about innovation, and about the enduring value of embracing change.

Alaska was very important to the world and to BP. But what was important to Alaska was Alaska itself. Little did it matter what the world wanted. Oil transformed the Alaskan economy. Oil revenue today accounts for more than all its other major industries – fishing, mining, timber and tourism – combined. Some 87 per cent of state revenues comes from taxes and royalties on oil production.

As oil started to flow down the pipeline, the state established the

Alaska Permanent Fund to benefit current and future generations of Alaskans. Revenue from oil has enabled significant investment and the Alaska Permanent Fund now stands at more than $33 billion. The principal is invested permanently and cannot be spent without a vote of the people. Fund income can be spent, and the decision as to how it is used is made by the legislature and the governor. No one in Alaska pays state income tax and every man, woman and child collects a dividend cheque each year.[19] For 28 years the individual dividend cheque has dropped through the letter box; in 2008 this cheque was $3,269.00.[20]

The Alaska Permanent Fund has been hailed as enlightened and a way of equitably distributing resource rents to people – avoiding the so-called "resource curse", so that everyone benefits from Alaska's natural resources. Yet it is also an example of how people who live off rents fail to appreciate the source of their wealth because it is not earned. If anything, the source of the rent is simply despised.

I started my career in Alaska and it would stay with me throughout my years with BP. In the last 12 months of my tenure as CEO, when the company had a series of oil spills on the North Slope, the spectre of the stricken *Exxon Valdez* came back to haunt me.

But back in 1986, I was about to head to Cleveland where I would have a battle on my hands.

3

CLEVELAND AND SCOTLAND

Enterprise

February 1986: "You will have to resign from BP, John."

My boss, Bob Horton, was not one for making jokes. So I knew this was for real. Bob was BP's chief financial officer, and he wanted me to be part of the new management team of the Standard Oil Company of Ohio, Sohio for short, a company part-owned by BP. I needed to leave BP and become a Sohio employee.

This move would give me hands-on experience in turning around a failing business and the experience of an important acquisition. But the boot would be on the other foot. I would not be with the acquiring company but on the target side, defending Sohio against BP. And that might well have put paid to my career with BP.

But before this experience, I had a lot of learning to do.

I returned in 1976 from San Francisco, and my involvement with Alaska, to work as a petroleum engineer, based in BP's head office in London. My initial task was to work on the North Sea.

BP had been looking for oil in the UK for 50 years. In April 1970, the chairman and CEO Eric Drake,[1] when asked about the North Sea, had said: "There won't be a major field there."[2] But within six months BP had announced the discovery of the Forties field, the first major oil strike in the British Isles. It was headline news in every British newspaper. And within 12 months Forties was confirmed as a world-class oil field.

Much had changed – both in BP and Britain. The company was now reliant on its two pipelines, Alaska and the North Sea, rather than the Middle East. And Britain had just emerged from the "swinging 60s". Yet BP was still a top-down, hierarchical organisation. And I was to find out that working in the UK was very different from the US.

I had a small office in North Britannic House in London, one of the buildings for head office staff. It felt as if I had walked into a government department. Authority was much respected; senior managers were "sir". Your grade influenced not just your office, desk and chair, but the cup in which your tea was served, and the type of biscuits, too. At my lowly grade, it was definitely a plain cup and saucer – not a china teapot on a tray – and a plain rich tea biscuit.

I never understood how decisions were made. We had no way of thinking of ourselves in comparison to other companies, the competition. And the pace of work was steady, even slow. My boss was the charming Michael Unstead, who had previously been a petroleum engineer with Shell. He taught me about the North Sea. I was soon learning about offshore engineering and North Sea tax and regulation, all very different from Alaska.

The Forties field, which lay under 350 feet of water, had been building up to its plateau production rate of 500,000 barrels a day. Its development had stretched the company's technical skills to the limit. The four Forties platforms had been built to withstand a once-a-century storm bringing winds of over 130 miles per hour and massive waves more than 90 feet high. The largest ever deep-water submarine pipeline had been laid. Within a few months, it would supply 20 per cent of the UK's oil requirements.

The company was now seen as *so* important that Tony Benn, then Secretary of State for Energy, was intent on nationalising BP, particularly as the government already owned a controlling interest.[3] I was too low down in the organisation, and too busy travelling back and forth to the North Sea, to understand the boardroom efforts to keep Mr Benn at bay. But Benn's hopes of nationalisation were dashed by the dire state of the British economy, when the government had to apply to the International Monetary Fund for a loan in the autumn of 1976.

BP continued to look for oil beyond its two pipelines and it was during this time that I was asked to go to China, but that is another story. In the late 1970s I went to Canada to look at opportunities in oil sands. My view then was that they were too inefficient to be viable. It was a viewpoint I continued to hold, for economic and environmental reasons, during the rest of my time at BP.

New chapter

The 1980s brought the start of a whole new chapter in my life – on professional and private fronts. It began with being selected by BP to go to Stanford to study for a business degree as a Sloan fellow. It was not something I had even considered.

While I was in Canada I got a call out of the blue from Frank Rickwood. Frank had been my ultimate boss when I was in San Francisco, and was now in charge of worldwide E&P. I always admired him as he was a brilliant geologist and managed to balance his work and private life well. Frank said: "I don't know much about business schools but I'm told there is kudos in going to Stanford so you just need to take this exam and get in." I think Frank knew far more. He believed that if scientists and engineers were to get to the top of the company they would need formal training in business. I agree with this view; perhaps that is why I have been the chairman of the advisory boards of three business schools.

There was no choice; as far as BP was concerned, I was going. This would change my whole working life.

However, on 1 August 1980, the month before I was due to go to Stanford, my father died after many years of complications from diabetes. He had started to suffer from diabetes shortly after we came back from Iran. He coped with medication for many years but the diabetes eventually became debilitating and he could then no longer work. In the last seven years of his life, he had undergone a series of progressive amputations resulting in the loss of both of his legs. My mother had devoted herself to him. She nursed him right until the end. It was a cruel time and a bitter blow when he died. He was only 64.

I was now my mother's only family. It seemed natural and appropriate that she should accompany me to the US rather than stay in the UK alone with her grief. I have no regrets, but I little realised then how dramatically that decision would impact my private life. My mother would live with me until her death in 2000.

The idea in 1980 was that she could keep busy in Stanford. It was something new and different, and something to look forward to. The experience was good for her. Together we found a convenient townhouse to rent in Menlo Park with a flower-decked terrace with three bedrooms, one of which became my study. A great hostess, she entertained in the large kitchen and became a very active member of the "gang of spouses".

The time at Stanford not only gave me a very different perspective on business – it was far richer and more complex than I had previously realised – but it also transformed my aspirations. Stanford's way of learning was characterised by its team approach. There was a belief that this team-orientation made Stanford very different from Harvard, where students "ate what they killed".

Certainly at Stanford you got negative points if you could not work in a team. Everyone on the Sloan programme had been in business for 10 to 15 years, bringing their own rich experience which we shared. We learnt to tackle problems together. I was one of the leaders of the out-of-class programme on decision sciences because of my background in mathematics.

The work was intensive, fun and, importantly, relevant. I was immersed in macroeconomics, global inter-relationships and finance. We looked at big problems and learnt how to resolve them, using case studies such as Love Canal which was topical at the time.[4] This opened my eyes. I saw how all the various pieces could fit together in very different ways and that in business you needed to think about things in a wide context. It began to make sense of my experiences in Alaska and the North Sea.

By the time I graduated, Stanford had permanently altered the way I thought about and wanted to do business. The West Coast had become a big and indispensable part of my life. And it was through Stanford and the dean, Michael Spence, that I became a non executive director of Intel in 1990 – but more of that later.

North Sea tax

My first role on returning to the UK in 1981, after Stanford, was managing the commercial unit of the E&P division. I was back at Britannic House, but business training at Stanford made me look at problems quite differently. I came up with a novel way of increasing the value of the Forties field by selling units to smaller exploration companies.

North Sea oil taxation – as is so often the case with tax – was a complex system. Companies were able to offset development and exploration costs against tax. The UK government's idea was that this would encourage more companies to explore and develop the North

Sea. But it did not. To make tax deductions you needed income, something that new entrants did not have. So here was our opportunity. As a large operator producing large amounts of oil, BP was paying a massive amount of tax; even our expenses left lots of tax unabsorbed. So our idea was to sell small units of the producing Forties field to independent exploration companies that could utilise the tax shelter of the production. That would indeed get more companies to come and explore.

It nearly did not happen. All planning and offering of the units was done in the utmost secrecy, hand in hand with a young and clever banker, David Verey of Lazard Brothers.[5]

Nowadays, I doubt if you could keep a secret like that with about 40 companies involved. We had kept the government informed at a technical level but, a few days before the announcement, the political leaders understood properly what was happening. On the one hand, the number of companies in the North Sea would expand significantly. That was good for the UK. But on the other hand, BP's "ingenious plan" meant the company would get close to a £400 million windfall from selling part of Forties for a big premium because of taxes, and the UK government would lose much more.[6] That was too much to be acceptable. It would look as if we had ripped off the UK Treasury.

Fierce negotiations involving Robin Adam, the chief financial officer of BP, and Nigel Lawson, the Chancellor of the Exchequer, ensued. The answer was a hastily drafted modification of the tax law, which took away a bit of the margin and preserved face all around. It was a lesson in mutual advantage.

So it went ahead and the next thing I knew I was up in bracing Aberdeen as manager of the Forties field, one of BP's most important production assets. I realised how much you learnt if – as Woody Allen says – you "just showed up". I found an apartment in one of the city's granite houses and spent every other weekend offshore with the team from a different platform (there were four and a mobile vessel by then). The 12 platform managers called themselves the "college of cardinals" and I was known as the "pope". Some years later I became "Brown with an E" in the irreverent bootleg North Sea magazine, the *Delta Free Press*.

Subsequently, Bob Horton, then chief financial officer of BP, asked me to become group treasurer. He telephoned me in Aberdeen and said the job, effectively deputy CFO, would be good for me although I had no experience and expertise in finance. I was to take over from Quentin Morris. "Q", as he was known across the City of London, had joined BP from the UK's Inland Revenue. He was a big man who liked big cigars and big deals. When I asked him about investor relations his response was to the point: "It's very simple, John. People can either buy our shares or sell them. It doesn't matter much. As the British government owns the majority, we don't actually care."

So with that introduction I went off to my first investor briefing in New York with a set of 35mm slides. Only to find when I arrived at the 21 Club, a well known but rather stuffy restaurant with large meeting rooms on 52nd Street, my assistant had dropped the carousel of un-numbered slides on the floor. The best I could do was to show the slides in the wrong order. Not that it seemed to matter.

In this new role, because of what I had learned about finance at Stanford, I set up an "internal bank", one of the very first in corporate history outside finance corporations tied to such entities as General Motors.

Our own bank

BP, like all international oil companies at the time, faced an uncertain future. In the past, big oil companies had been vertically integrated. They had owned the oil resources and controlled production, refining and selling and marketing of the final product. That vertical chain began to break down as independent refiners started to buy oil from producing nations and independent producers sold oil on an increasingly deep global market.

After the OPEC crisis in 1973, BP had to think very differently about the different parts of its operation. It might have been making large profits from the North Sea and Alaska, but other parts of the business were struggling. In the winter of 1981–82 its European refining and marketing operations lost £1 million a day and petrochemicals a further £500,000.[7] Significant investments, in transport, refining and marketing, needed to be profitable in their own right or be sold off. We had to close refineries as we had too much capacity. And there was a move to diversify.

Oil major Mobil bought the retailer Montgomery Ward. Gulf Oil even tried to buy a circus. BP, under the new chairman and CEO Peter Walters,[8] invested heavily in hard-rock minerals and coal; in telecommunications, including one of the predecessors of Cable & Wireless; and in food, including a sausage company. Peter created a structure in which these units operated as autonomous businesses.

While I am a great believer in decentralisation, it can go too far and verge on anarchy. A loose structure can be motivational but some things, like the flow of finance, need to be glued together tightly, particularly because shareholders regard a company as a single entity and not the sum of its separate divisions.

In 1984, the financial markets had yet to be deregulated but financial techniques were already changing. The team of financial experts who worked for me were full of ideas, which they had never been able to implement. Among them was David Cobbold, whose father had been Governor of the Bank of England, and who understood banking through and through; Peter Smythe, a corporate finance expert; and Alan Beale, an expert on banking relationships. They were each brilliant in their own field. They had experience but they were not risk takers. I had no experience in finance, so nothing to hold me back. We had the idea of creating an in-house "bank". I knew we could pull it off.

With this small team of experts, we started to change BP's finances. No other company was doing this at the time. We created BP Finance International as a profit centre and began to make money for BP on very simple things, such as centralising foreign exchange transactions and borrowing centrally at lower cost than at divisional level. I learnt a great deal about finance during a time of great change, the lead-up to "Big Bang" in October 1986 when financial markets were deregulated in the UK. Initially there was internal resistance but, with persuasion, people began to realise a central unit could manage finances better and so improve profits over all.

Finance brings opportunities, people, ideas and resources together in a business and so people started coming to us for advice on risk management. Soon I had a well-worn sofa – and a call from the Governor of the Bank of England. He wanted to know why I was running a "bank" without a licence. It was obvious that we were not a bank but merely a treasury. So we changed the name. And the lesson learned? Be careful with important words.

Cleveland and the massacre

My next stop was Cleveland, Ohio, which was the headquarters of the Standard Oil Company of Ohio (Sohio), a powerful fragment of John D. Rockefeller's dismembered empire. This was when I had to resign from BP.

The name "Standard Oil" still counted for a lot in the industry and indeed Cleveland was the very place where John D. Rockefeller, the most important figure in shaping the oil industry, had started his business. In the 1860s Rockefeller could see the growing importance of the oil business and had a clear vision of what he could achieve. He owned one of Cleveland's most successful oil refineries and bought out his more cautious partner. Within a decade he had got rid of most of his competitors, too. He would go on to build the world's first multinational corporation.[9]

No blood was spilled in the Cleveland Massacre but in 1872, in less than six weeks, John D. Rockefeller effectively killed off the competition. Standard Oil managed to acquire 22 out of 26 of its Cleveland competitors to dominate the burgeoning oil market. Realising that the railroads were vital for effective transportation of oil and held the key to competitive advantage,[10] Rockefeller used his shrewd negotiation skills to persuade three railroad companies to discriminate on freight prices in favour of a group of refineries. This group was in effect a cartel, the South Improvement Company, led by his company Standard Oil.

Rockefeller's competitors, faced with a seemingly permanent disadvantage in transportation costs, saw little prospect of staying in business. They decided to respond to Rockefeller's approaches and sell out, typically at scrap value and in return for Standard Oil stock. Sellers included the largest refinery, owned by his first employer, and a refinery owned by a former partner. This was Standard Oil No. 1 refinery, which I discovered was still on our balance sheet when I went out to Cleveland.

It was an extraordinary achievement, both in the scale of its ambition and ruthlessness of its execution. Even Rockefeller's largely sympathetic biographer condemned the South Improvement Company as "an astonishing piece of knavery, grand scale collusion such as American industry had never witnessed".[11]

Defenders of Rockefeller argued that through his action he stabilised the price of oil, which then made the rapid development of the oil industry possible. Certainly Standard Oil went on to dominate the oil industry across the US. Rockefeller himself argued that vertical integration and consolidation ensured the economies of scale that enabled Standard Oil ultimately to reduce the price of oil.

Rockefeller was admired by a few for what he had achieved but had become the most reviled businessman in the US.[12]

The exposure of Rockefeller's business practices in the early 20th century, by a tenacious journalist, Ida Tarbell, paved the way for the downfall of Standard Oil.[13] Tarbell was the daughter of an independent oilman and 14 years old at the time of the Cleveland Massacre. She revealed underhand business practices which included secret deals to restrain competition, the use of spies and bribes to win votes, and favourable reporting. She accused Rockefeller of being the pre-eminent representative of "commercial Machiavellianism" in which success was the justification of every practice, and commonly accepted values were separated strictly from business practice.[14]

Newspapers were full of Tarbell's story. This exposure helped lead to the widely publicised break-up of Standard Oil into 34 separate companies, each with its own distinct board of directors, under the Sherman Antitrust Act in 1911.

In time, BP would come to acquire more of those separate companies than anyone else: Sohio, Amoco and ARCO.[15] It started with Sohio.

By the early 1980s, as the result of a deal done in 1970, BP owned 55 per cent of Sohio.[16] But it was clear that the relationship between BP and Sohio was not going well. Returns were bad. Sohio seemed bent on spending an expected mountain of money in advance of it materialising and on pursuing expensive and largely unsuccessful exploration programmes – including losing more than $300 million on the dry hole, Mukluk. Sohio, like BP, had diversified, investing $6 billion of revenues from Alaska in unprofitable investments in the US. And Sohio was competing with BP on the international exploration stage, in places like Algeria.

In London there was a growing feeling that we had to take some action. As group treasurer, I put together a plan to take over Sohio in one fell swoop: by using BP's shareholding to outvote the minority shareholders, simultaneously change the Sohio board and have the board recommend a merger with BP. Bob Horton was supportive but Peter Walters thought this too strong-armed and came up with a different tactic.

In February 1986, the BP board asked long-time Sohio chairman Al Whitehouse to resign along with the chief operating officer and the chief financial officer. Bob Horton, Colin Webster and I were asked to go over to Cleveland to turn Sohio around. We all resigned from BP.

Leaving BP and London for Ohio was a wrench, particularly as Cleveland was then regarded as the "mistake on the lake". I am convinced it was the butt of so many jokes because numerous entertainers and comedians, including the legendary Bob Hope, were associated with the city.[17] People used to joke that the difference between Cleveland and the *Titanic* was that Cleveland had a better orchestra.

Nevertheless, I was determined to enjoy the new opportunity. My mother went with me and I bought a house in the once fashionable Shaker Heights area, but thought that it might be the first time I would lose money on property.

You can imagine the frosty reception on arrival. We were viewed with deep suspicion. We were the "bad guys" from the UK. I was viewed as particularly dangerous since a rumour about my strong-armed plan to take over the company had already reached Cleveland. Bob was chief executive and I was chief financial officer. We were nicknamed "Batman and Robin" by one city analyst.[18] In his particular way, Bob knew how to get results. He had sorted out BP's chemical business, and in Cleveland he took a direct approach. He set about making himself and Sohio liked.

He invested in Cleveland, which we soon learnt was at rock bottom. Some years earlier the debris-filled River Cuyahoga had caught fire; Randy Newman wrote his song "Burn On" about it.[19] Even past mayors came in for ridicule as one had accidentally set his hair on fire at a ribbon-cutting ceremony.[20]

People in the company, in the local community, and in the US more generally soon began to view us positively. So much so that the then mayor, George V. Voinovich, said: "If I were going to point to a model of the way foreign owners ought to behave in terms of public responsibility I would say, 'Find out what Bob Horton did in Cleveland'."[21]

The house I bought came with a huge basement and my mother had the idea that we could turn this into a space for entertaining. Soon we were holding parties. She was making friends and we became part of the community. People were very friendly and we began to see the real and good side of Cleveland.

Sixteen-hour days were common. A lot of effort went into changing the attitude of the people in Sohio. In a short time we turned the company's negative cash flow to positive. This was in spite of the drastic collapse of the oil price in 1986, when Saudi Arabia decided it could no longer restrain its production to keep the price of oil up. Sheikh Yamani, the oil minister, concluded that it was better for his country to produce more oil at a lower price. That is what happened, but meanwhile Sohio's stock price was rising.

January 1987: Just when things were back on track in Cleveland, BP made a move to buy out the minority shareholders and take over Sohio. It was probably inevitable, but Bob and I were taken aback at the speed. I should have guessed; I had noticed people were trying to avoid me, when I was in London at the end of the year. As I was now a Sohio employee, BP's plot had to be kept from me.

The news came through as Bob and I were holidaying separately in the Caribbean. We found out a few hours before the market and had to fly straight to New York for the first meeting of the special committee of Sohio's board, chaired by Doug Danforth, the CEO of Westinghouse. Doug was recovering from a problem with his ears, which were heavily bandaged, so he was hard of hearing. The meeting was somewhat confused. None of the committee members had ever had the experience of being attacked by a majority shareholder.

I was in a very difficult position. Where did my allegiance lie?

I had left BP to join Sohio and now BP wanted to take over Sohio. I decided that I could not ride two horses at once. I was the chief financial officer for Sohio so had to represent its interests. And that meant defending Sohio against BP. My role – even though I might be working myself out of a job – was to get the best price possible for minority shareholders from the majority shareholder. There were lots of potential conflicts but it was clear what our approach should be.

I wrote a paper for the Sohio board which set the direction for getting what we believed would be a fair price. As always in the oil business, the upside is the key and I wrote not only about the strong upward potential of oil prices but about the mysterious promise of the Arctic National Wildlife Refuge (ANWR). Sohio had some rights to acreage in ANWR and claimed that this added to the company's value. BP discounted that notion. Nobody knew ANWR's true value so it became the football that was passed back and forth.

We picked First Boston Corporation to represent Sohio as its financial adviser. And with First Boston arrived the larger-than-life deal impresario Bruce Wasserstein, who had a strong track record of getting more from an acquirer. He was known as "Bid-'em-up Bruce".

This was when Bruce was in his heyday and knew how to use the media, law and his financial skills to drive up any bid. Bruce was driven by a sense that he was representing the minority shareholders directly. But his advice was compelling and so, however heroic, we went along with it.

I knew this could put my career with BP in jeopardy. Just before the takeover was done, Peter Walters came over to the US and made a rather chilling comment to me: "I am sure you can get a job elsewhere."

Our defence, spurred by Bruce's efforts, meant the price BP had to pay was very much higher than they had first offered. And, eventually, all the shareholders agreed, with little legal comeback. The incident made me realise that business is, of course, business. You must pick your side, you must fight, and you have to see it through to the end.

As it turned out, Peter asked me to stay on in Cleveland as chief financial officer and also to take on the running of BP's North American E&P operation. Because Sohio merged with BP's other US interests to form BP America, the country's 13th largest industrial corporation, I was now responsible for the largest oil producer in the US.[22]

I was delighted to take on the new challenge. I had support from both Bob Horton, with all his energy, and Peter Walters, who made you feel that nothing was an effort. He was always calm, projecting a sense of "we can get this done" and so commanded great respect.

In my new role I started to focus on what BP needed to build a future. We had very little in the Americas apart from Prudhoe Bay and Kuparuk in Alaska; later we would acquire the Milne Point field. ANWR was now closed. We had been unsuccessful in the Arctic Ocean; Mukluk had proven the risk of E&P in that area. And we had inherited years of fruitless exploration in the lower 48 states, from Sohio, with little or no significant results. Because of the poor quality of the mixed assets in the US, I decided we should create a special unit for all the E&P assets in the continental lower 48. This was called TexCon, which we eventually sold off.

Then with Chris Wright, Ralph Alexander and the team, we began to expand our horizons. We decided to go where no one else had gone.

This would turn out to be an important strategic decision. BP's success in the Gulf of Mexico deep waters stems from this era.

When we looked at the Gulf of Mexico hardly any other companies were operating there. That was not surprising. The water was more than 3,000 feet deep – so deep that you could not fix anything to the seabed. Exploration wells cost a fortune to drill. There were few discoveries and even if a discovery was made, there was no proven technology to develop it.

But our geological studies were promising. The Gulf seemed to have all the attributes of an oil province. We reasoned that there were a number of different ways oil and gas could have accumulated there. It was far more stretching than the North Sea but we decided the Gulf had enormous potential. Oil was likely, but the risk of failure was very high.

We made the decision to take a big acreage position. And we began to test the different accumulations. Many companies came to co-operate and compete. Some lost heart but we were determined to keep building our knowledge and experience there. Someone once described the engineering challenges in BP as "Isambard Kingdom Brunel revisited 100 times" and that was never more true than in the Gulf of Mexico.[23] Importantly, we saw that we could pursue a strategy without having to follow other dominant players, as we were forced to do as a late entrant into other oil-rich states such as Texas.

One company that was in the Gulf of Mexico was Shell. In a moment of strategic weakness, they let us into one of their discoveries called Mars. Shell in Houston was instructed by their head office not to develop Mars without a partner because it was too risky. So along came BP. And that added to our new deep-water opportunities in the US.

Discovery after discovery followed in the Gulf of Mexico. "Sticking to our knitting" had paid off. By the time I left BP, the decision to pursue the deep-water strategy had proved to be highly successful. Today BP is the largest producer of oil and gas in the US Gulf of Mexico with net production of more than 400,000 barrels of oil equivalent per day.[24]

Integration

One of the things we did not do well with Sohio was to integrate it with the rest of BP. And we made the same mistake with the next acquisition. But then there were very different reasons.

In 1988 BP bought Britoil, a company established in the 1970s from the UK government's direct interests in the North Sea. It doubled our exploration acreage there and got us some properties overseas. But the deal was weakened by the many conditions attached to its completion. It proved to be a monumental struggle from the very beginning.

Before this happened, I had my eye on another opportunity in the US. If it had gone ahead, it might have changed the course of business history for the better.

Deregulation of the energy market was under way and I believed that gas transmission was a good business for the future. I made a case to buy Houston Natural Gas (HNG) and put a paper to the board, which eventually decided in favour of Britoil. We could not afford to do both.

I had started discussions with someone called Ken Lay. He was the chief executive of HNG who went on to sell his business to Omaha-based Internorth. The combined business then changed its name to Enron Corporation. Ken became chairman and CEO of Enron and was eventually brought to trial for fraud and corruption which led to the much-publicised and far-reaching downfall of Enron in 2001.[25]

The HNG deal did not happen. However, Britoil was now part of BP and there were issues to deal with when I returned to the UK in 1989. But, before I left the US, a horrific accident shook the industry.

6 July 1988: Piper Alpha, a North Sea oil-production platform which was operated by Occidental Petroleum, caught fire, killing 167 men. A pipeline had ruptured under the platform causing an inferno. It was the world's worst offshore oil disaster. It changed the way offshore operations were conducted across the whole world.

Lord Cullen, who led the inquiry into the disaster, took an enlightened approach. New safety recommendations were to be enforced not as rules and regulations, but as principles. Operators were expected to assess and manage the risks peculiar to each field. And for BP it meant that we had to understand the risks to the safe operation of each of our offshore production platforms and make investments to reduce the risk of a catastrophe. BP was now the biggest operator in the North Sea and this became a very significant activity. This was about understanding and managing the safety of the production processes, a topic which would dominate my agenda again after a fatal explosion at the Texas City refinery almost 20 years later.

I returned to the UK to find that BP had made significant commitments to the UK government in order to win its approval to take over Britoil. As a result, the government did not exercise their "golden share", a device which could have stopped the takeover. BP persuaded the government by arguing that it had plenty of cash flow and good technology so it could explore more and develop faster than smaller Britoil. The government seized on this argument and converted BP's statements into legally binding commitments – drill so many wells a year, develop so many barrels, spend so much money, invest in Scottish technology, keep the Glasgow office open, and so on. Every month the Britoil exploration manager had to report to the UK Department of Energy on how many wells he had drilled, not on whether he had found oil. The purpose seemed to be drilling for drilling's sake rather than exploration. It became almost impossible to integrate Britoil into BP.

BP was now three completely separate companies – BP, Sohio and Britoil – all part of one group but not integrated. This had to change.

It was clear that we needed to get out of some of the Britoil commitments otherwise we could never make the business work. So some serious renegotiation with the government got under way. As with any government, political trade-offs were made; for example, we were allowed to close the Glasgow office but we had to form an advisory board of the great and good from Scotland to monitor our activities in the North Sea and the Scottish mainland.

We sold some Britoil assets that did not fit. This was all part of a wider divestiture plan to consolidate the upstream into one entity and get it in line with the new E&P strategy which we began to develop in 1989. We had to start to reduce our costs and focus our activity. Oil prices were low and we felt that these low prices were here to stay. The company could not afford to behave as it had; it needed to change.

So began a long period of day-to-day supervision of our activities and ways of managing that I would use for the rest of my career with BP: delegation of clear targets, monthly and quarterly detailed reviews of progress, going to talk with the people actually operating in the field and making sure everyone remembered the purpose of their job and knew that they were valued.

By the time I became CEO of BP in 1995 I could see that the company needed to do more than just explore in order to grow. I started looking at even bigger opportunities.

4

TRANSATLANTIC

Consolidation

February 1998: I phoned Larry Fuller from my London office. We hardly knew each other, and had never met, but I thought he would take my call.

After a discussion on our joint venture in Azerbaijan, I said: "What are your thoughts about the future of Amoco? Because it seems to me it's a good time for a few oil companies to get together."

He might have been surprised but Larry, chairman and CEO of Amoco, responded swiftly: "Well, it's not on my agenda, but why don't we talk?"

"When would be convenient?"

"How about the day after tomorrow?"

Two days later we met at Kennedy Airport, in New York. And so started discussions for what would become, at $110 billion, the world's largest industrial merger. It would prompt a wave of consolidation which would change the shape of the oil industry.

My call might have seemed out of the blue to Larry, but mergers and acquisitions had been on BP's agenda for some years. It was what we needed if we were ever going to be anything more than middle-ranked. We had been through a decade of change and yet we were still not able to play in the top league.

By the time I came back to London to head up the whole of E&P in 1989, I knew that BP controlled insufficient reserves and opportunities to secure its future.

In the 1970s BP had been squeezed out of many countries by the wave of oil nationalisation. Our exploration track record was poor, with only a handful of discoveries. We had few places to go and what we had was beginning to decline. Our two producing areas were the North Sea, with Forties and Magnus past their prime; and Alaska, with Prudhoe Bay starting to decline, though Kuparuk, the oil field we nearly sold, was still producing at a good rate. The only other place from which we had significant production was Abu Dhabi.

BP had no option but to get its legacy sorted out, get faster on its feet, do more deals and become more innovative. But most of all, BP had to make more money. We needed to have "a distinctive set of assets" – low-cost reserves, sustained by a flow of sizeable, low-cost discoveries.

As luck would have it, two big developments, which happened around the time I came back to the UK, provided the platform to reformulate BP's exploration strategy: the fall of the Berlin Wall and the rise of the microprocessor.

9 November 1989: Few who watched events unfold will ever forget the sense that this was the beginning of the end for the Soviet empire and the entire Eastern bloc. I watched the scenes on television with my mother in our home in London. She was moved deeply and said that now she could go back to visit her birthplace, Oradea. That was something she had refused to do when Hungary and Romania were part of the Soviet bloc. In fact she never went back.

Months before, anyone attempting to cross the Berlin Wall would have been shot. Now jubilant crowds were clambering atop the concrete divide. Others were taking sledgehammers to hack large chunks out of the wall. The world watched as the powerful symbol of the Cold War was torn down by the people.

Story after story followed over the next few months as the Eastern bloc crumbled – from the Velvet Revolution in Czechoslovakia to bloodshed with the execution of Ceausescu in Romania. In Moscow dissatisfaction with *perestroika* took hold and Gorbachev became increasingly unpopular as food shortages grew and living standards fell.

By 1991, the Iron Curtain and the USSR were gone. Countries such as Armenia, Azerbaijan, Estonia, Kazakhstan, Tajikistan and Turkmenistan were now independent. These countries, although still in a state of transition from communism to free market, could now be added to our exploration map.

In parallel, rapidly improving technology meant we could now reduce the costs and risks of drilling. Advances in techniques, such as seismic signal acquisition and processing, allowed more accurate images of the shape and internal configuration of sub-surface structures to be made. The risk of dry holes was significantly reduced.

I determined we should use the moment to sell off what we did not want and to go and explore new and different places. But there had to be one of two reasons why we would do that: either political change opened up the opportunity to get licences in a new area, or application of technology allowed us to identify new prospects in an old area. And if it was neither of those reasons, we would not go in and explore.

So the exploration team, lead by David Jenkins, started to scan the world and go to places which would previously have been impossible.

We also looked to our competitors to see what we could learn from them. We scored different companies on different aspects of their exploration performance. Shell was by far the best, and Amoco by far the worst. In many ways Shell was our paragon and paradigm.[1]

What Shell did brilliantly was to be consistent and focus on material opportunities. They knew when to go into a place and knew when to stop and come out. And, based on their observed success and other companies' failures, we developed a set of principles for exploration.

We were smaller than Shell but could still emulate them. We knew we had to change our focus to those areas which were most likely to succeed. In that way we would spend *less* money to find *more*. Our agreed new exploration strategy would focus on a small number of the most attractive basins where we could potentially control a billion barrels of oil and gas. In these we would take big positions. We reasoned that costs would be lower per barrel for big fields, and it would be easier to attract and retain good staff for the large long-lived projects. Success would be based on giant prolific fields and related infrastructure, not on a collection of small fields.

This strategy was novel at the time. Today most oil majors have adopted a similar path; even Shell has rediscovered its old strategy and called it the "Big Cat" approach.

Bob Horton was now chairman and CEO of BP.[2] The E&P approach fitted with the new corporate strategy of rapidly divesting unrelated businesses and focusing the organisation on three clear businesses: upstream oil and gas exploration and production, downstream petroleum refining and marketing, and petrochemicals.

Other badly needed changes in BP were under way. We were no longer part-owned by the UK government but the company was still riddled with internal politics, top-heavy, burdened by bureaucracy, had a cumbersome matrix structure, and performed poorly. The company was also significantly indebted because of the purchase of the additional 45 per cent of Sohio and the purchase of Britoil. But there was another big factor.

Privatisation

When the British government decided to sell its remaining shareholding in BP, as part of Prime Minister Margaret Thatcher's privatisation programme, the timing could not have been worse.

As it would be the biggest private share sale ever seen on the London Stock Exchange, BP assumed that the government would sell its holding in instalments over a number of years. However, Peter Walters, then chairman and CEO, was alarmed to discover that with so many privatisations in progress, the Treasury had decided to sell all its BP shares at once. I was in the US at the time and, with Bob Horton, gave presentations to persuade investment analysts and big institutional investors of the attractiveness of these shares.

On Thursday, 15 October 1987, Royal Marines abseiled down the face of BP's head office in Moorgate, London, to reveal a huge poster with the price of £3.30 per share. That night, the south-east of England was struck by a great storm. It was an omen. On 19 October stock markets around the world crashed on what became known as "Black Monday" and more than £50 billion was wiped off the value of the London Stock Market. BP shares had plunged well below the £3.30 offer price.

The sale of BP's shares should have been a triumph in Margaret Thatcher's privatisation programme. Instead it was a flop.

The Kuwaiti government spotted the opportunity and swooped to buy what threatened to be a controlling interest in BP. Under pressure from BP, the UK competition authorities ruled that Kuwait, an oil producer, had to cut its holding back to 10 per cent. BP bought the shares from Kuwait but this increased the company's debt considerably.

The consequence of privatisation and poor performance, in a world of surplus oil production and refineries, led Bob Horton to start a project of radical change when he took the helm of BP in 1990. This project sought to reduce the role of the head office, eliminate layers of

management and devolve financial authority down the flattened hierarchy. The idea was to improve the speed and effectiveness of managerial
decision-making and importantly to get people to feel a sense of purpose;
they were encouraged to take more responsibility and exercise initiative.
All of this was just what was needed, but it proved too much for the
company to take in one go.

In the face of a deepening global recession and falling oil prices,
BP had to cut jobs and capital budgets. BP needed to change, but
Bob's energetic style became out of step with the organisation. He
had good reason to be self-confident as he had the most extraordinary
intellectual capacity but sometimes he just went too far. In 1992 *Forbes*
magazine printed an interview where he was quoted as saying:
"Because I am blessed by my good brain, I tend to get the answer
rather quicker and more often than most people. That will sound
frightfully arrogant."[3] Unfortunately it did and this eventually led to
his undoing.

In June 1992 the board, led by non executive director Lord Ashburton,[4]
asked for Bob's resignation. As Lord Ashburton said, Bob was asked to
go because events built up, rather like snowflakes in a snowdrift. The
suddenness of his departure led to a lingering suspicion that Bob was
dispatched without due process.

Bob had been chairman and CEO. The role of chairman and CEO
was then split. Lord Ashburton became non executive chairman and
David Simon became CEO.[5]

The company experienced the first loss in its 80-year history. The
dividend was slashed, the share price fell and staff felt battered by the
recent downsizing and organisational upheaval. David, with his calmer,
more measured approach, announced his new "One-Two-Five" targets
to the market. He promised that BP would achieve $1 billion in debt
repayments, $2 billion net profits and no more than $5 billion a year
capital expenditure by 1995.

In 1992 E&P, which I ran, was responsible for more than half of
BP's spending and earning power. The new exploration strategy was
beginning to pay off. However, it was clear we needed to generate better
performance from existing assets. That meant lowering operating costs,
getting more production out of oil and gas fields and controlling capital
expenditure, while still finding and developing new hydrocarbon
deposits.

Reorganisation

For more than a decade, BP had been organised on a so-called "matrix structure". In this structure people had different and distinct roles: to do with activity in a country or group of countries; to do with so-called "functional" content, for example engineering, technology, or accounting; or to do with the operation of a business activity.

This sort of organisation was designed to have specialists do specialised work. To a lay person this looks confusing – and it was. To get something done, you had to negotiate with people with different roles and different objectives. The objective of the manager of a country was to make that country the most important place, the manager of engineering wanted to get the best engineering done, and the business manager wanted to get the highest profit and lowest cost. It seemed to me that we were often more interested in debate rather than action.

After this experience, something different had to be done to divert all the energy expended internally towards more productive external activity; that was very necessary since BP needed to forge some new distinctive external relationships to expand its business.

The themes of Bob Horton's reorganisation of the early 1990s were a reaction against the "matrix": reduce internal negotiation; simplify everything; reduce costs; get enterprises outside the company to take on some activities they could do better, so-called "outsourcing"; become more entrepreneurial; and so on.

And that was exactly what I believed that the E&P division should do. We devised a new decentralised organisation that abandoned the matrix and gave real authority to managers who ran the business units. Each of the 40 business units consisted of a major oil or gas field or a group of co-located fields. We pushed decision-making and resource control down to the individual managers of these units. This was not simply a reshuffling of the cards, as many company reorganisations might appear to outsiders. It was a move that would radically change the way people thought about and actually did business. Much of this reorganisation and culture change has been well documented in business case studies and other books.[6]

People work better when they know that they, personally, have made something possible rather than feeling that they are just employed to do something for someone else, as "hired hands". This was in touch with the times. I had a sense that people did not want to live in a centralised culture of conformity. Everyone recognised the need for clear direction and limits, but they wanted to manage their own agenda and to be entrepreneurs, even in a large company. To achieve that, everyone needed to understand exactly what they had to do to create value, had to see the result of their actions and, importantly, would stand accountable for the results they created and take the consequences, good or bad. People needed to say what they were going to do, get this agreed, and then get it done. And that was the purpose of performance contracts.

Business unit managers agreed performance contracts directly with me, in a session that was wide-ranging. It covered not only what their business units could do but also an evaluation of what they had previously done, and their view of themselves and their staff. It was as much about coaching managers in the techniques of management as it was about operational and financial performance. The agreed performance contracts empowered them to deliver, making their own decision on things like suppliers, staff and when and how to drill. And when it came to relationships with suppliers and governments, the business unit managers were tasked with the job of forging relationships which could enable them to do business with the same party again and again. Good and lasting business should never give one party an unfair advantage.

To ensure support across the assets and to avoid building barriers between them, we created "peer groups". These were based on the life stage of the asset. Although the assets in a peer group were geographically dispersed, they were likely to face similar issues. Within each peer group, we encouraged assets to call on support from individuals with relevant expertise. There was no reward for this. The process worked because of a cultural shift valuing mutual interdependence and collaborative learning. Peer group members could challenge each other on targets they intended to recommend for their performance contracts; this further fostered a culture of knowledge sharing and collective responsibility.

We invested in extensive educational and training activities. These allowed us to check the quality of the management and ensure that they understood their roles and responsibilities. That would prove to be even more important as BP expanded and we had to ensure that distant operations were run safely and in line with strategy. We also invested in measurement and information systems. We developed one of the first knowledge management systems. Learning is at the heart of a company's ability to adapt to a rapidly changing environment so I wanted BP to be able to capture, share and apply knowledge faster and more widely.

One aspect of this entrepreneurial approach was to encourage innovation and breakthrough thinking. I asked people to challenge the status quo and to look for a better way to achieve objectives. That led to the development of the Andrew field in the North Sea, which had been dormant for 17 years and had been studied by a couple of generations of engineers, including me in the late 1970s. We got government, contractors and BP working together, rather than against each other, by implementing incentive systems which aligned everyone around one goal.

Another example was at Wytch Farm in Poole, England. We were planning to build an artificial island in Poole Harbour to drill part of the oil reservoir. We had mounted a campaign to get a Private Members' Bill through the House of Commons to allow us to do this. The oil in the Wytch Farm field extended under the outer limits of the harbour; the only way to recover it was to drill wells in that area. So creating an island seemed the best option because wells could not be drilled from the shore. At least, that was what people thought.

But the island seemed a very bad idea. Poole Harbour is one of the world's largest, and most beautiful, natural harbours and the site of a sensitive ecosystem. So we needed to invent a new technology to recover the oil.

Using our experience, we developed a method to drill wells, starting from the land and reaching out into the harbour. This is called "extended-reach drilling". The length of the well was a world record. And we did not need to build the island.

News of the success of performance contracts reached the ears of a young politician, Tony Blair. We had started talking when he was leader of the opposition as he was keen to learn from business. He was looking, in particular, for a way of ensuring that political commitments were delivered. Our conversations were mostly about how to get individuals and teams to meet targets. I explained what we were doing.

"In BP, performance contracts are just a way of agreeing what you are going to do. Because targets are written down and personalised, people feel committed. We keep the contracts short and simple, and with only a handful of meaningful targets."

I have a penchant for things in fours, whereas Blair seemed to talk in fives.

"You can have five targets if you like, but ten is too many," I told him.

I also explained that if you set the wrong targets you get the wrong results; the targets must be designed to achieve the required outcome and in the right way. Some years later, hospital waiting lists in the UK proved the point. The target was achieved as the lists were indeed reduced. But this was done by spending less time with each patient and did not achieve the best outcome for patients.

I did not realise the media storm I would create when I made this point at the World Economic Forum in Davos, 2004. Things have come a long way since then and the understanding of how to target effectively has improved enormously. I still think, however, that you cannot assume that the techniques used to get businesses to perform are the right ones for the public sector. The goals of public service are not tied together with a single objective. In business, that objective is sustainable profitability. Without that a business will disappear.

A new exploration strategy, new organisational strategy and a new way of thinking led to a step change in the performance of the upstream business. We went to places which previously would have been unthinkable: Algeria, Azerbaijan, Kazakhstan, Venezuela and Vietnam. And we expanded our operation in the deep waters of the Gulf of Mexico using drilling technology which only years earlier would have been in the realm of science fiction. We tried to get into Russia, but that would take more than one attempt.

In late 1994, David Simon, then CEO of BP, wandered into my office one day and told me that the board had decided I would take over as CEO when Lord Ashburton stepped down and he stepped up to become chairman. It was a great piece of news but, curiously, the day felt no different from the one before. This was just another step; I had never had to apply for the next job in BP, I just got promoted. It was only later that I realised how big the job was and that it would occupy almost every waking moment. My life would be under the control of the company and, in many ways, under the control of other people.

The transition was smooth. David was there to guide and coach, and my team members were the peers I had worked with over the previous five years. We were to carry on with managing the company as we had previously done.

But despite the continuity, it did not mean everything had to stay the same.

Changing the game

10 June 1995: I knew even before the day I took over as CEO that we had to change the game. BP was stuck as a "middleweight insular British company". It was either up or out.

There was no doubt that the financial and organisational disciplines we had put in place had secured the short-term improvements but we were still unable to compete against the top tier of the industry. We did not have the size to give us the strength and endurance to withstand the volatile trading environment while making investments which took a long time to pay back.

There were many important missing pieces or strategic gaps. We had inadequate natural gas reserves relative to competitors. In the US and European downstream businesses we had weak competitive positions and poor returns. Our portfolio was too narrow in chemicals. We had insufficient access to growth markets, and limited exposure to Asia. For BP to compete on the global stage we needed scale and reach.

David and I agreed that organic growth could only take us so far. The obvious solution was a merger or acquisition. The timing was right. Oil prices were low. In our view, the industry structure was unsustainable as low oil prices meant oil companies could not deliver shareholder returns comparable to other industries.[7] Costs needed to come down and even more focused strategies pursued. Consolidation seemed inevitable.

For a new CEO, embarking on such a strategy was a big gamble but we had no other options. The decision seemed very straightforward. Three years previously, BP's weak share price had made it ripe for takeover. Some would say we were lucky to have remained independent then. And even in 1995, despite significant improvements, our share price was still relatively low. If BP had not actively sought to merge with another company, it was my firm view that we would have been taken over.

David and I agreed if that we moved first we could pick the partner we wanted and drive the process. But before we had an opportunity to engage, we risked losing the lead.

Cor Herkstroter, chairman and CEO of Shell, called me: "I wonder if you would like to get together for a chat?"

I immediately saw this as code for "I wonder if you would like to get together as a business?" Shell was an admirable company but this was a most disagreeable prospect. Nonetheless the best way to deal with it and keep Shell at bay was to keep talking. So I flew to The Hague in some secrecy and had dinner with Herkstroter and then kept the discussion going with a further dinner.

I was also invited to Shell's senior leadership conference to talk about what we were doing in E&P. This was highly unusual because we were major competitors, but I was happy to go and present what we were doing in some areas such as outsourcing and research.

Luckily for BP the conversations did not get very far. For Shell it would have been a cheap way of getting a presence in E&P areas missing from their map. There would have been lots of issues to resolve and these slowed down the discussions.

September 1996: The board meeting at the Four Seasons Hotel in Berlin was a turning point for BP.

Over two days I presented the plan, which had been worked on for some time, notably by the creative genius of David Allen, the planning manager, and Ellis Armstrong, his deputy. It outlined how we would go about a significant merger. I made it clear that if BP was going to be among the top tier we had to step up to the game.

Admittedly I was a little nervous about talking to the board on the subject of mergers. BP had taken some knocks in the previous five years. With the cost-cutting exercise and redundancies, there had been some tough moments. And the board had been presented with several merger ideas by Bob Horton. The ideas were not liked because the board believed that BP was doing well by itself and we should "not rock the boat". That same thinking would return, but not for at least a decade.

My big worry was that the board would dismiss these ideas, too. They might even think we had lost our senses and try to put us back in our box and tell us to just get on and attend to the day-to-day.

But David Simon "got it", as did non executive director Chuck Knight, chairman of Emerson Electric, and with their support the board began to see the logic.

BP needed both physical and technological economies of scale. We could employ our technology over a larger number of assets and thus get more value from it. As a big company we could drill more wells than a smaller company and hence we could learn far more through greater experience. The bigger we were the more we could leverage knowledge and experience and do the same things better. So scale and reach seemed like virtues worth having just on this basis.

But there was more. We believed governments of oil-producing nations would increasingly prefer to work with very big and influential oil companies. They did not think small was beautiful – that was clear when you spoke to them. They wanted to see a big balance sheet, global political clout and technological prowess, and they wanted to be sure that you would be around for a long time.

In the Four Seasons Hotel, discussions continued in and out of the formal meeting, in twos and threes, but the upshot was agreement to pursue a merger strategy and we set our course.

First choice was Mobil. Second choice was Amoco. And third was ARCO.

Courting Mobil

Mobil was the obvious first choice. Around this time we had started a joint venture with Mobil combining both our competitively weak European downstream operations. By combining these refining and marketing activities – including terminals, tanker fleets, refineries, depots and retail sites – together we got a bigger share of the market, significantly reduced costs and improved returns.

Neither side saw it as a first step to total integration but it was a good start. So, following the Berlin meeting, I began to chat to my friend Lou Noto.

Lou, chairman and CEO of Mobil, and I started to meet regularly. We had always got on well. A warm, friendly person and "bon viveur", Lou smoked cigars, as I did then. We talked, we planned, but without any conclusion. BP's board was keen to take the discussions to the next stage and we got lawyers and bankers involved. Many secret meetings concluded with a big session in the offices of the law firm, Davis Polk, in New York. Much was agreed but it soon became clear that Lou did not have his board with him.

BP had proposed a merger of equals with a complex structure, a dual-holding company which would satisfy internal and external opinions.

But Mobil had a developing view that theirs was a better business and their future was better than ours. When the price of oil recovered to a small degree, discussions ceased.

28 March 1997: I had the final meeting with Lou in Mobil's plane hangar in Washington DC. It was clear that we could go no further. I felt I had wasted a lot of time and effort. I flew back to the UK with my policy adviser, Nick Butler, in silence. As we landed, I said to him: "Well, we'd better think of something else."

So we did. Amoco was our next target.

When we started looking seriously at Amoco the price of oil was collapsing. My view was that we had to use the uncertainty and the low oil price to our advantage. Would Amoco be interested in talking to BP? We had no idea how they viewed their future. To us the two businesses seemed a good geographic and strategic fit, but would their view be the same?

What appealed to us was that Amoco was very much a US business and it would give us access to great US refining and marketing operations and US natural gas production.[8] We knew we were stronger on the global E&P side. Amoco had not found anything noteworthy, despite significant investment in exploration. They had some good assets, including oil discoveries in the Gulf of Mexico, the North Sea and Trinidad, and a strong petrochemicals business. Like us they would be hurt by the low oil price. Natural gas in the US was cheap but we believed it was about to increase dramatically.

I suggested to the board that I pick up the phone and find out what Larry Fuller was thinking. I did not know him well.[9] Nonetheless, it seemed like a good way to ask him for a meeting and so I did.

That is how I came to call Larry in February 1998. When we first met at Kennedy Airport, I soon understood that my phone call had been timely. As it turned out Amoco did not see much future upside in the industry and so were interested in exploring options, including merging. After years of unsuccessful explorations and, in particular, the reduced value of its significant gas production because of very low gas prices, Amoco was a company that had lost its way. Larry and I agreed, at the end of that first meeting, to get our lawyers and bankers involved.

We then met as often as possible. Details were discussed over many dinners at London's landmark restaurant, Pont de la Tour, where we could meet unnoticed in a private room. Larry could smoke his cigarettes and we could all drink Puligny-Montrachet. If two "Big Oil chiefs" had been spotted together there would have been much speculation, but remarkably no one noticed.

This was to be a merger although it was not a joining of equals. BP was the bigger party; matched against Amoco, the ratio was 60:40 rather than 50:50. But the decision on how to combine ultimately depended on practicalities. Initially discussions were on the basis of a dual-headed structure in two locations, as different expressions of the same underlying company.

Ben Stapleton, from one of our advisers Sullivan & Cromwell, and, in my view, one of the best lawyers in the world specialising in mergers and acquisitions, said such a structure would not work for tax and other reasons. And it became increasingly clear that BP did not need to concede on this point. I had never really liked the idea and, as the talks progressed, I realised we were far bigger, much stronger and so had more cards. Amoco was desperate to do the deal and we had in effect thrown them a lifeline. This would be their way out.

A week before the deal was announced, on a hot August afternoon, I called Larry from my home in South Eaton Place, London. The whole BP merger team was there. I had ten people drinking Coca-Cola, talking on my phones and making a mess. There was huge tension in the air. Months of negotiation now hung on a single point.

I told Larry we could not do the dual structure. "This only works if it's a British company, based in London, and we get one more director on the board. That's it. Let me know in the next 24 hours if you are happy, otherwise the deal is off."

We all waited in my house. The tension increased. A few hours later the phone rang. It was Larry and he agreed. The deal was on.

Across at Amoco's headquarters in Chicago, they had about a dozen people working on the deal. BP had about the same number on the front line. But we also had a whole team working behind the scenes not only on the merger transaction but, importantly, also preparing for post-merger integration. The lesson learned from the Sohio and Britoil acquisitions was that it was important to have a plan for the day after as well as the day itself. More than 250 people in BP knew about the deal. The sense of trust and deep responsibility meant no one talked.

11 August 1998: The deal was kept so completely under wraps that when we made the announcement, on a bright August day at the

Honourable Artillery Company in London, it took the world by surprise. The new company was to be called BP Amoco and Larry would stay on for a year as co-chairman. It was front-page news with headlines such as: "The biggest industrial deal of all time" and "The UK's largest company created". And it catapulted BP into the top tier of the industry.[10] The share price rose dramatically and the increase even touched 60 per cent at one point.

By the time the deal was completed on 31 December, oil had reached a low of below $10 a barrel. A well-developed plan for merger integration was then implemented with what seemed to be military precision. But a sharp and painful lesson seven years later would make me realise that, at least in one place, our integration with Amoco did not go deep or far enough. I will return to this later.

The BP Amoco deal triggered merger agreements which consolidated and reshaped the industry, creating a new group of what the analysts called "Supermajors". It was as if the industry had been standing by waiting for someone to make the first move; it felt like we had broken a dam. Exxon reacted swiftly by making a move for Mobil on 1 December 1998, even before the BP Amoco deal was completed. Other mergers followed to reshape the industry: Chevron merged with Texaco, Conoco with Phillips, and Total with Fina and Elf. Only Shell would stand apart.

When the dust settled, I spoke to Lou Noto and asked him whether he would have preferred BP or Exxon. He told me: "BP, of course, but I couldn't make it work. When you bought Amoco it was inevitable that Exxon would buy us. It was only a matter of time."

ARCO and trouble with the US Federal Trade Commission

But almost before the ink was dry on the BP Amoco deal, another interesting call came through to my office.

This time it was Mike Bowlin, chairman and CEO of ARCO. He got straight to the point. "We would like BP to buy ARCO." It seemed too good to be true.

The Atlantic Richfield Company (ARCO) simply wanted to drop into the lap of BP. Mike told me that he had agreed with his board that he should sell the company. The rationale was that there was no room for ARCO to compete in a period of low oil prices. Oil was at $10 a barrel. Media commentators were focused on how low the price might go – would it reach $5? *The Economist* predicted it would go to that level and stay there.[11]

Mike said that there was a good fit between our two companies in assets and culture; selling out to BP offered a rational exit strategy. It all seemed so logical. The only outstanding issues were price and conditions – so we thought.

1 April 1999. We announced that BP and ARCO would combine in a $26.8 billion deal.[12]

Shareholders of both companies approved the deal, as did the European Commission's competition watchdog. But what we had not anticipated was that we would run into trouble with the US regulators. And I had made a big mistake. To minimise uncertainty, ARCO had included a "hell or high water" clause. I had agreed that the contract to purchase ARCO was almost unconditional.

ARCO and BP each had sizeable positions on the North Slope of Alaska, and one of the main attractions of the deal was the opportunity for synergies from combining North Slope production. This took me back to the start of my career with BP in Alaska. ARCO had been one of the companies that had first discovered oil in Alaska in 1968. Both ARCO and BP had gained new life from their collaboration in Alaska and now their future would be together.

But the Federal Trade Commission (FTC) said the deal would violate antitrust laws on the basis of a theory that the merger would give BP an unacceptable level of market control, because controlling 75 per cent of Alaskan North Slope oil production would allow BP to charge higher prices for oil sold to West Coast refiners. The open question was whether they had a case.

BP argued strongly against this theory, on the basis that the price of oil was set in the international market, and any attempt by BP to raise the price of supply to West Coast refineries would simply cause them to source supplies elsewhere. Jeremy Bulow, director of the FTC bureau of economics, apparently agreed.[13] But soft-spoken Robert Pitofsky, chairman of the FTC, did not.

All our advisers had told us that the ARCO merger would not be a problem. Now it appeared to be just that – and a big one, too. Our error was in not thinking through all the possibilities, but then if you could foresee all the potential obstacles you would never do anything.

We believed that the difficulties we were facing were more about the industry context than about the FTC's case. There was a shift in public mood around this time, to which the FTC was sensitive. The series of prominent mergers had aroused concern about growing concentration in the oil industry. I think, too, there was particular unease in the US at a foreign company taking over a second major US oil company. And the difficulties were exacerbated by disclosures of email exchanges within BP relating to the trading of oil; these reinforced the FTC's position.

The question was whether to take the FTC to court or try to negotiate with them. We knew that the court process would take too much time and in any event we were bound to proceed with the deal with ARCO. So I undertook a prolonged and intense negotiation with FTC chairman Pitofsky.

It took more than a year for the FTC to finally approve the BP Amoco/ARCO deal. We had to agree to sell ARCO's Alaskan assets and we subsequently sold them to Phillips Petroleum.

This made the merger significantly less attractive to BP, although we got some good downstream assets in California and leases in the Gulf of Mexico, North Sea and Indonesia. The ARCO deal should have been a blockbuster. The FTC intervention made it more ordinary. I recognised that I had no choice but to accept it and move on. From a personal perspective it was a real blow; it was my first setback as CEO. It made me very aware that, no matter how simple and attractive an opportunity may appear on the surface, you have to think deeply about all eventualities.

Nevertheless, it was a new millennium and, with the acquisition of ARCO, BP Amoco was now a bigger, stronger business. It would become leaner and fitter as it safely pared its activities down to the essential, realising more than the promised economies of scale. This, combined with the fact that the Amoco merger took place when the price of oil was in single digits, generated an enormous amount of value for BP shareholders. We discovered hidden value in both the Amoco and ARCO deals. With the Amoco deal we got Trinidad and Tobago, which turned out to be one of the combined group's "crown jewels"; we increased production there by a factor of four. We also grew the US natural gas business significantly. And we realised significant value from Tangguh in Indonesia, the Gulf of Mexico and the North Sea – all through the ARCO deal. In both deals, synergies achieved were much greater than expected.

And a further acquisition in 2000 would take the company full circle. As part of the ExxonMobil deal, we had to unravel our joint venture with Mobil in Europe, which then left us without a worldwide recognised lubricants brand. Castrol was the last-remaining independent lubricants brand. So we started discussions with the chairman of Burmah Castrol, Jonathan Fry, and we bought the company.

When the deal was completed on 7 July 2000, it was an extraordinary moment. Ninety-five years earlier Burmah Oil, a small Scottish company based in Glasgow, had come to William Knox D'Arcy's aid when he ran out of finance during his early explorations in Persia. When Anglo-Persian Oil Company (the company which eventually became BP) started trading in 1909, Burmah Oil owned 97 per cent of the company.[14] Now BP owned Burmah Castrol.

5

CALIFORNIA

Climate

19 May 1997: You would expect the temperature in Northern California in mid May to be around 20° C. That day it must have been touching 30° C. I had been CEO of BP for just two years and I was now about to deliver what would turn out to be a seminal speech on climate change and alternative energy.[1] I was aware of the blistering heat; it was as if the sun wanted to demonstrate its ultimate power.[2]

Staging the event outdoors had seemed a good idea during the planning phase in the London office. The impressive open-air Frost amphitheatre at Stanford University would accommodate the large audience and we could erect demonstration solar panels around the auditorium – old hat now, but then still quite new. But I had not reckoned on the sun.

As the audience began to wilt, they hardly needed me to talk about science showing average temperatures were rising.

My starting point was the common interest and shared responsibility that people, institutions, employees and consumers had for the global environment, as citizens of one world.

One world. It was more than seven years since the fall of the Berlin Wall. People had witnessed the collapse of communism in Europe and the break-up of the Soviet bloc. We were living in very different times and I alluded to two views of history that had been put forward, that of Francis Fukuyama with *The End of History*[3] and that of Jacques Delors, then President of the European Commission, who had talked about the *Acceleration of History*.

"History has neither accelerated nor stopped. But it has changed," I said. And BP wanted to be very much part of that change. I announced that since the link between man-made carbon emissions and global warming could not be discounted, BP had decided that it was time "to go beyond analysis to seek solutions and take action".

On that day, a Big Oil company broke ranks with the rest of the oil industry. We took our first tentative steps to going green. BP was then at the start of a very different road. And it was only a start.

Two options would have been possible in response to the emerging challenge of climate change. One would have been dramatic, sudden and surely wrong. Actions which sought, at a stroke, drastically to restrict carbon emissions or even ban the use of fossil fuels would have been unsustainable because they would conflict with the world's desire for economic growth. The second option, the one we chose, would be a journey taken in partnership by all those who wanted to get involved. We would get started on a step-by-step process involving both action to develop solutions and continuing research to build knowledge through experience.

Cynics would say, since BP is in the oil business, I was unlikely to be a proponent of the first option. "We must stop using fossil fuels," was a demand I had heard many times. But, like it or not, the reality was that we were going to be dependent on oil for many years to come. There was no viable alternative. And even if there were, how could we in the developed world turn round to other countries and deprive them of a key source of revenue? How could we deny people all over the developing world the opportunity to have fuel for heat, light and mobility? Both would be morally wrong and politically futile.

On that scorching hot May morning I expressed the view that business can play a key role in finding and delivering new ways of achieving both environmental stability and economic prosperity. The two must be inextricably linked. I saw BP as the right vehicle to turn such a possibility into reality. Our global reach enabled us to cross borders and cultures, encompass diverse regulation and policy and spread best practice effectively.

Through practical, focused research we could identify and develop alternative energy sources and test the different possibilities in commercial markets. Meanwhile, in order to satisfy growing world demand, we had to continue with oil and gas. But we had to do this a lot better.

Understanding the issue

In some ways BP had ventured on to this road seven years before that Stanford speech. We were just unsure of the direction we were taking.

Then, as a leading oil and gas company, we were very aware of both our need to be safe and to protect the environment. Bob Horton wanted to position BP in a leadership role in these areas. He was anxious to do the right thing and got BP involved in the Earth Summit in Rio in 1992.[4] Was BP "the" environmental leader or "an" environmental leader in the oil industry? There had been quite a debate; the executive management danced on a pinhead trying to work out where we should be.

Our discussions became more intense as the "environment" began to encompass the issue of global warming. But many people said that climate change was not proven. One of the problems was noise in the data. It was difficult to isolate cause and effect. However, it was clear from an early stage that climate change was a large, complex challenge involving uncertainty and probability, just like many business challenges. A considered judgement was needed.

I began to interrogate my team and outside experts. What does the science tell us? What happens if this is true? How much damage are we doing? What are we going to do about it as a company? How long have we got?

I started with our own scientists. David Jenkins, then BP's head of technology, said: "You know, as we are in an interglacial period, we either warm up or chill down. But I do have a feeling that what humans are doing now is really affecting the rate at which the earth is warming."

Jake Jacoby, a world expert on global environmental issues at the Massachusetts Institute of Technology (MIT), gave me a perspective on what was happening in the US. At the time, more of BP's assets were located in the US than in any other country. The US was crucial to our future. And the US was then emitting around 25 per cent of the world's greenhouse gases.

I had a couple of private meetings with President Clinton to get a more rounded picture of US policy. You cannot help being overawed by Clinton's presence, charisma and focus; he creates a sense that he is dealing only with you and effortlessly remembers every individual and detail. I felt that on climate change Clinton was being pulled in two opposite directions. I began to see the tension between what the Clinton administration wanted and what US industry was prepared to do. The administration was clearly keen on taking action on the environment, but US industry was concerned about what this would mean and how it would impact their business.

Many of the wider US population saw climate change as an important issue. But they did not want it solved at their expense, certainly not at cost to their own lifestyle alone – and definitely not with other nations, chiefly China, taking a free ride.

After the Kyoto Treaty in 1997, I was invited, with other business people, by Clinton to meet with his Cabinet to discuss what industry was doing on climate change and what actions the US government should take.[5] Punches were pulled, or at least the gloves seemed very soft. I think Clinton genuinely believed that the US could meet the Kyoto targets but was neither convinced nor prepared to persuade everyone that the US economy would not be damaged. This was one of the reasons why the treaty was not ratified by the US.

Before giving the 1997 Stanford speech, I met with George W. Bush, then Governor of Texas. At that time he seemed to take a positive stance on mitigating climate change. His view clearly changed once he was in the White House. In the end, because so many other nations did not like him, Bush's resistance to Kyoto inadvertently made the Treaty more significant to the rest of the world.

These and other discussions made me determined that BP should never be labelled a "free rider". They also helped me to reach the view that climate change was far too big and complex to be solved by any one group in isolation.

So I began talking to environmental NGOs in the US and Europe. I wanted to see the issue from their side and to ensure we avoided being viewed as simply good at rhetoric. Any time BP identified a problem, I was keen to say that we had also identified a solution.

One of the most influential US NGOs was highly sceptical. It was the Pew Center, headed by Eileen Claussen.[6] Eileen was a very seasoned player and she wondered about the credibility of a Big Oil company coming along saying they had come out of denial. She was, however, at least prepared to enter into a refreshing dialogue. Her approach was constructive. The Pew Center's standpoint, that protecting the climate and economic growth are not mutually exclusive, aligned with mine. And so they gave us ideas of what actions BP might take and their likely impact.

The Pew Center's view was not shared by many. For most, particularly the oil industry, talk of climate change was considered as scaremongering and a threat to the very existence of their business. They became very concerned as the NGOs were starting to point the finger at them. "Culprit" was the accusation, as the link between the burning of fossil fuels and rising levels of carbon in the atmosphere was made.

BP decided that it had to distance itself from the rest of the industry. For a start we had to get out of the Global Climate Coalition.

The Global Climate Coalition had been set up by the American Petroleum Institute (API) in 1989 to lobby against anything that might adversely affect the oil industry when it came to climate change.[7] Being a member of API, BP was signed up to the Global Climate Coalition by default. We often did not agree with the actions of the coalition and were increasingly concerned about the amount of lobbying under way. On more than one occasion I asked our API representative to get a rebate on our membership fee because we wanted to opt out of the campaigns. We did not get a rebate. I decided there was no question; BP had to leave. And we eventually did so in 1997.

In 1996 the Intergovernmental Panel on Climate Change (IPCC) published its second report.[8] I felt we could no longer ignore the issue of climate change. Internally the debate was whether we could go out and admit the possibility that fossil fuels were creating global warming. Would that be like the cigarette companies admitting that smoking causes lung cancer? How would our industry colleagues react? And how would our customers feel?

We asked the IPCC for a number of meetings. John Houghton, co-chairman of the scientific assessment group, came into BP's London office several times.[9] He educated us. You simply could not ignore his passion and credibility; John spoke in our language of probabilities. The IPCC data was – and still is – voluminous, complex and incomplete. And in many ways it will never be conclusive. As Karl Popper[10] noted, almost all science is provisional and research can never end.[11] It is all about uncertainty and probability and, with climate change, about scale and response.

The IPCC had run a series of models and these demonstrated that mankind was doing something that was very likely to put its future existence at risk. That concern triggered a much bigger question in my mind about the fundamental purpose of business. I firmly believed that BP should do more than just focusing on short-term profits to maximise shareholder value. Profit was important but how we contributed to society in making that profit was just as important.

I was also concerned about how people viewed the industry. In a speech at an oil and gas industry conference in Houston in 1996, I said: "It's an industry, so they say, which has remained stuck in the century in which it was born – the 19th century. They say the industry damages environments and communities and that it generates pollution and waste. They say those involved in the industry are secretive, arrogant and driven solely by profit."

My deputy, Rodney Chase, was a great ally. He understood; he was very involved with the World Business Council for Sustainable Development (WBCSD) and became the organisation's chairman in 1995.[12] He and I were determined to set BP on a new path, and position it as a force for good, while improving its profit potential.

Rodney said: "You can't motivate people to get up every day and come through those doors just to increase shareholder value."

He was right. Taking a lead on climate change had some big benefits in terms of having a voice in the debate and employee motivation. We needed the oil industry to offer a career, excitement, challenge and that intangible but crucial reward of *pride* for employees and potential employees. If we were seen as dirty, old-fashioned and short on ethics or environmental principles, we would not be able to attract the brightest and best of the next generation.

But for me there was a much bigger issue at stake. This was a strategic imperative for BP.

If the needs of society were changing, and we were in the business of meeting that need, we had to change, too. If the scientists were right about climate change being in some way caused by carbon emissions, then our industry was unsustainable in its current form. At that industry conference in 1996 I said: "The industry, they believe, is in decline. Shrinking. Being overtaken by other sources of energy and vulnerable to the fall of the last bastion of demand – the transport sector." With that air of doubt, the imperative was to work out how to turn BP into a sustainable business.

One of the first steps was to convince the board. That was not easy. Some felt there was no need for BP to go out on a limb; we should just ignore the issue. One of the key non executive directors was Robin Nicholson.[13] He had been scientific adviser to the Prime Minister, Margaret Thatcher, and she had already spoken of the need to combat climate change. Robin clearly knew how to get action taken on important issues.

David Simon, then BP chairman, was supportive but was concerned at how the big players in the oil industry would react. He told me: "You know if you start to support climate change, Lee Raymond is likely to come over and lecture you about how you've got it all wrong." Lee was chairman and CEO of the world's biggest oil company, Exxon.

Innovation

We needed a deadline to make something happen. Organisations, large and small, like to avoid making difficult decisions. They hope that somehow the decisions will make themselves. They do not. So I decided to force the pace by giving a speech to the outside world. It was to become the speech at Stanford in May 1997.

I discussed the idea with Michael Spence, the dean of Stanford graduate school of business. Although Mike was not at Stanford when I was there in 1980, I was chairman of his advisory board for the first six of the ten years of his tenure (1990–96). I had grown to know, like and, most importantly, trust him. He was a good sounding board.

Some years earlier I had discussed with Mike how I might maintain my involvement with the West Coast in the US after leaving the advisory board. I wanted to keep in touch with the rapidly changing technology and thinking. Mike suggested that I become an independent director of a little-known company called Cisco, or a slightly better known, but smaller, company called Intel. I had met Andy Grove, one of the founding employees of Intel, and was very impressed with him and what he was doing, taking the company deeper into the new microprocessor area and out of the manufacturing of memory chips.

Andy and I met again and, after what I eventually realised was a typical interrogation, I was introduced to the senior founder and chairman of the board, Gordon Moore. It was clear from him that there was no limit to the future. *Electronics* magazine had quoted Gordon in 1965 as saying that the power of microprocessors would double every 18 months. This became known as Moore's Law.

My final interview took place when I met Arthur Rock, some say the inventor of venture capital. He was an early investor in Apple, Microsoft and Intel. Arthur is a shrewd businessman and understands that fine line between engineering perfection and profitability. He also understands what motivates people. We met when he was in London and he pleasantly asked me why I wanted to be part of Intel. I told him it was so I could help them become global and they could help me learn. They took me on. They were very US-focused then; now they are mainly in "most of the world" outside the US. And I learnt a lot.

Andy Grove firmly believed that only the paranoid survive.[14] He predicted that there would be a billion connected personal computers within a decade. He could see the power of the IT revolution. He believed in the power of strategy, in discussing and communicating it widely and then implementing it. That, and his out-of-the-box thinking, altered my approach to many things in BP.

And so because of this, California was the obvious location for the speech. We booked the date, agreed the venue and invited the guests. The die was cast.

No other speech in BP has probably undergone so much scrutiny and so many iterations. I was the chief executive of an oil company and I was about to become an environmental activist. The message had to be clear and there had to be no doubt that BP was set on creating a new future. I was also very aware that, no matter how well a speech is written, people do not always hear what you intend to say.[15]

Alan Watson,[16] then chairman of Burson Marsteller, was a great friend and I asked for his advice. As a former BBC *Panorama* presenter and a communications expert, Alan was both witty and honest. His view was: "It's a very good paper but it won't persuade anyone. It doesn't give people a reason to believe you. You need examples. You need to demonstrate that you are going to do things differently."

More rewriting and more rehearsing followed. By the time I walked up to the Stanford podium I was confident the message was right.

I committed BP to five specific actions to get us started on the road: first, to reduce our own carbon emissions (a Kyoto-style target of reducing carbon emissions to 10 per cent below the 1990 baseline by 2010); second, to fund research and development to create greater understanding about the issues; third, to take initiatives for joint development of activities in the developing world to reduce carbon emissions in those countries; fourth, to develop alternative fuels and energies for the future; and lastly, to contribute to the public policy debate in the search for wider global solutions.

Rarely have I known journalists stuck for words. But on that blisteringly hot morning, my sense was that few reporters seemed able to frame a decent question. It was as if they did not know what to ask and were unsure as to how they should report the news.

Some welcomed BP's action; most said it had not gone far enough. Comments ranged from: "BP's stance sets a higher standard against which to judge other companies' readiness to co-operate with governments to fight climate change"[17] to "Browne, not heretofore known as a flower child, also talked about solar power".[18]

We were less interested in what the media said than in getting our message out to thought leaders. Eileen Claussen came along and, as I expected, she maintained her open mind. "Well, I won't buy it all, but I'll watch what you do," she told me.

Within the oil industry, the API accused us of "leaving the church". David Simon was right. Chief executives of other oil companies did come to see me and asked if I had "lost the plot". Lee Raymond had a very clear but very different view to mine and we never agreed on this issue.

Outside the oil industry, the NGOs were vocal. Some were supportive. Others said what we had done was simply "greenwash". Greenpeace were adamant in maintaining their stance that only phasing out oil and gas would stop climate change. They had a point, but I could not agree with it on practical grounds. BP had to start reducing its carbon dioxide emissions. As a business that was ready to commit its resources behind its actions, BP would be an important player to have around the table as the future of carbon was debated. BP did not have an exclusive viewpoint but one that needed to be debated with NGOs. That was good for us and society.

In 1997 BP was out on a limb, but within ten years there was, at least on the surface, a broad consensus on climate change in the industry, even in the US. Among major oil companies, Shell left the Global Climate Coalition[19] shortly after BP, and Chevron and Total now accept the risk of climate change. Economic cycles and legislation will test the reality and the longevity of this.

More recently, a group of NGOs and US businesses came together to form the United States Climate Action Partnership,[20] with the sole aim of countering climate change while continuing to expand the US economy. This partnership has the opposite aim of the now defunct Global Climate Coalition.

Making it happen

Returning to a somewhat cooler London in May 1997, I was aware that I might have announced publicly that we would monitor, measure and reduce our own greenhouse gas emissions. But we had not actually worked out how to do this.

We understood the issue, we recognised the problem and I had created a vision. The next thing was to involve and engage BP's leadership team, about 500 people at the time. We asked for ideas. "Here is the challenge: we want to reduce greenhouse gases. How can we do it?"

I could not simply direct a fundamental shift like this from the top and then move on. I had set a clear direction; there was no substitute for that. But how you create that direction is also important. Setting the context and creating the right boundaries are vital. But you need to allow people the space to determine themselves how things can be done and, importantly, you need to listen and support people while they get on and make things happen. That was the purpose of asking the leadership team.

Not everyone responded, but we did receive some superb ideas from energetic and enthusiastic team members. Some held discussions or workshops and came back with ideas, others replied individually: "This is what we should do. It's about time."

And the ones who did not respond? They were sceptical. They did not believe the science around climate change and did not want BP to have a role in tackling the issue. Slowly the number of sceptics reduced but there were always some, and some were in the top team.

In order to know where to reduce carbon emissions, we wanted to develop a simple emissions trading scheme within the company. It would become the very first of its kind. And the person instrumental in helping us set this up was Fred Krupp, head of the Environmental Defense Fund, an environmental NGO.[21] We had come full circle. This NGO had virtually single-handedly halted the construction of the Trans Alaska Pipeline in the early 1970s.

The emissions trading scheme allocated quotas of emission permits to BP's business units across the world and allowed them to trade with each other. Each business unit had a choice: it could comply with its emission targets by internal actions, or buy emissions permits from other business units. If a unit more than met its targets, it could sell its excess permits to other units that were above their emissions targets.

Targets, measurements, incentives and bonuses; they worked.

In little more than four years, we met our goal of reducing our greenhouse gas emissions by 10 per cent. This was achieved by reducing flaring and venting of natural gas and improving the energy efficiency of our operations. BP generated $650 million of value. It was impressive. We had demonstrated that being environmentally friendly did not mean a trade-off with profitability, quite the opposite.

Like many big problems, tackling carbon emissions was a matter of progressive action. The easy and quick wins, the low-hanging fruit, were taken first while working out what next to do with the more complex and difficult problems. There is danger in waiting for the perfect solution.

A big component of cutting greenhouse gases is making things more efficient; emitting less carbon dioxide means using less energy. But BP was well aware that reducing emissions would require more than just efficiencies. Transportation, for instance, accounts for around 13 per cent of the world's total carbon dioxide emissions.[22] So we worked with our customers on a number of initiatives.[23] For example, in Australia a purchaser of gasoline could make a contribution to forestry by planting a tree rather than receiving a set of free glasses or table mats as a promotion. Individually these were small efforts – some would say like swatting one mosquito to eradicate malaria – but collectively they added up.

In the autumn of 1997, some six months after the Stanford speech, I delivered a similar address in Berlin. It went even further. It was time to say we needed to have not just business involved but governments, too. The important point was that governments should engage with business to understand what is possible. I put forward ideas on incentives for more rapid turnover of capital stock to remove outdated and polluting equipment.

Because of our position we gained a seat at the table of government policy debates, not just with Clinton's Cabinet, but in many different places. This enabled us to contribute and improve our understanding, and spread the best practice in policy formulation. Building on our experience, BP was involved in developing carbon cap and trade policies in the UK in the late 1990s, then carried out the first trades in the UK Emissions Trading System (ETS) when it was launched in 2002, and helped customers trade in the market. The UK ETS went on to inform the European scheme (EU ETS).[24] These will be important markets for the future as the world puts carbon-free and fossil fuel energies on a level playing field.

It was because of this knowledge and understanding that I became involved in discussions in California and got to meet some very distinguished and colourful characters.

A seat at the table

31 July 2006: "Emissions Terminator" Governor Schwarzenegger and the Prime Minister, Tony Blair, were just two of the influential people on the platform with me at Long Beach, California. A BP tanker served as a backdrop for the agreement between the UK and California to collaborate to fight global warming. Part of a major round table on climate change and clean energy, the event involved key business leaders including Richard Branson of Virgin and Sergey Brin of Google.

Schwarzenegger is far more than a movie star; I watched him preparing his speech that day and he was not learning the lines as an actor. When he took the platform, he engaged the audience not merely with a skilled performance but with his own powerful and proficient mix of passion, communication and leadership.

I got to know Schwarzenegger because of BP's big interest in California after we acquired ARCO. The leading retail gasoline brand on the West Coast, with more than 1,400 gas stations, ARCO was the volume supplier in areas such as Southern California and Sacramento, and owner of the *ampm* convenience store brand.

Schwarzenegger and I had a number of things in common; our interest in climate change was one thing, fine cigars another. But merely being a cigar aficionado was not sufficient to warrant an invitation to Schwarzenegger's famed cigar tent. This was where the serious business got done. And so I found myself under the canvas in the Sacramento Capitol's quadrangle as he wanted to pick my brain.

The tent, with its espresso machine, was a good place to puff away while discussing possible climate change programmes and policies. This was in the build-up to AB32,[25] a landmark bill to reduce greenhouse gases in the state.[26] My advice was that for California to succeed it needed: "targets, measurement, incentives – and regulations".

The outcome was that Schwarzenegger announced a target of 25 per cent reduction on 1990 levels in carbon emissions by 2020 – and a more ambitious 80 per cent by 2050. The bill required the California Air Resources Board (CARB) to develop the necessary regulations and market mechanisms and to start to measure emissions. He called on all businesses to "harness their entrepreneurial spirit" to help achieve California's climate change goals.

A month before I left BP, I went to say goodbye to Schwarzenegger. This time we met in his private office where he was surrounded by memorabilia from his *Terminator* films. You cannot help but admire the man. Relaxed and accessible, his underlying determination is not threatening. And in that way he is a great advocate for climate change.

Making progress

26 April 2007: I returned to Stanford to deliver a second speech on climate change, some ten years after the first speech.[27] Climate change was now hard to ignore. I was preoccupied with my own concerns. I was to resign as CEO of BP a few days later. But none of that got in the way of this important task.

The IPCC had just published its fourth assessment report, which stated: "Warming of the climate system is unequivocal ... Most of the observed increase in global average temperatures since the mid-20th century is *very likely* due to the observed increase in anthropogenic greenhouse gas concentrations."[28]

In my speech I said BP had made huge strides from those first small steps in 1997. Actions ranged from research and development in many forms of new energy technologies to developing new low carbon bio-fuels. We had also made significant investments in solar energy, wind power and natural gas. All of BP's interests in developing new energies had been combined into a new business, BP Alternative Energy, in 2005.

I talked about advances in carbon trading, carbon taxes and regulation. I had seen a lot of people searching for a silver bullet, but I believed an effective solution required a combination of many things.

The Stern Review *The Economics of Climate Change* had also recently been published, which provided an understanding about the costs of action or inaction in respect of climate change.[29] I referred to the fact that Stern had said climate change was the greatest market failure: "This will only be solved by the introduction of a market mechanism. Such a mechanism can only be introduced by governments."

I was clear – and my view has not changed – that societies cannot solve climate change on their own. Nor can the business sector succeed in isolation. Only governments can create and police the framework within which true progress can be made.

Today we understand more about the causes of greenhouse gas emissions, more about the effects, and more about the changes that need to take place to mitigate the degree of climate change.

We will still need to use fossil fuels as part of our energy mix for some years to come. But we have reached a position when we might reasonably look forward to a time when energy crises are a thing of the past and where energy is clean and locally generated.

After I left BP, the quest to achieve that would take me to many new and different places. But back in 1995, a very different quest had got me involved in one of the most violent societies in the world.

6

COLOMBIA

Big picture

February 1995: It felt like an enormous milestone. We had reached the official commissioning of the Cusiana production facility, in the lush Llanos foothills of the Andes Mountains.

Going into Colombia had been like stepping into a maze of fire. There was a tantalising prize of rich resources but the polarised society, violent insurrection and dark undercurrents in politics had disorientated me. I had become embroiled in a country more complex than I had ever imagined.

On this day, I tried to put all that out of my mind. In spite of thick perimeter fencing, stringent security and a heavy military presence, it was a moment to celebrate. Here, about 120 miles east of Bogotá, BP had made vital new oil discoveries, which would secure its future beyond its two pipelines, Alaska and the North Sea. Production would soon be on stream, pumping money into the Colombian government, back into development for the local region, and into BP's treasury.

As the largest recent discovery of oil in Latin America, it was a landmark event for the country, attracting many Colombian dignitaries and politicians, including President Samper. Everyone assembled was well aware that getting to this day had not been easy.

I was still the chief executive of the E&P division and my appointment as CEO of BP had already been announced. I had flown over from the UK with BP's chairman, Lord Ashburton, for the event. It was a great surprise to all when he unexpectedly launched into fluent Spanish for his opening speech. The delight on the assembled guests' faces was obvious. He could not have gauged the mood better.

We had gone into Colombia because the pressure was on to find more oil. Existing assets were declining and finding new oil fields was vital to

Colombia was a venture into the unknown

secure the company's future. We had started to look outside our traditional OECD stronghold and in 1987 began to explore an area in the eastern province of Casanare in Colombia. Prospects were good but the geology complex; getting to the depth where the oil was to be found involved drilling to more than 15,000 feet. In 1988, BP completed the first well that hinted at a major oil find but big technical challenges meant the scale of the find was unclear – in fact, so unclear that I was close to selling the property in 1990. I was stopped by a questioning head of exploration, David Jenkins. But by 1991, we confirmed that we had indeed found something very exciting.

It was the first success of the new big field exploration strategy. It seemed like a gift. The Cusiana field, in the eastern province of Casanare, a remote region near the Venezuelan border, offered what we believed was more than one billion barrels of oil reserves.[1] This was followed by the Cupiagua field in 1993, with slightly lower reserves. The oil had been a struggle to find and I knew it would be a technical stretch to develop, but I did not anticipate the struggle in which we would become embroiled.

Perhaps it was because we were foreign and underestimated Colombia's complexity, legal system and intellectual heritage. Or perhaps we just did not appreciate how much there was to know.

Society characterised by conflict

Colombia is characterised by a high level of endemic violence, including guerrilla warfare, paramilitary activity, drug trafficking and narco-terrorism.

For more than half a century,[2] an armed struggle, originally supported by revolutionary Cuba, has been under way between guerrilla groups, right-wing paramilitary groups and the government.

The two large, well-organised, left-wing guerrilla movements, the *Fuerzas Armadas Revolucionarias de Colombia* (FARC) and the smaller *Ejército de Liberación Nacional* (ELN), have been seeking to overthrow the government by armed force since 1964. Their activities are financed by ransom kidnappings and protection rackets. They are part of the "Grand Coalition of Simón Bolívar" of which I doubt Bolívar would have approved.[3]

At the other end of the political spectrum, right-wing paramilitary groups, largely organised in the mid 1990s as the *Autodefensas Unidas de Colombia* (AUC), operate in a similar fashion beyond the law. Their roots are in the vigilante groups organised years ago by landowners as protection against the rebels.

Colombia also reportedly has the largest cocaine industry in the world which, the CIA estimates, supplies the majority of the US and international market. This lucrative drugs trade seems to be linked to many elements of the different armed groups. The civilian population are merely caught in the crossfire and, as a consequence, suffer poverty, violence and displacement.

Yet this conflict sits alongside 5,000 years of extraordinary cultural development. Sixteenth-century Spanish conquistadors were drawn to Colombia in search of legendary riches. Colombia's sophisticated Muisca Indians, for example, developed skills in mining, smelting and working the local gold. Utilitarian and ornamental gold pieces were common-place; many survive today in the country's abundant archaeological museums. The El Dorado legend is said to have its origins in Colombia.[4]

This history is at the heart of the conflict as, like much of Latin America, Colombia developed to become a highly segregated society. There is a marked divide between poor mixed-race Colombians and traditional rich families of mainly Spanish descent, who mostly run the country. I saw clear evidence of this in Bogotá, for example, where vast swathes of "informal housing" are juxtaposed with wealthy guarded properties, housing the great families and works of art.

In the mid 1990s, I was invited to the wedding of BP's company physician in Colombia. As I walked into the monastery, near Cartagena, I could see that the whole refectory was glowing pink with thousands and thousands of roses. Everyone was dressed well and talked of a bright future for business, of pleasure, and of family. No one really talked of Colombia as it was then. With such lavishness and beauty, it was hard to imagine anyone in this country could be poor or corrupt. But that is the danger of impression. With its lush rainforests, vast savannahs, and snow-capped Andes Mountains, Colombia's natural beauty belies the endemic violence.

Colombia had its dark side but it also had its strengths: a thriving business sector; a well-educated, professional class; functioning national institutions; and a long-established democracy, uninterrupted by the coups and military governments of its neighbours. And to the best of our knowledge, Colombia had never defaulted on foreign debt.

Colombia was seen as the big, new, exciting opportunity that could change the company's fortunes. My quarterly report to the board focused on technical and practical issues. How fast could we get the field on stream to start paying back on the investment? How would we process and transport the oil from the field? We had to construct major processing installations in a remote rugged mountainous region, and a 120-mile network of flow lines connecting wells to facilities. We were also involved in the OCENSA pipeline to be constructed across 500 miles of extremely mountainous terrain from Casanare to the Caribbean sea port of Coveñas.

What about security? Thick barbed wire and security personnel were initially the obvious answer. And the army was always close by.

Just as in Alaska, our questions should have gone beyond money and operations and considered the longer-term social and development issues. That learning would come only after violence and hard-won lessons.

My role was to keep everyone aligned – in Colombia and back in the UK – but more than that, I wanted to be involved. At first the board was nervous and reluctant when I said I wanted to go out and see things first-hand. But as we already had people in the field there, I saw every reason to go myself.

On the first of many visits, I flew up to the Cusiana field from the closest large town of Yopal. I was struck by the sheer beauty which opened up before me: the lush territory with sweeping plains, small foothills dotted with forests, and soaring mountains. We spoke to a few of the residents; I had a strong sense that we were not welcome. We would have to work hard to gain people's trust.

In the field

We did not help ourselves. Colombia was far more advanced than we thought. Yet, in spite of the experience in Alaska, we still believed that we were opening up a frontier and could write the rules. The first incident was a near miss with Colombia's environmental laws.

We tried to drill a well without the right permit in what turned out to be a dried-up river bed, not realising that special permission was required. It was an honest mistake but, like many companies stopped in their tracks, we were affronted. We blamed the bureaucratic, legalistic environmental agency rather than recognising that we had actually been in the wrong. Then we became entangled in issues to do with who had what rights over the land we needed for our activities. Everything seemed to be riddled with complexity and confusion.[5]

By now a very seasoned player, David Harding, was heading up the Colombian operation for BP. One of the geologists working for David was Tony Hayward, later to succeed me as BP's CEO. David brought great experience from the Middle East and North Sea. He was able to command the respect of the government and its oil company, Ecopetrol. He was a leader and could get things done.

What he, and others in BP, could not have foreseen was the dramatic change that oil brought to the Casanare area and how swiftly community relations would deteriorate.

Casanare was a new administrative body, only formed as a department by the 1991 constitution, and little more than a peripheral and isolated location in a country of about 42 million people. Before the development of the oil fields, this sleepy backwater had little infrastructure or institutional strength, and minimal central government financial support. Ninety per cent of its economy was based on rural activities such as cattle breeding.

BP's arrival changed everything. The project was massive in relation to the local economy. We brought jobs and infrastructure but the overall impact was not straightforwardly beneficial, since the project changed the relative balance of economic activity and created local inflation. Not everyone was benefiting from the project. The local economy had not yet felt the impact of oil revenues, employment and procurement.

The project had a honeypot effect, attracting a huge inflow of migrant labour, often single young men, with the associated problems of assimilation, housing and prostitution. Some came to get a slice of the oil action, others came to protest. Guerrillas and illegal armed groups came simply to cause trouble and extort money. Despite our efforts to build harmonious relations locally, underground forces were at work to terrorise anyone connected with oil. It was unlike anything any of us had ever experienced before.

In Aberdeen or Alaska, BP would have been far more aware of such imminent problems because our staff would have been deeply integrated into the local community. In Colombia, however, the constant threats of kidnapping or assassination made that sort of contact almost impossible.

During construction, BP facilities and staff were repeatedly attacked by different guerrilla groups operating in the area. BP's facilities were not the only targets of guerrilla attacks. In the early 1990s the strategic Caño Limón-Coveñas pipeline (owned by Occidental and Ecopetrol) was repeatedly blown up.[6]

More than 30 BP contractors were kidnapped, and many police and military guards were killed. We decided it was safer for expatriate staff and Colombian professionals to live "offshore" and fly into Casanare for short stretches. While there, they worked in a protected compound behind a perimeter fence, and travelled around in armoured cars with armed bodyguards. Barbed wire and segregation had seemed a pragmatic solution. But, as it turned out, this approach created an even greater division between BP and the community. You cannot make friends while living behind fences.

As security deteriorated, we recognised we were caught up in one of the most violent societies in the world. There was some discussion with Total as to whether we should get out. BP's press and government affairs people began to say the situation was too difficult to handle. We had made the decision to go into Colombia and I was convinced that it was right to stay to see our endeavour through. That would give BP credibility to do more.

Development and diplomacy

After a while, the Colombian government seemed satisfied with what we were achieving. We were getting production on stream so that revenues could flow through. Security was still a perpetual and serious threat. Agreements with the government on how to tackle this threat were changed repeatedly. This became such an important issue that negotiations were escalated up to the highest level. I had to go to see successive presidents of Colombia. We had difficult and often ethically fraught discussions.

I was adamant that we would never take any actions that could make us look as if we were taking sides in the country's continuing political struggles. We were clear with the government that we would not make any payments that could be interpreted as being used to provide weapons to the military in their conflict with the guerrillas. With no experience of this type of discussion to draw on, we merely kept muddling through.

In 1993, in response to unceasing attacks, President Gaviria created a set of special military units to guard the oil pipelines, production facilities and exploration sites. Oil companies needed to have troops to protect people and plant but there was nothing in the national budget to pay for them. Because of the scale of BP's fields and because we had made the most representations about the lack of security, the president turned to us for money and equipment. Lack of experience and naivety led us to provide some minor non-lethal items. But we quickly realised the serious error and stopped. So then the president established the unfortunately named "war tax" on each barrel of oil produced ($1.10 per barrel) to raise the money.

This created a big dilemma. Because we were producing more than anyone else we found ourselves responsible for paying most of this tax. It would now look as if we were funding lethal aid. What should we do? We decided that we could pay on the narrow basis that this was a "tax" and we had to pay it to stay legal. We also agreed to build accommodation for military units stationed near to our facilities. This was to make sure that the troops, mostly conscripts from poorer families, actually stayed near us and did not wander off. We recognised we were walking an increasingly fine line. We would pay the tax, pay for the accommodation, but not make direct payments for military operations.

President Gaviria seemed fair to deal with but he was followed by President Samper who was not so straightforward; he was alleged to have used money from the drug cartels to finance his presidential campaign. I recall at least one fruitless conversation with Samper, at the presidential palace, *Casa de Nariño*, about landowners who we thought were taking on the guerrillas. It seemed to us that the government and military was taking sides with the right-wing paramilitary and this was resulting in increased violence; BP and the Casanare community, as a result, were caught in the crossfire. We were stuck. Our investment was made and security was deteriorating.

Meanwhile, relations with the local government were getting tense. It took quite a time for the oil revenue to arrive in the region. We tried to get the national government to give Casanare an advance but they would not. We did what we could to expand local employment and services but it was not enough. Resentment built and the guerrillas made more headway.

Kidnappings were our living nightmare. They were undertaken by the guerrillas simply to make money. We knew it was illegal to pay ransom for a hostage's release but of course many companies did. The Colombian government made it clear, after the guerrilla groups expanded in size and effectiveness through extracting protection payments from foreign companies, that BP's licence was dependent upon not making any such payments. To the best of my knowledge, we never did.

In 1994 the residents of El Morro, a small hamlet west of Yopal, launched a blockade of the only road to the main production facility at Cusiana. They demanded more social investment, a paved road and more jobs. After several weeks of negotiations, the blockade was lifted, and activities resumed. But that was not the end of the matter. Subsequently the leader of the community and the blockade, Carlos Arrigui, was murdered at home by gunmen.

It was unclear who exactly had been responsible for the incident – thugs, right-wing vigilantes, or possibly left-wing guerrillas trying to frame BP. The Colombian government launched an investigation, culminating in a report in July 1995 compiled by the Colombian government bodies, which cleared BP of involvement in the incident.[7]

This bad local problem now became a matter of worldwide attention. In Europe there were heightened suspicions of the motives and behaviour of oil companies, following Ken Saro-Wiwa's execution in Nigeria in the autumn of 1995. Accusations about any oil company, especially about human rights, fell on understandably fertile ground.[8]

Media nightmare

May 1996: Negative stories started to appear in the European press about BP's activities in Colombia. The main source was the government report about the El Morro incident. Specific allegations in the news stories included charges that: we were complicit in the assassination of community leaders by the military; we were involved in hiring mercenaries; the military, which BP supported, was aiding and abetting paramilitaries in Casanare; and BP's security contractor was importing arms for the Colombian military and gathering intelligence on individuals opposed to the company.

We were outraged but showing anyone this emotion would not help. We needed to understand how people had come up with all this and to develop a practical response. An internal audit was launched and I asked for a further investigation by the human rights unit of the Colombian prosecutor general's office (*Fiscalía General de la Nación*) into the allegations.

Watching the media campaign gather momentum was rather like being under siege. BP thought it was a responsible company. We were dismayed to find ourselves accused of complicity in human rights abuses, frustrated that we could not refute the charge of complicity with clear and credible evidence and – because fact and assertions were hard to untangle – fearful that we might never actually find out what truth lay behind the allegations.

The situation took an inordinate amount of senior management's time and energy. Up until this point in my career, I had not been fully aware of NGOs. Now I could not ignore them. They became very vocal. We took every allegation seriously and investigated each one. As far as the NGOs were concerned the story was very plausible. Colombia was a lawless place, controlled by drug cartels, where human rights were abused routinely. BP was there and hence complicit in these abuses. To the NGOs it was black and white. We were in the wrong.

The reality was a tapestry of grey areas. How could we explain the complexity of trying to do business in Colombia? The damning press coverage culminated in three extremely negative British television programmes. The storyline was predictable but excruciating – a multinational in league with a brutal military regime, which in turn relied on a shadowy paramilitary to do its dirty work. BP was accused of complicity in human rights violations and, more broadly, of supporting a footprint of oppression in Casanare.

I felt particularly despondent after watching the June 1997 *World in Action* documentary with colleagues in the boardroom. There was little hard evidence to back the allegations. But there was little hard evidence to refute them either. The programmes had been carefully filtered for anything defamatory and relied on emotive circumstantial footage, including blurred images of the Colombian military shooting somebody.

We had been asked for a comment before the programmes were broadcast but chose not to do so because it was clear we could not win any points. A full crisis team, based in London, was set up to manage our response.

Internally, I was briefed to ensure I could respond and not sound defensive. Media people came in to test and rehearse me. One very distinguished interviewer put me through the paces. His opening line was: "Now, Mr Browne, do you like murdering people?" That was the sort of opening line I had to be prepared to counter without blinking.

Did I ever feel personally threatened? There were often small protests outside my apartment but I never felt that people would physically attack me in the UK. In Colombia I had close protection, with my bodyguard, Fritz Fahrenholz, in an adjoining room but alert to my panic button. Fritz, and the other security guards, seemed to have stepped out of *Miami Vice*.

They wore loose Hawaiian floral shirts with revolvers tucked inside the waistband of their trousers. It was some time before I realised that the string bags they carried over their shoulders also contained machine guns.

BP people never went anywhere without close protection. We could never use the same-coloured car for two trips in a row. I only walked freely in Bogotá on one occasion – the day of President Samper's inauguration. The city streets had been sealed off and military sharp shooters were positioned on every building's roof. The everyday danger of crime and violence in Colombia was real, as was brought home to me on two specific occasions.

On one visit I went across to Cartagena, a lovely resort town on the Caribbean coast, which by all appearances seemed safe and unthreatening. The San Pedro Claver square looked particularly inviting. I was keen to see and experience something of the real Colombia so said to the driver: "Do you think we could stop in the square and find a coffee?" Fritz interjected: "Sure we can stop somewhere." He then made a number of hushed calls.

Ten minutes later we arrived at a very modern, remote building with no windows. Inside there were no people – the whole place had been cleared merely so that I had could enjoy a cup of coffee. It was hardly what I had intended.

On another occasion Lord Ashburton was with me in Colombia and we had both expressed an interest in visiting San Augustin, with its extraordinary pre-Columbian stone statues.[9] I had not appreciated how complicated a request this would be, or how dangerous. Not only was the site difficult to access, but it was in a FARC stronghold. So the trip involved a helicopter journey with military escort. We arrived at this stunning archaeological park, reputedly one of the most important ancient sites in Latin America, to find we were alone save for an extraordinary variety of anthropomorphic and zoomorphic figures, some more than 20 feet high, with military sharp shooters on every horizon.

More scrutiny

While we were considering how to resolve the issues with the Colombian community, we were subject to yet more scrutiny. In 1997 the issue of BP's activities in Colombia was investigated by the foreign affairs committee of the UK's House of Commons and raised in the European parliament. We knew we had nothing to hide so invited British and European ministers to visit our Colombian operation.

Some companies freeze in the face of extreme criticism and they are unable to make progress. I was determined that BP would not get dragged down by Colombia. Companies have to be careful not to chase every negative comment. You have to keep things in proportion and only be concerned where comments deeply affect the reputation of the company and its ability to do further business. The only time negative comment should become a company's biggest concern is when the board or executive team knows they have done something wrong. This should have been the case, for example, at Siemens, a large German engineering conglomerate, when senior management knew there was a problem concerning bribes. It was only later that the management admitted the company had violated the Foreign Corrupt Practices Act.[10]

In our case, the criticism continued. It began to affect the share price and it became clear that Colombia, despite our well-managed crisis response, was threatening the company's reputation. Understandably, the board was extremely concerned.

In Colombia less credence had been given to the allegations. Fabricated accusations were commonplace in the polarised environment. Even so, BP was under pressure, particularly since a government report was the source of many of the allegations about BP fostering paramilitary activity, which was exactly what we had suspected rogue elements of the government of doing.

In 1998 the Colombian prosecutor general cleared BP of any wrongdoing.[11] Neither our own internal audit nor the prosecutor found any specific supporting evidence for the serious allegations against the company.

Within BP, some people suspected that the allegations were motivated by a desire – either on the part of a journalist with an agenda, or on the part of ELN – to cause trouble or even frame BP. That same year ELN admitted that its members were responsible for bombing the OCENSA pipeline in October causing a horrific firewall and 78 deaths, almost wiping out an entire village.[12]

Our own investigation found relations with BP were good in some communities but were characterised by wide distrust of BP by many in the communities near the oil fields. At least things were clear. BP was not complicit in human rights abuses but we were widely mistrusted.

Rebuilding trust

The fundamental challenge BP faced was to regain an adequate level of trust in the communities in Casanare. I was unrealistic about how long this would take. I thought we could resolve the issues in a year or two; the long, difficult process took almost a decade.

We had talked at length about how BP and its people must behave consistently with the will of society; that is what people call corporate social responsibility (CSR). We had not, however, understood what to do when corporate responsibility deviated from responsibility to society. In Colombia we learnt that the issues of human rights, land ownership and environmental impact are not add-ons but integral elements which must be well managed to make the business sustainable over the longer term. These elements had to be regarded as actual contributors to profit. They were not simply an expression of BP's "citizenship". With hindsight it seemed so obvious. We now realised we had to ensure we considered social responsibility as an integral part of everyday business operations. That would give us our licence to operate.

In Colombia we had thought we were playing a constructive role in the local society, but we had not understood the complicated tensions that our business had set in motion. In 1998, because of that painful lesson, we determined we would consider the social impact of our business wherever we were.

It was essential for us to have simple principles to guide the way we would do business again and again over many years. BP needed to be able to say what it stood for, and what values it had, in a way that was the same for all places and circumstances.

BP's inability to articulate clearly what it stood for when it found itself in a fast-moving situation of considerable uncertainty had left the company looking insensitive, naive and amateur. David Rice, the individual inside BP who advised on our relationship with NGOs, started to look at statements of corporate values of companies we admired – notably The Body Shop and The Co-operative Group in the UK, and Johnson & Johnson in the US. He assembled an internal group to work together to create a statement of what BP stood for and how we would operate.[13]

That learning meant we had to change our approach completely in Colombia.

BP Colombia had to position itself as a non-partisan local company. This local company had to have a more representative mix of staff with a modern and inclusive outlook, and avoid alignment with any particular faction. The challenge was to strike the right balance between being part of the fabric of the place, tuned in to local concerns, and going native and adopting local customs inconsistent with global standards. This worked. The head of BP Colombia has been a national for the last seven years, the number of expatriate staff is down to a handful, and the main internal language of communication is now Spanish.[14]

BP had to think of security as more than just physical measures, which we had discovered can actually make things worse by creating a barrier. We realised that no large piece of infrastructure can be made secure from an external threat at reasonable cost without the active support of the local community.

Engaging the local community involved a range of different strands, such as increased local procurement from Colombian companies. And we began to focus on helping communities in the immediate neighbourhood of BP's operations. The villagers of El Morro had been consistently suspicious of BP, and the source of many allegations. We sought to tackle their isolation by agreeing to pay army engineers to improve the road to the local capital, Yopal, and to improve security by persuading the army to provide a permanent presence in the village.

We established separately governed funds to support social entrepreneurship, housing and education.[15] But what was really needed was a more professional and informed approach to the development of the region. So in 2000, once the immediate problems were resolved, we funded independent studies[16] to establish a development baseline, and to examine the causes of violence in the province, and used these to develop a strategy aimed at supporting broad-based development and the strengthening of Colombian institutions.

This work informed the design of community programmes. For instance, one independent report[17] had identified a weakness in the management of oil revenues, and subsequently BP supported projects to improve financial administration in Casanare. Another report identified violence and conflict as a major problem in Casanare, with murder and domestic violence cases well above national averages.[18] In response, BP supported the construction of a local human rights training centre, which trained over 4,500 soldiers in human rights and international humanitarian law. It also supported the establishment of a House of Justice and Peace to provide a mechanism for resolving cases through conciliation, without the expense and difficulty of going to court.

Human rights

The Ken Saro-Wiwa incident had started a broad international debate about business and human rights. Internally this and the specific accusations against BP were the catalyst for a major re-evaluation. Did we as a multinational have multinational accountability for human rights that would transcend national law? The United Nations Universal Declaration of Human Rights had been written for member countries' agreement.[19] Could we as a company subscribe to it?

I went through the declaration line by line and annotated what we could agree to. I got to know more about that declaration than I had ever realised before. The upshot of many discussions was that we said we believed we could subscribe to the declaration, but needed to understand the implications. It would mean that wherever we went in the world we had to build in human rights considerations as a fundamental part of the operation.

But how far should we go? Was it just for the people who were directly affected? And if it was people indirectly affected – to what extent? We decided we had to be pragmatic; we should focus on what we directly controlled.

How would this work practically? I had the long-held view that the most important thing was to treat everyone with respect and dignity, including people in communities affected by our operations. One manifestation of this would be to give employees every opportunity to develop within the company such that a Colombian could not only aspire to run the Colombian operation, but also to hold senior appointments in any geography in BP. We proved this could be done, as a few years later the operations manager in Alaska was someone who had risen through the ranks in Colombia.

Thinking through human rights issues made it clear that we needed to develop a fresh approach to the security challenge which the company continued to face. That approach had not only to be effective on the ground but enable us to demonstrate that what was being done was honest and fair.

What was needed was an external review of our conduct. In the longer term we needed some independent third party to establish a code of conduct to provide a benchmark against which performance could be credibly assessed. We tried but we could not find anyone credible to become the external reviewer. Perhaps we did not try hard enough because we did not have the confidence to be examined, or the understanding of how to get that done.

The NGOs were not keen to be third-party reviewers, understandably, since they were worried about compromising their credibility. So we tried a different tack. In conjunction with Human Rights Watch, we floated the idea of establishing a set of international standards or code of conduct for multinationals wanting to provide security in developing countries.

The timing of this idea turned out to be fortuitous. It was enthusiastically taken up by Bennett Freeman, the US Deputy Assistant Secretary of State for Human Rights. As almost the last act of the outgoing Clinton administration, the US government encouraged a coalition of NGOs, governments and companies to agree to what became known as the Voluntary Principles on Security and Human Rights.[20]

These principles are now an international industry standard. They require companies to make a security risk assessment, to establish procedures for public and private security forces, to provide security in a way which respects human rights, and to implement monitoring and reporting procedures.

Talking with NGOs

BP's media battering showed that the company needed to improve its capacity to communicate with critics. For me, it was a sharp lesson in the new power of both the media and the NGOs to damage reputations and to alter the course of events. BP clearly had to put new effort into building relationships with NGOs, particularly those involved with human rights, to ensure that it was more attuned and responsive to the concerns of civil society. But at the time BP had no regular contact with NGOs and had no idea how to begin to establish such relationships.

A breakthrough came when David Rice saw a well-written letter from a Catholic relief agency in the UK newspaper, the *Independent*, which criticised BP's operations in Colombia and demonstrated some genuine knowledge of the situation. David, in his proactive style, looked up the organisation and phoned the surprised letter writer to ask for a meeting.

The call put us in touch with a network of London-based NGOs. They had been discussing BP in Colombia among themselves for some time. At the initial meeting, understandably highly suspicious of BP, the NGOs felt they had the opportunity to get their collective frustration off their chest. David later told me: "It felt like being put in the stocks and pelted with tomatoes."

Although David did not have the opportunity to respond at the time, the tomato-throwing smoothed the way for a constructive dialogue. From BP's perspective, the dialogue was helpful. The NGOs had good information on community concerns in Colombia, often better than BP's, because they were trusted. And, importantly, they had ideas worth listening to. This was the start of my understanding that we could work with NGOs and that they could form a valuable role in society. But I also realised that we had a long way to go before they would trust us.

I like to think that BP's investment in Colombia brought about some positive changes. I really cannot prove this, however, as no one knows what would have happened if BP had not been there. But I do believe that if there had been no oil, the situation would have been much worse. We increased oil production at a time when the economy needed a boost, creating jobs and changing the way Colombia was regarded internationally.

One of our independent studies in 2001 showed Casanare had doubled in population and GDP since the 1990s, had lower unemployment than other regions and significantly improved utility coverage (water, electricity and telephone), school enrolment rates and healthcare coverage.[21]

Before I left BP, BP Colombia was a highly successful business unit, and a substantial net exporter of internal labour, sending more than 100 BP Colombians to work for BP abroad. It had one of the best operational and health and safety performances and one of the best reputations for dealing with human rights. And as for security, BP had had no major security incidents in the three years up to 2007 and never had to stop production. The operation turned out to be very profitable for BP and the Colombian government now receives a large income from oil. BP, like other oil companies, has to pay a significant percentage of its oil revenue directly to the government.

The big lesson I learnt in Colombia is just how easy it is for observers to misinterpret the actions of a company, assume that what is being done is wrong, and believe that profits are put before human rights and the needs of civil society. I recognised that BP would always risk some of its goodwill and reputation when building a business in an unfamiliar country, particularly one with a reputation like that of Colombia. What I had underestimated was the degree of risk. So I began to think of a way we could minimise that risk and a way that would ensure we never again made the same mistakes that we had in Colombia.

Leaders are not perfect; they are bound to make mistakes as they do new things. But they must never make the same mistake twice.

Transparency in Tangguh

BP learnt a lot in Colombia. We had not fully understood the society in which we were operating. And when we had made mistakes people had assumed that our motives were bad.

To avoid this in the future, we decided that we had to open ourselves up for inspection, to report our actions as they happened without editing and to have an active dialogue with the communities in which we were operating. To make this effective we would go one step further; we would make the effort and have the confidence to appoint a panel, independent from BP. The first time we did this was in Tangguh.

When we acquired ARCO, one of its assets was the massive natural gas field, Tangguh, near the Bintuni Bay region of West Papua in Indonesia. The fields had the potential to become one of the world's premier natural gas supplies but, looking beyond those reserves, I could foresee many problems and ways that people could easily misinterpret our activities.

Formerly known as Irian Jaya, Papua is Indonesia's largest and most-eastern province, on the western half of the island of New Guinea. Annexed by Indonesia in 1969, for years the province had been unsettled with claims for independence and a promise of autonomy, which was not followed through, plus land rights issues, human rights abuse and military intervention.

The area is home to a mix of indigenous ethnic groups and migrants including Javanese and Bugis. Construction of the processing plant required relocation of two village communities, Tanah Merah and Onar. In addition, the environment around Bintuni Bay, close to the gas field, was already despoiled by the activities from a copper and gold mine. I saw the vivid orange and purple effluent in the river flowing into the Bay on my first visit out there.

After our experience in Colombia, I knew we had to ensure that people did not think BP had anything to hide. We had to tackle problems head on and avoid matters building into a crisis. We appointed an independent standing commission, The Tangguh Independent Advisory Panel (TIAP), to examine our activities, to listen to people, to encourage debate and to report its findings and recommendations for improvement in a public way.

The key was to find people of the right calibre and standing for this panel. They needed to have the time, capability and experience to observe and sometimes resolve conflicts. With so many different groups who had vested interests, we knew that the chairman had to be someone who recognised that the person who shouts the loudest, or is most persistent, is not necessarily the one with the right answer. A distinguished former US Senator George Mitchell – for a number of years Senate Majority Leader, and currently President Obama's Special Envoy to the Middle East – took on the chairing of the panel.[22]

Initially, not everyone in BP saw the appointment of the panel as a good thing. I thought the panel would be an important source of guidance and be able to give an independent view to people who were concentrating solely on the often daunting, huge and complex technical challenges that have to be met every day. But initially it was viewed with suspicion. Internally, people felt that they should be given a chance to correct a mistake or error of judgement before it was made public. They missed the point. I insisted that we reported things as they were – mistakes, errors, failures and successes. This would help us understand the broader economic, political and social impacts of the Tangguh project and we would commit to improve where necessary.

In Colombia, we had not understood the honeypot effect which attracted a whole circus of undesirable people to the Casanare region. The panel helped us develop ways to minimise the impact of inward migration on the villages near our Tangguh project. We had to start with understanding the society. We commissioned social anthropological studies to help us understand the complex problems of inward migration. And using this knowledge, we then developed appropriate management and recruitment policies. This meant recruiting people from outside the affected areas, returning them to these areas for rest periods and at the end of their employment, and paying wages in the place where they were originally hired. We also set up closed camps for workers to minimise disruption on the local community. This was all part of a broader integrated social programme, designed to help the local people decide for themselves what to do during an extraordinary period of economic growth.

Our response to security concerns in Colombia had been to build a massive fence. In Tangguh we deployed the Voluntary Principles on Security and Human Rights and, working with the panel, developed the idea that the community would police the area. After all, they had a stake in protecting us because we provided jobs and tax revenue. We reached an agreement that the police and army would stand away and only come in when called upon by the community.

In Colombia, we had got into big problems over land rights as it was hard to identify who owned the different pieces of land used for the pipeline right of way and field development. In Tangguh, to avoid the same problems, we devised and announced, before any land acquisition took place, a detailed plan to guide activities. This plan adhered to Asian Development Bank and World Bank standards. A group of experts worked with the panel to help the company maintain these standards, with reports published regularly on the BP website.

Few people trust what a powerful company says, especially when that company has a strong vested interest in making money from a particular location. An independent panel provides a dispassionate view. It helps to anticipate issues and hopefully head them off before they become problems. And it provides credibility.

Being open as things are happening is tough for the company leadership. It is so much easier to report on events, tweaking and reordering to create a more comfortable story. But I could see it was a way to get on and do business in a difficult place.

In other countries I could see that the way to try to do business – or to try to do business in a better way – was to go toe-to-toe with the leadership.

7

ANGOLA TO LIBYA

Leaders

Early 1990s: The drive through Luanda's war-torn streets was harrowing. On every street corner, groups of ill-clad young men loitered aimlessly. Nearly everyone was missing a limb. Men, women and children, mutilated by landmines, bore the scars of the continuing civil war.[1]

In the distance I could hear the sound of occasional gunfire. The roads were potholed and the buildings crumbling or in total collapse.

The political and ethnic conflict in Angola began after the abrupt end of Portuguese rule in 1975. Different factions had fought colonialism for independence but then turned on each other as long-standing ethnic divisions, suppressed under colonial rule, erupted. On one side was the ruling party, the socialist MPLA (*Movimento Popular de Libertação de Angola*), latterly headed by President dos Santos. On the other side: anti-communist group UNITA (*União Nacional para a Independência Total de Angola*), headed by Jonas Savimbi.[2]

The war was further complicated because the opposing socialist and capitalist sides were supported by various foreign governments as part of the Cold War struggle. The MPLA was backed by Cuba and the Soviet Union, and UNITA predominantly by the US and, at one stage, by China.

A battle for control of the country's "blood diamonds" was involved and, of course, for the country's oil. In particular large oil fields off the coast of Cabinda, Angola's exclave province, added extra impetus to that region's secessionist demands. Hundreds of thousands were killed and many more made homeless. Despite various peace negotiations and attempts to establish democracy, the war dragged on.

I was on my way back to my hotel – where running water from the taps or a flicker of light were a bonus rather than a certainty – to collect

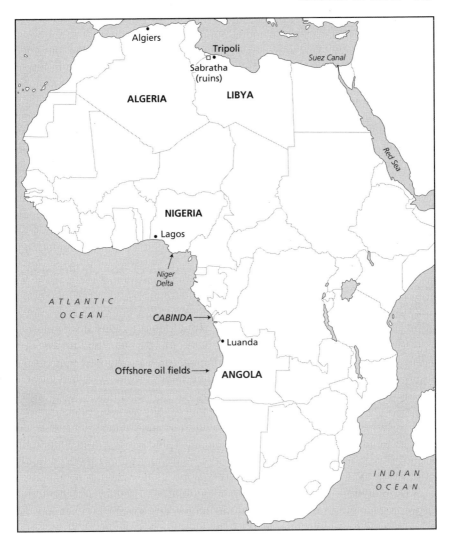

Africa: many countries with unfinished business

my bags and head for the airport. The interior of the old black Mercedes had the fusty smell of stale cigarettes and mildewed leather. Outside it was hot and humid; clouds loomed. The visit had not been a success.

I had been invited to Angola to discuss BP's potential involvement in offshore prospects. But the situation on the ground was confusing and how to do business was unclear. Meetings with strange people, many of whom were intermediaries or agents with an office registered in a strange country, had left me none the wiser. Everyone seemed to want a bribe.

The country was in turmoil. Its institutions, health and education services and infrastructure had been virtually destroyed. The street scenes were evidence of the plight of the majority of the population, who lived in dire poverty.

By the time I reached the airport I had made a decision; it was best not to get involved. I was torn by the appalling plight of the people but had to be pragmatic. The ruling chaos was a big obstacle and so was the complex geology.

Over the next few years I went back and forth to Luanda a number of times. I did not look forward to these trips. The best thing was to fly in for a brief visit and get out as quickly as possible. I was not going to give up. But it would take a long time before I was prepared to invest in Angola.

By the mid 1990s, I began to be more interested. International peacekeepers in the country offered some hope. And the scale of Angola's potential offshore reserves was becoming increasingly clear. Oil had first been discovered onshore in Angola in the 1950s and now we expected to discover billions of barrels more lying off its coastline under the Atlantic. The National Ministry of Petroleum had divided the deep-water areas into blocks. Sonangol, the state oil company, was seeking investment from international oil companies. Drilling in such deep waters was high risk, requiring the advanced technology of international oil companies, and this would minimise Sonangol's upfront investment. Oil companies from across the world, particularly the US, were looking at options.

Angola had its troubles but offered an opportunity for big discoveries of oil. The Middle East remained closed for investment and sources of oil in the West were declining.

I was still concerned by the continuing conflict and political disorder, but BP was offered interests in two offshore licences that seemed reasonable. We introduced Statoil, the Norwegian state oil company, as our partner. They were neutral and beyond reproach. We had been working with them in other conflict areas, including Azerbaijan and Nigeria. They helped pay for some of our exploration commitments which, for a company of BP's then small size, were too big for us to handle.

I had foreseen all sorts of problems in Angola but not the one which surfaced.

Caught out in Angola

This was around the time that we were undergoing public castigation for our activities in Colombia, so I was aware of the risk of going into another country with a bad international reputation. All activity in Angola would be offshore, entailing very different problems – there would be no land rights issues and fewer concerns about security. But the board was still concerned.

Before we committed ourselves we had been very thorough in our studies. The social impact assessment report commissioned from a well-known consulting firm, Environmental Resource Management (ERM), in November 1997 confirmed our concern that "oil revenue to government fails to benefit the wider society".

In our analysis of the ERM study, we noted that there were: "risks to the reputation of BP and Statoil if the government of Angola fails to live up to commitments made to increase democracy, accountability and transparency, and if oil revenues continue to be the main source of income to the government, although anticipated increases in oil revenue could potentially finance investment in the human capital and infrastructure necessary for economic and social development".[3]

Initially we made only a small investment so there was not too much at risk for the business. But things changed with the Amoco deal. By 1999, BP Amoco had become a major player in Angola as the operator of blocks 18 and 31, and an investor in blocks 15 and 17. It had participated in more oil discoveries than any other international company.

The war was there in the background. But I believed we could do some good; we had plans for community investment, to build a sustainable business and boost the local and national economy with employment and contracts for local suppliers.

But the thing that caught me out was the money we had paid to the Angolan government.

To get our offshore licences in Angola, we had to pay so-called "signature bonuses". And the international focus on the country, triggered by the plight of its people and its reputation for corruption, meant we began to be on the sharp end of criticism from some British NGOs.[4]

Just what exactly was BP doing in Angola? Why were we paying money to a corrupt government? "Signature bonuses", though unfortunately named, are not illegal. In fact, they are standard practice in the industry. Perhaps that was why it had never crossed my mind that they might cause an issue.

Signature bonuses are lump sums paid by companies to foreign governments when they sign a contract for a licence to explore and extract oil from a specified area, or block. In many countries around the world, including the US, such payments are the norm as they provide upfront revenue to national governments in advance of royalties and taxes, which only flow through when production starts. In Alaska, licences in the Prudhoe Bay area had been awarded in 1965 to the highest bidder, in effect, an auction with an upfront payment.

BP pointed out: "It would be very difficult to refuse to pay Angola what is standard practice elsewhere."[5] But the NGOs were not going to let us off the hook.

1 December 1999: Global Witness, a campaigning NGO, published a report called *A Crude Awakening*, which accused the banking and multinational oil industries, including BP, of complicity in the mismanagement of Angolan oil revenue.[6] The report stated that: "Rather than contributing to Angola's development, Angola's oil revenue is directly contributing to further decline."

This perspective was so different from mine that it was painful to read. I could see it was well-written and had some significant merit. It was not only a polemic against oil companies but also came up with recommendations. I had never even thought of some of these ideas.

One recommendation was phrased as a challenge: "It is simply not good enough to continue in the same vein, so we are challenging the oil industry to adopt a policy of 'full transparency'." Global Witness singled out BP, quoting from the ERM report, and challenging us to set a benchmark for corporate responsibility and accountability by publishing a full set of Angolan accounts, as well as details of past payments made and contracts signed with the Angolan government and state oil company Sonangol.

With Colombia ever present in my mind I wanted to show that BP was not making any illegal payments. That is what full transparency would do. But the real merit in the Global Witness proposal was the idea that if we could publish what was paid to governments then this might increase the pressure on those governments to use the money in ways that would benefit a broader population. And it might help us by improving political and economic stability in the country.

That report sparked action. Much internal and external discussion followed, including a meeting, convened by Peter Hain, the UK Government Minister for Africa, with two NGOs, Global Witness and Transparency International, along with a number of other oil companies.

Some of the other oil companies were less concerned. But I decided that BP would take a lead on the issue. As a company incorporated in England, which had to file its accounts in Companies House,[7] we could be explicit about what we had paid to the Angolan government. Global Witness was right in suggesting it was time for a radical rethink of international business practice. And we would make a start. We would break the mould because we had nothing to hide.

6 February 2001: In an open letter to Global Witness we committed to publish the total net production by exploration/production block, aggregate payments made by BP to Sonangol, and the total amount in taxes and levies paid to the Angolan government.[8] We also pointed out that in the accounts of our Angolan subsidiary we had disclosed a payment of a $111 million signature bonus to the Angolan government. In our previous accounts, payments to foreign governments had been aggregated.

NGOs responded favourably. Other oil companies waited to see the response from the Angolan government. They knew, as we did, that our contract stated that such payments had to be confidential, except when the law or regulation determined that they needed to be published.

My view was that since we were obliged to report these significant payments made by our English registered subsidiary, publishing the financial information did not breach the contract. Angola had a different view.

Shortly afterwards, I received a cold letter from Manuel Vicente, chairman and CEO of Sonangol, which was copied to other oil companies working in Angola.

Dear Sir

It was with great surprise, and some disbelief, that we found out through the press that your company has been disclosing information about oil-related activities in Angola, some of which have a strict confidential character. According to the media, your company promised to continue to supply further such information . . . thereby seriously violating the conditions of legal contracts signed with Sonangol . . .

We are aware that some oil companies have been under pressure by organized groups that use available means in an orchestrated campaign against some Angolan institutions by calling for "pseudo-transparency" of legitimate government actions. . . . Finally, and in the hope of maintaining the good relations that we have always had with the oil companies that operate in Angola, we strongly discourage all our partners from similar attitudes in the future.[9]

It was a warning shot. I was then summoned down to Luanda to see President dos Santos.

Surrounded by makeshift shanty-style dwellings, the luxurious presidential palace seemed far removed from the struggle of everyday life in Angola. President dos Santos was angry; he made it clear that because we had broken our contract he could kick BP out of Angola. I made the point that we were within our rights as we were obliged to disclose the information in the UK. There then ensued a very robust discussion.

I decided to push my point. I suggested that he should seize the opportunity. "It's obvious that you need to disclose this information. You can't have groups like NGOs as your enemy forever. You have to get them on side and get the world on side. Otherwise you will be subject to ongoing criticism and you will have even bigger problems." He did not reply.

We had stepped out of line with the industry again, just as we had four years earlier, when I acknowledged the oil and gas industry's leadership role in climate change.

Most oil companies disagreed with our action. Some, chilled by Sonangol's letter, hid behind contract confidentiality clauses; others claimed that the payments were competitive information. Lee Raymond said BP had made things difficult for ExxonMobil in Angola.[10]

Clearly a unilateral approach, where one company or one country was under pressure to "publish what you pay", was not workable.

Different groups began to point in the same direction. There was pressure from the NGOs. The IMF and World Bank strongly advocated transparency. Financier and philanthropist George Soros was garnering support for a "publish what you pay" campaign. Academics reminded everyone who would listen of the research done on the impact of the resource curse. And business was cautious, but quietly expressed the view that transparency might improve governance and hence might protect them from tax increases.

It was clear that we needed a global standard for companies to publish what they paid to national governments and for governments to disclose what they received. It all seemed like a good idea but without support from the other big oil companies, efforts began to waver.

I sensed the initiative needed bolstering and went to see the Prime Minister, Tony Blair, to explain the importance of this initiative from an international perspective. This was about far more than one oil company. I also talked to his chief of staff, Jonathan Powell. Blair could not enact the initiative but he could take a leadership role, which is what he did.

The result was the formation of the Extractive Industries Transparency Initiative (EITI),[11] announced by Tony Blair in October 2002 at the World Summit for Sustainable Development in Johannesburg. The EITI's objective would be to support improved governance in resource-rich countries through the full publication and verification of payments by companies to governments and government revenues from oil, gas and mining.

In June 2003 the EITI was formally launched at a conference at Lancaster House, once one of London's great private mansions and now used for government receptions and international summits. Some 140 delegates – representing 70 governments, companies, industry groups, international organisations, investors and NGOs – attended to agree a statement of principles and actions to increase transparency over payments and revenues in the extractives sector. There were plenty of very pious statements by oil producers and host governments. Blair reiterated his support. The US government was less supportive, wondering whether it would make any difference at all. We had a long way to go, but at least we had made a start.

However, transparency was just one aspect, accountability was another.

Slow change

In February 2002, Jonas Savimbi, the UNITA leader and government enemy, had been killed in a skirmish with Angolan government forces. It was an opportunity for change and stability after 27 years of war. But the much hoped-for change has been slow in coming. For me Angola is unfinished business.

My clash with President dos Santos in 2001 was the start of the country's recognition that it needed to address transparency. But it has not gone far enough.

Today, the nation's daily oil production is more than 1.8 million barrels.[12] It is Africa's third largest producer of oil.[13] Yet despite the wealth generated by its oil and other resources, it is still one of the poorest countries in the world. According to the 2009 UNDP Human Development Report, Angola ranked 143rd poorest out of 182 countries.[14]

Are oil companies to blame? Some would say so. But why would oil companies want to contribute to a country's decline rather than to its development? Purely from self-interest this would be wrong. Oil is a long-term business, requiring investment over a 30- or 40-year horizon. Enlightened companies recognise that, if they are to benefit from any society, they have to contribute to its wellbeing. That contribution to society needs to be more than just philanthropy. It needs to be about capacity building and governance. Otherwise the business of a company is not sustainable.

Companies need robustly to support transparency as part of good governance, with proper checks and balances. If it is clear where the revenue comes from and how it is spent, the chances of the revenue being well managed increase; and with increasing oil revenues, governments are less likely to come after business for more money.

In a world of sometimes vague but well-meaning initiatives, EITI is proving to be a practical success. Thirty countries, including major producers like Nigeria and Kazakhstan, are implementing the EITI to improve their management of oil, gas and mineral resources, through transparency and tackling corruption. Emerging evidence shows that the countries implementing the EITI have seen an increase in trust between citizens, companies and the government.[15] The strong support for the initiative by the big international companies and institutional investors suggests they see it as part of a country's efforts to tackle the resource curse and improve stability, predictability and sustained growth. That was certainly the case with BP. Azerbaijan, with encouragement and help from BP and the other oil companies operating there, is already compliant with the indicators of the EITI global standard. Angola, however, has yet to sign up.

The Angolan government has been repeatedly accused of corrupt

My parents' marriage in post-war Germany. My mother is wearing a suit and hat she had made herself. May 1947. (Author's collection)

Above right: With my mother, a few weeks after my birth. Hamburg, 1948. (Author's collection)

Below: My mother and I dressed for a wedding in the UK, some time before we went to live in Singapore. (Author's collection)

Right: Getting ready to board, with my mother. Singapore, 1953. (Author's collection)

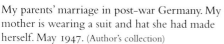

Ready for school in my St Luke's uniform, with my mother. Cambridge, 1956. (Author's collection)

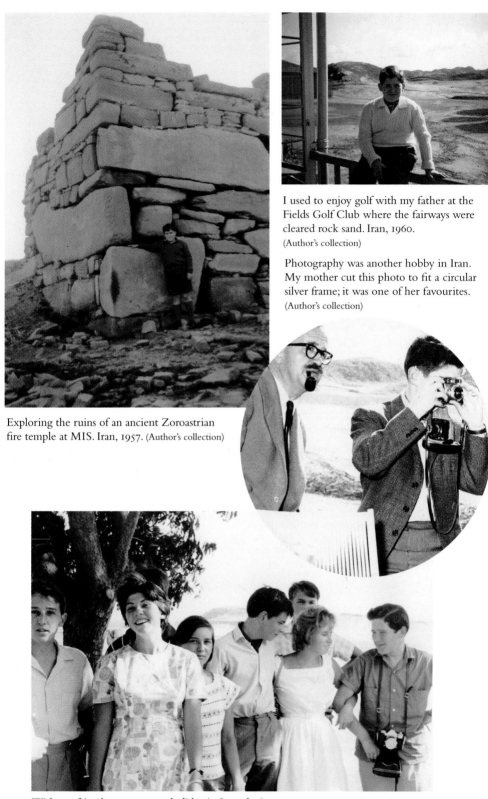

I used to enjoy golf with my father at the Fields Golf Club where the fairways were cleared rock sand. Iran, 1960. (Author's collection)

Photography was another hobby in Iran. My mother cut this photo to fit a circular silver frame; it was one of her favourites. (Author's collection)

Exploring the ruins of an ancient Zoroastrian fire temple at MIS. Iran, 1957. (Author's collection)

With my friends one summer holiday in Iran, during my teenage years. (Author's collection)

Another trip back to England, from Iran. (Author's collection)

Right: With my parents, outside their home in Stansgate Avenue, where they lived on return from Iran. Cambridge, early 1970s. (Author's collection)

Above: Renting a CDC 6600 computer (in the background). Palo Alto, California, 1971. (Author's collection)

Right: Making good use of the time on my hands. New York, 1972. (Author's collection)

The table set for dinner at Waverley Place, with one of my Hockney prints on the wall. New York, 1973. (Author's collection)

Trip to the Ming tombs, with a China Airlines' 'Picnic pack', with BP colleagues (l to r): Ian Robertson, Simon Downs, John Norman, John Grundon and Colin Davis. Beijing, 1979. (Author's collection)

A fishing trip in Alaska with BP colleagues (l to r): John Bramley, David Jenkins, David Harding and Rodney Chase. (Author's collection)

Exploring Egypt in the late 1970s with (l to r): Peter Cazalet, then a director of BP and later deputy chairman; David Steel, chairman of BP; and a BP official. (Author's collection)

'Batman and Robin' – as Bob Horton and I were described by one London City analyst in 1986. (BP)

Discussions with President
Gaviria (right) with
General Sir James 'Jimmy'
Glover, a non-executive
director of BP. Colombia,
early 1990s.
(Author's collection)

Visiting a community nursery project with Business in the Community,
as part of the *Seeing is Believing* programme, started by HRH The Prince
of Wales. London, early 1990s. (BP)

Visiting an oil platform in North America with colleagues; we are wearing
hats with the old 'colonial-style' BP shield logo. (Author's collection)

With Larry Fuller, chairman and CEO of Amoco, after the announcement of the largest ever industrial merger to form BP Amoco. London, August 1998. (BP)

Ringing the bell at the New York Stock Exchange with (l to r): Rodney Chase, deputy CEO of BP Amoco; Dick Grasso, chairman and CEO of NYSE; and Larry Fuller, co-chairman of BP Amoco. February 1999. (Used with permission of NYSE Group, Inc. © 1999 NYSE Group, Inc.)

My mother launching the Petrojarl Foinaven oil drilling tanker for the North Sea. Spain, 1996. (BP)

Al Gore visiting BP's solar panel plant in California, after my 1997 climate change speech at Stanford. (BP)

Learning about local boat-making in Indonesia with Chris Wright, a senior BP executive. (Author's collection)

Opening BP's first filling station in China, in Guangdong Province. September 1996. (BP)

Above right: Zhu Rongji asked for BP's support when China wanted to float some of PetroChina's shares. (Author's collection)

Right: Wen Jiabao's visit was a demonstration of the strength and significance of BP's relationship with China. London, 2004. (BP)

Jiang Zemin seemed to believe that BP was an arm of the UK Foreign Office and could resolve issues such as Hong Kong. (Author's collection)

practices and not using oil money for the benefit of its people. Despite verbal commitments from President dos Santos, the government had consistently failed to demonstrate that it was prepared to reform the management of its oil revenues. From 1997 to 2002, $4.22 billion of oil revenues were unaccounted for.[16] However, there are signs that things are beginning to change. For example, the 2009 Ibrahim Index of African Governance, from the Mo Ibrahim Foundation, showed that Angola's governance has improved over the past three years.[17] Perhaps those early steps towards transparency helped.

There is a limit to what any one company or a group of companies can do. They cannot, in these post-colonial times, throw their weight around with impunity. If they do, they cannot expect to be a respected partner. Nor can they instruct governments on how to spend their revenue. They can, however, work through bodies such as the EITI which can then apply pressure for change by demonstrating to a country what the best of its peers are doing.

I now think that some Angolans are benefiting from BP's presence. Almost half of the people employed by BP in Angola are nationals, including Jose Patricio who heads the business. Born in Angola, Patricio served his country as a distinguished diplomat in the US and Portugal, and at the United Nations. He is a good and honest man. Patricio is implementing a programme of "Angolanisation" to create a wider, deeper pool of local BP leaders, individuals with the capacity to address local needs, local sensitivities and local issues. People outside BP are benefiting too – from education and broader community investment. In my time, BP started training programmes for Angolan engineers, created a business centre to encourage local enterprise and provided education for children, particularly female war orphans.

From a business perspective it was a huge success. By the end of 2010, it is expected that BP will have invested in excess of $8 billion in its Angolan business. This would place it among the largest foreign investors in the country.[18]

I pushed things in the right direction in Angola. However, in one country I found it was not possible to make any headway. That country was Nigeria.

Nigeria and the resource curse

BP and Nigeria had a very chequered history. BP was thrown out in the 1970s. More importantly, Nigeria is often quoted as the leading example of a country affected by the resource curse.

It has been widely documented that many countries derive little benefit from natural resources. Logic says that large mineral deposits should be a benefit for a country. Natural resources should attract additional investment which creates jobs and generates revenue for the government. These revenues should increase the fiscal capacity of the government, allowing it to increase spending, reduce taxes or even establish a national savings fund. All or any of these choices would benefit the wider population. But that is not always the case. Of the ten biggest oil nations in the world (measured by reserves), seven are ranked in the bottom third of Transparency International's Corruption Index.[19]

Former US Vice President Dick Cheney, when he was CEO of Halliburton, famously said: "The problem is the good Lord didn't see fit to always put oil and gas where there are democratic governments." The real problem is that oil or gas – or indeed any natural resource – does not encourage democracy or an open society. In fact the real *curse* of natural resources is that they can undermine the nation's economic and political institutions.

In a country with rich resources, particularly one undergoing significant change, such as the transition to independence after being a colony, there is a risk that one single political caste will get into power. Those in power will then control the revenues generated from resources and nothing stops them from using these solely for their own purposes. This encourages bad governance, poor economic development, and poverty, all in the face of fantastic wealth. Apart from the few who are involved in the resources industry through employment, the population as a whole sees very little benefit. Typically, the other industries outside the resources sector are neglected and eventually fall away.

These other sectors are not only affected by changes in behaviour but also by economic factors, the "Dutch Disease".[20] This phenomenon makes the economy's traded sectors less competitive, and leads to a boom in services and construction. The economy can then lose some of its previously competitive non-oil industries and may suffer significant inflation. In extreme cases, with the presence of an incompetent and corrupt government, the bad economic side-effects of the natural resource discovery can outweigh the economic benefits.

Oil revenue is unearned income or rent. Governments that gather oil revenue do not have the incentive to promote wealth creation among the broader population since they are not reliant on general taxation.

In Angola, we tried to make change happen by encouraging greater transparency. But history, geography, culture and economics got in the way.

In Nigeria, the problem was the resource curse. Some 99 per cent of Nigeria's export revenue is generated by oil and gas, resulting in billions of dollars flowing to the state every year.[21] However, much of the country remains impoverished and underdeveloped. Between 1970 and 2000, Nigeria's poverty rate – measured by the proportion of the population living on less than a $1 a day – increased from 36 per cent to 70 per cent. This meant that 19 million poor in 1970 had grown to 90 million in 2000.[22] A small group of political oligarchs holds the power and controls the country's entire resources; the wider population sees no benefit.

Nigeria became independent from the UK in 1960. And from the end of that decade, the country saw much strife with the Biafran war of secession, the assassination of two leaders, numerous coups and 30 years of military rule. Nigeria's economic and political problems and institutional deterioration have often been laid at the door of oil companies.

After the Biafran civil war (1967–70), the victorious Colonel Gowon's military government blamed "the expatriates, the ex-imperialists, and the oil companies" for the country's inherent problems.[23] By the early 1970s, BP and other oil companies were forced to accept new terms.[24] And by the end of the decade, BP was thrown out and its assets expropriated by General Obasanjo during his first time in office. The basis for this action was BP's alleged involvement in South Africa; it was, in effect, a trumped-up charge.

Some years later, in the early 1990s, under President Babangida, we were invited back. My immediate reaction was to decline. There was too much bad history. And there was too much conflict in the Niger Delta.[25] The invitation was: "We want you back. If you come down we will give you some licences virtually for free." The reality was we were not *wanted* but *needed*. Nigeria, like many countries after 15 years of nationalising their oil, was seeking help with technology and people skills.

So I got on a plane and went to discuss opportunities. I met the oil minister and we had a convivial discussion about the award of exploration licences. Then he suddenly said: "Fine. If we're going to do this there are certain conditions. You have to come on television with me and apologise for your company's past misdeeds." I would not agree to it.

Eventually we got the licences anyway. We undertook a joint venture with Norwegian partner, Statoil. Harald Norvik, Statoil CEO, and I went down to Lagos to celebrate our award. But my heart was not in it. It was as if there was a cultural block; the past was just too vivid. Nigeria had far too many problems and the leaders did not have the will to change. I felt we just could not operate in Nigeria. We sold our Nigerian licences and I never wanted to go back.

Madness in Algeria

Some companies felt the same about Algeria, although I saw it quite differently. The opportunities were new and I felt that first-movers could influence things. But it required a great deal of nerve.

BP had a limited history in Algeria but had never been involved in upstream activities; the company had run gasoline stations and distributed lubricants in the 1950s, during the final years of French colonialism. When the country had embarked on mass nationalisation of the industry, we had sold these downstream activities and left.

My first foray there was in the late 1980s when the country again opened up for foreign companies to conduct exploration and production. Post-colonial problems had set the country back for many years and it was still very troubled. A tough bureaucratic one-party regime existed. There was civil unrest and the rise of two opposing protest movements. By 1988, President Bendjedid conceded to the end of one-party rule and this led to an election in December 1991.

The FIS (*Front Islamique du Salut*) won the first round of elections but the opposing party the FLN (*Front de Libération Nationale*) cancelled the second round, deposed President Bendjedid and imposed military rule. The FIS was banned and thousands of its members were arrested. Islamist guerrillas emerged and began an armed campaign against the government and its supporters. A brutal civil war ensued, which some now believe was the first act in the rise of Islamic extremism.

To my knowledge, all the foreign companies left or shut up shop. But BP stuck it out through all these troubles. At times it seemed impossibly difficult and sometimes foolhardy. But it turned out to be the right decision because support given in difficult times is never forgotten. Business can be more easily developed in turbulent times provided you can see the possibility of peace in the future.

Algiers, once a picturesque Mediterranean town, was dangerous and unpleasant. We had a "safe house" there and at one time were reduced to a few trained people. The house had a swimming pool but it was never filled with water; it would not have been safe to be outside.

But Algeria had sizeable natural gas reserves and we needed access to these to get BP involved in marketing gas in mainland Europe. We had many conversations about gaining access to the identified reserves with the leader of Sonatrach, the state oil company. But it was hard to button down a specific agreement.

In the mid 1990s I thought we were close to something. Abdelhak Bouhafs, then head of Sonatrach, spent an afternoon at my house in Belgravia discussing a deal. The surroundings were pleasant but the negotiation was tough. I thought we had everything agreed and then it all fell apart. Deals were agreed and re-agreed.

Initially I had my eye on a business in the north but because of the troubles we focused on the south. Eventually our tenacity paid off; we got agreement to develop the In Salah gas field, deep in the Sahara desert. BP is now the largest foreign investor in Algeria.[26] And, of course, nearly all the major international oil companies are back in Algeria.

I had to be realistic about another country but for very different reasons.

Venezuela's political weapon

It was clear when I met the Venezuelan President Hugo Chávez, shortly after he had been elected in 1998, that he would use oil as a political weapon.

Venezuela's rich oil deposits have been developed for almost a century and the country was one of the founder members of OPEC in 1960. I first went there in 1979 as part of a delegation led by the executive director in charge of E&P, Jack Birks. A man aware of his position and very English, he found the trip trying. Everyone told us how well things were done in Venezuela and how delighted they were to see us but we could only advise as the oil industry was fully nationalised; there was no likelihood of business.

We went to see the heavy oil areas in the Faja, near the Orinoco River; that was my responsibility because I was running the heavy oil project in Canada at the time. We went to the exotic operations at the polluted Lake Maracaibo and to the refineries that produced large amounts of fine coke as they broke down the heavy oil. The coke blew all over the place and made the air black. We went to parties with the rich but we also saw the poor who live in the *rancho* (slum) dwellings, the red cinder-block houses with corrugated tin roofs, which cling to the sides of the valley of Caracas.

This was an extraordinary country, with stunning varied natural beauty and little recognition of its history and past culture. It was run by an elite of the rich and technocratic. Those running the fully nationalised oil industry seemed to be stuck in the ways of behaving they had learned from the American companies which they had expelled a few years earlier.

Years later when I went back it seemed that little had changed. Even the hotel in Caracas, the Tamanaco, retained its 1970s decor with shag pile carpet. BP had maintained a small presence through the 1980s and early 1990s trying to find ways of creating a business. We had carried out lengthy studies of potential field developments and campaigned with various presidents to encourage the government to allow us to get involved in developing the country's reserves.

The first time I got to an agreement was with President Carlos Andrés Perez in 1993. Shortly after he signed, he was imprisoned for corruption and we had to start again.

The oil business was run as a monopoly by the state company, Petróleos de Venezuela (PDVSA). Venezuela had a law prohibiting foreign investment in natural resources. But in 1994, the government developed a new strategy which allowed foreign companies to develop oil fields which were past their peak, so-called "field rehabilitation" projects. They were generally third-rate fields, which meant that there was a strong risk of not recovering the initial investment. But we felt that it was worth going in as it would give us a foothold in the country. We began to operate part of the Pedernales field, which had stopped producing in 1986; and we had other fields in eastern Venezuela.

Pedernales was in the middle of the Orinoco Delta. As I flew in on my first visit, I was taken by the vast expanse of water and mud with trees alongside. The colourless trees seemed to turn red before my eyes. Thousands of scarlet ibis were taking flight, their plumage coloured by the consumption of shrimps from the water.[27]

Political tensions meant that BP, like many other international oil companies, could not prosper. There was widespread corruption, a stifling bureaucracy and political paralysis as the two main parties, completely out of touch with the population, waged internal battles.

In February 1999 Hugo Chávez came to power as a man of the people. The election of Chávez, who challenged the existing political structures and their leaders, should not have been a surprise. I had met him before he became president and could see immediately that he had unshakeable views with his own strong ideas of Bolivarianism.[28] Coincidentally, I had been in Caracas on 4 February 1992 during his failed coup, though I had slept soundly through the early morning activity at the airport and only heard about it the following day.

My particular meeting with him, after he became president, was in a London hotel in 1999. Initially I felt I was doing quite well. I spent a few minutes telling him how good a job I thought we were doing in his country and that we had all sorts of plans to invest. But I was mistaken. He launched into a lecture about the "evils of foreign oil companies" and the "end of devil colonial activity". I was berated for more than an hour.

It was clear that this was the beginning of the end for BP in Venezuela. Chávez was probably going to be the first leader in the new millennium to rediscover resource nationalism. Despite all the tremendous difficulties we had encountered in neighbouring Colombia, the leaders there were not in the business of confiscating the assets of private oil companies. Slowly but surely, however, Chávez set about changing the rules for oil companies.

Some of the headlines were: increased taxes; demands to hand over more of the oil produced; stipulations that exploration and production projects must be joint ventures with PDVSA, which in turn seems to be increasingly aligned with Chávez's Bolivarian revolution;[29] and selective cancellation of contracts deemed to be undesirable. Chávez was lucky since oil prices rose early in his presidency. A populist, his hold on the country relies on high prices continuing to keep the electorate happy.

In Venezuela, we applied what we had learned about corporate social responsibility. We invested. We employed plenty of local people. But we had to accept that, when a government's mood changes, so does your standing.

However, as one door closes, sometimes another opens; that is what happened in Libya. I was probably one of the last people left in BP who remembered exactly what had happened with Colonel Qadhafi in 1971.

In a tent in Libya

19 June 2005: I assumed that we were meeting Qadhafi in Tripoli. But that was clearly not the case. We were merely kicking our heels waiting in a hotel in the capital. Our hosts had us driven out of the capital to visit Sabratha, the magnificent Roman ruins with its well-preserved theatre, near the sea. We had the site to ourselves. Magnificent though it was, the polite efforts to kill time were a poor substitute for getting on with business.

It would have been unthinkable, a decade before, that Qadhafi would want to meet Western diplomats or businessmen, or that they would want to meet him. Qadhafi had started the process of oil nationalisation. He had played a key role in the oil crisis in the 1970s.

In September 1969, Qadhafi had seized power, overthrowing the ageing pro-Western King Idris in a bloodless coup. Initially Qadhafi said he would respect existing agreements with oil companies, but it was obvious that oil would be a political weapon in his radical stance against the West and particularly the US.

Libya was uniquely placed to challenge Western oil companies. First, in 1969 Libya was the largest Arab oil producer; its oil was high quality, low in polluting and corrosive sulphur, and cheap to transport to nearby markets in Western Europe.[30] Second, King Idris had encouraged competition in the Libyan oil industry and many international oil companies and smaller independent companies had concessions. BP was in Libya with the US independent oil operator, Bunker Hunt.

Third, Qadhafi knew that, with its small population and already high oil income, Libya "could live with reduced oil exports more easily than the West could live with reduced imports".[31]

Qadhafi began by negotiating with the competing oil companies, including BP, for an increase in the posted (official) price of oil and an increase in the tax rate. Once he began to succeed with one company, it started a ripple effect until the status of all international oil companies had changed. On 7 December 1971, Qadhafi nationalised BP's Libya operation.

In OPEC countries a wave of so-called "participation negotiations" got under way. The result was participation rates of 100 per cent for the country, and nothing for the companies. These oil-rich nations, dominated by foreign countries and foreign oil companies for years, were now their own masters. They could set the prices and call the tune.

In 1973, having seized control of their own resources, the OPEC nations could now use them as a political weapon. Libya was one of the nations that played a key role in the oil embargo in response to the US's role in the Yom Kippur War. This sent oil prices rocketing and created real concern about energy security in the West, particularly in the US. This was what finally got the Trans Alaska Pipeline the go-ahead, while I was in New York.

And oil was not Qadhafi's only weapon. In his actions against the West, Qadhafi supported terrorist organisations including the Irish Republican Army (IRA). The country's connection to terrorism and incidents, such as the killing of PC Yvonne Fletcher in London during a protest against Qadhafi outside the Libyan embassy in London, in 1984, and the West Berlin disco bombing two years later, led to President Reagan's bombing of Libya in April 1986. Forty people were killed, including Qadhafi's adopted baby daughter. In December 1988, a flight from London to New York was blown up by Libyan terrorists over Lockerbie, Scotland, killing 270 people. Libya was subject to a variety of sanctions for more than a decade.

In 2003, Qadhafi announced the end of Libya's weapons of mass destruction programme and opened up the country to inspection. It was a dramatic change of course, made possible by secret negotiations by the UK and US and hastened, perhaps, by the overthrow of Saddam Hussein in Iraq. By agreeing to compensation for the families bereaved in the Lockerbie tragedy, Qadhafi began to re-establish diplomatic ties with the West.

It was important for Britain to work on bringing Qadhafi back into the fold. And in 2004 Tony Blair was one of the first Western leaders to visit Libya in decades. Qadhafi also began to reopen the country's oil and gas reserves to international oil companies. I followed as one of the first Western businessmen in June 2005.

When we returned from Sabratha we went to the central market in Tripoli and sat and drank coffee. You would think that three Caucasian men dressed in blue suits would stand out. But no one seemed to take much notice of us. Suddenly, a messenger appeared to take us back to the hotel. There we were told that we were to go back to the airport. It soon became clear that we had to make another flight to an unknown destination. Our pilot was not happy.

We landed in the middle of the desert and could see nothing except the leader's plane. A beaten-up old Mercedes pulled up at the foot of the plane steps. The car smelt, the driver was smoking a cigarette, and without a word we were whisked off to a place that was used as a "conference centre". We were given keys and shown to rooms. I thought we might have to wait a few hours but we were there for the night – and without any luggage or change of clothes.

Everyone knew that Qadhafi's location was unpredictable. He was apparently always on the move for security reasons. All of this heightened the drama and increased the frustration. My colleague, Mark Allen, spoke fluent Arabic and made sufficient fuss to get us food – bananas, peanuts, and coffee. I still smoked cigars at the time. Sitting on a balcony overlooking the desert while Mark smoked his cigarettes, I puffed away for the whole evening. It made the time pass peacefully.

Next day we were told to be ready first thing. Another Mercedes picked us up. As we were driving along, an armoured car appeared in front of us. It was in this military convoy that we reached a semi-permanent military camp in the middle of the desert.

Finally, in a large Bedouin tent, we met Qadhafi, slightly unkempt and dressed in his colourful garb. I was given orange juice, tea and a bunch of birch twigs bound together with aluminium foil at the end. Qadhafi was holding a similar contraption and was using it to waft away the persistent flies. My travel companions were dismissed and I was left alone with Qadhafi and his interpreter for a long meeting, almost two hours, to agree some broad principles of our re-entry into Libya.

I was concerned that requests or threats to do with the UK's relationship with Libya would be the subject of our discussions. I had often been in similar situations and had always successfully refused to engage, whether with Jiang Zemin on Hong Kong, or Putin on Russian exiles in England. But nothing of the sort came up then or in future meetings. Rather, it was very telling when he said: "Tell me why, when I look at Algeria, I see that foreign companies left trained people. When foreign companies left Libya there were no trained people. Why not?"[32]

Qadhafi, once the young revolutionary, was now an older, seasoned person. He too needed foreign companies back in the country. He recognised that they provided a service. They would help him re-skill his people, get new technology into the country and get people working again. Generating economic activity and effectively rebuilding Libya's human capital was vital for the country's future.

Qadhafi was elliptical in his conversation. People in Libya were reluctant to do much without understanding what the leader wanted; this was, and still is, slightly Delphic. Increasingly, his English-educated, second son Saif is involved in the interpretation. Without continuous input from Qadhafi, processes in Libya slow down just like a clock that needs winding up. So some months later I found myself in another tent, on a plastic chair, talking to Qadhafi again. This time we were closer to Tripoli and we were in a field, rather than a desert.

This was a shorter meeting to cement a specific point. All this led to a joint venture with the Libyan National Oil Corporation which was announced in June 2007 shortly after I left BP. I was disappointed not to see the effort through, but at least I started it off.

Rebuilding the relationship with Qadhafi was a rare modern example of where political diplomacy opened up trade. Without Tony Blair's intervention, I doubt BP would ever have been as significant a player as it turned out to be in the re-opening of the oil and gas industry of Libya.

In Russia, I never wanted Tony Blair to get involved but I did want him as a witness to a deal. However, I did not expect that I would have to ask him twice.

8

MOSCOW

Wild east

April 1990: McDonald's would not have been my first choice for lunch but we needed food and that was the best available. So we bought two hamburgers and ate them in the car, outside the Ministry of Oil and Gas.

The opening of the "golden arches", the symbol of globalisation, in Pushkin Square, just a few blocks from the Kremlin was a real sign that times were changing. The USSR was close to meltdown. President Gorbachev's liberal reforms under *perestroika* and *glasnost* had resulted in an economic freefall. The remnants of communism were becoming a new order with new power and rules. How that order and power would develop was unclear.

But we had just heard something remarkable. Had we understood correctly? The car windows became increasingly steamy as we replayed the day's conversation.

Vagit Alekperov, then Russia's First Deputy Minister for Oil and Gas, had told us he was going to set up an oil company. Fashionably dressed in well-cut trousers, black roll-neck sweater and leather jacket, with his dark good looks, Alekperov was clearly powerful in this rapidly shifting society.

"So, do you want to be involved?"

I was naive, assuming he was talking about setting up a new company to explore a new prospect. "It sounds interesting. How are you going to do that?"

"Well, we'll give it some assets to start with."

"What sort of assets?"

"Basically some of the assets that I'm controlling now as a minister."

"How will you do that?"

BP had to be in Russia – it has one of the
world's largest combined oil and gas reserves

He did not respond.

Was he really suggesting a straightforward privatisation of state-owned assets? It seemed too incredible. Since 1987 small private businesses, erroneously named *kooperativs*, had been allowed in Russia, but natural resources were patrimony of the state. Even information about natural resources had been treated as a state secret.

Secrecy was part of the problem in Moscow. It was hard to get information, difficult to find the right people to speak to, and impossible to find anyone who could make a decision.

Alekperov clearly was one of the right people, but I had not gone to see him to talk about oil in mother Russia. I wanted to find out more about oil in Kazakhstan and Azerbaijan.

Kazakhstan was our first topic of conversation. The Kazakh Soviet Socialist Republic, like all countries in the Soviet Union, had been closed to the West until relations began to ease after the fall of the Berlin Wall. I was one of the first Western business leaders to go to Almaty, the Soviet-era capital, to start discussions about potential opportunities.

I had made great efforts, just a few months earlier, to get to know Nursultan Nazarbayev, then the ruling communist leader. This entailed immersion in traditional Kazakh customs and hospitality. Sheep's eyes would definitely not have been my choice for dinner but, wearing local ethnic costume, I had eaten one trying not to think of its texture or origin but simply of BP.

I had gone to Kazakhstan to talk about the massive Tengiz field. It turned out to be one of the largest oil fields in the world with more than 25 billion barrels of reserves. Now, in Moscow, Alekperov was telling me that Kazakhstan would be bad for my health and that we would not succeed there. When I asked him about Azerbaijan he was more positive, saying it was a "good place", but then he was originally from Baku.

And that was why we were plotting in the car, with the hamburgers. Should we pursue opportunities in Kazakhstan? Should we see what was happening in Azerbaijan? How could we get involved in what was happening in Russia? What was our next move?

These early conversations with characters like Nazarbayev and Alekperov were guarded and tough. Everyone knew the stakes were high.

Even in the face of Alekperov's chilling remark about Kazakhstan, I remained very confident; it was the confidence bred of ignorance. As the country gained its independence and Nazarbayev became president, our talks continued. Things waxed and waned. Projects were on and then they were off. Different oil companies tried to curry favour. We entertained Nazarbayev royally, took him to Alaska to show him the breadth and depth of our Arctic experience, and even helped him arrange his medical care. We looked at another field, Karachaganak. But in the end we could not agree the terms wanted by the Kazakhs. Their aspirations were sky high. At one stage Nazarbayev even asked the oil companies to help fund a soccer stadium for his new capital, Astana.[1]

Meanwhile, we began to make some tentative moves in Azerbaijan, but that is a separate story.

Feeling our way in Russia

Although Alekperov had said that we could get involved in something in Russia, trying to make that happen proved frustrating. I went back and forth to Moscow in the following months, but to no avail.

However, we did learn a lot. We discovered two things. First, Russian oil production was dropping rapidly and faster than we had expected. There was talk of ten million barrels a day falling to four million barrels a day. This had to be a management problem rather than a physical one. While we did not know the exact level of their reserves, we knew that they were substantial and more than adequate to support at least nine million barrels a day. Second, we discovered that getting a new project started would be a great challenge. The prevailing Soviet view was that nothing would work unless they had invented it. There was no incentive to change. And sourcing capital equipment would be a major problem. It was badly needed since the whole oil industry was decaying. Equipment was broken, corroded and often quite unsafe. Pipelines leaked. Gas produced with oil was routinely flared because it could not be collected for sale.

We went back to Russia and explored countless ideas. Many trips on old Soviet helicopters took us to one oil field after another in Tyumen province. We stayed at a mansion on the shores of the lake reputed to be the actual Swan Lake of the ballet. I got to know the Governor and his brother, who purported to control assets which would apparently be "just right" for us. Unfortunately, they were either not available or not appropriate. We looked at the Shtokman gas field in the Barents Sea but decided that it would be too costly to develop. I travelled to Timan-Pechora and found plenty of opportunities there but breaking into the local politics proved to be too difficult.

There were many colourful characters. Our plan was to keep talking to as many people as possible to find out what was happening and to spot the right opportunity. You can never do business by sitting behind a desk waiting for a call. You have to be in the flow of people and information. And that was never more necessary than in Moscow in the early 1990s as the stage, plot and cast all changed.

Following the fall of the Berlin Wall, Germany was reunified in October 1990 and by summer of the following year the Warsaw Pact crumbled and dissolved with little resistance from the Soviet powers. For some, Gorbachev's moves towards democracy and free markets went too fast and too far. Communist hard liners staged a brief coup in August 1991. It was not successful. And its failure was vividly illustrated by Yeltsin climbing aboard a tank, outside the White House in Moscow.

By December 1991, Gorbachev had resigned; the Soviet Union had ceased to exist. Yeltsin was now the President of Russia. He brought the promise of an even faster move to a free market economy.

Deciding to get rid of the centrally controlled communist economy was an important step. However, few people in Moscow had the economic skills or commercial experience to make this change happen. Institutions were ill-equipped to make a smooth transition to a free market economy and democracy. What followed was, not surprisingly, chaos – a "wild east". In the vacuum, wealth and power were seized by a handful of astute, driven and tough people. Widespread corruption, social dislocation and economic collapse ensued.

One of these "astute" people was Vagit Alekperov. I met him again in the middle of 1991 at a palace close to a dacha we had rented, west of Moscow. The palace at Arkhangelskoye was beautiful but deserted. It looked as if no one had been there for some time. The faded surroundings were the right setting to talk about change. And that is what we did, but to no concrete conclusion.

By November 1991 Alekperov had indeed set up an oil company, combining three separate state oil businesses into the vertically integrated state-owned oil concern Langepas-Urai-Kogalymneft. With privatisation in 1993, this would become private company Lukoil and Russia's largest oil company, with Alekperov as president and a major shareholder. He became one of the richest people in the world.[2] Meanwhile, with assets still under state ownership, our interminable discussions went nowhere. It felt as if we were banging our fist on a closed door. It was clear that things were changing but the mood in Moscow was up and down. I would go to one meeting and come back elated, and then go to another meeting and it was a disaster. The worst time to go was in the winter; it was dark, cold and depressing. It affected everyone; it reduced hope and made everyone miserable.

Since we could not find a way to get involved in exploration and production, we decided to try something different. We set up a joint venture with long-time Mayor Yury Luzhkov to build a chain of BP gasoline stations around Moscow. We got some of the best sites. The hidden hand of the mayor must have been at work to acquire them. The smart new forecourts with shiny signage, and shops with goods on the shelf, were an enormous contrast to the drab and decrepit gasoline stations of Moscow at that time. Everybody noticed them – including President Yeltsin.

This was an important move. It brought the BP brand to the attention of the big decision makers. We made some money too, by making it a "cash-only" business and the well-located sites became a valuable asset. Today those gasoline stations are still branded BP, although they are now owned by the TNK-BP joint venture.

Meanwhile, we were not going to give up on other options. We kept talking to government officials and eventually got agreement from the Ministry of Oil and Gas to undertake a study of the super-giant gas field, Kovyktinskoye, in East Siberia. It probably contained as much gas as the whole Norwegian continental shelf, one of the world's largest gas production areas. But, at the time, we had neither the right technology to produce it at a profitable rate nor the pipelines to get the gas to a market. The gas was a long way from the two big markets of the day – Europe and Japan. Rather than waste our efforts, we gave our study to a grateful but disappointed local administration. That gas field would later come back to us as part of the package of assets of our first Russian venture. And that venture was Sidanco.

One of the people we met when we were involved in the work in East Siberia was Boris Jordan. Boris was a lively American banker, Russian by birth, who would go on to set up Renaissance Capital and the Sputnik Group. I told him BP wanted to invest in Russia.

"You should buy a piece of Sidanco. I want you to meet Vladimir Potanin," he said. Potanin was one of the astute people who would become one of the so-called "oligarchs".

The oligarchs were made through privatisation of the state's assets. In late 1992 many in Moscow thought the move to a free market economy was not happening fast enough and that the country might revert to communism. Boris Jordan was one of the people who advised the government, including Yeltsin's minister Anatoly Chubais, on a scheme called voucher privatisation.[3] The idea of the scheme was to create widespread popular demand for privatisation. Everyone born in Russia before 2 September 1992 could, for a nominal fee of 25 roubles, purchase a voucher with a face value of 10,000 roubles (then worth approximately

$25). This could then be used to acquire shares in state-owned companies which were being privatised.[4]

Few people understood the scheme; many were happy to swap their vouchers for more immediate benefits – cash, cigarettes or vodka. As a result, when the companies were auctioned off, they ended up being highly undervalued and falling cheaply into the hands of well-placed management and the embryonic oligarchs. Some companies were deemed "strategic" and so the state kept a majority interest in them. Others were sold off completely.

In 1995 privatisation went a step further with a new scheme called loans-for-shares. This became the aptly named "sale of the century".[5] The loans-for-shares scheme involved the privatisation of some of the most valuable strategic assets of the Russian economy, including several large oil companies. Under the scheme, a few businesses or individuals made loans to the government in return for taking the shares of companies as collateral. Technically, the state could have repaid these loans within a certain period and hence redeemed the shares, retaining ownership of the companies. But it did not. It either did not have the money or the will.

There were no open or competitive auctions to establish the values of the businesses. Few people were involved and ownership passed silently into the hands of incumbent management, as with Alekperov and Lukoil, or into the hands of the embryonic oligarchs, such as Vladimir Potanin.

There are different theories – many of the conspiracy type – about what happened behind closed doors. What is not in doubt is that a political rather than market process transferred ownership of these companies at bargain prices.

With the economy in freefall, the government needed these sales to keep the budget deficit and inflation under control. The money met the needs of businessmen and reformers, led by Chubais, who were worried that the communist-led Duma could still regain control. The loans-for-shares scheme was a way of making sure that the capitalist revolution in Russia was irreversible. Others said that Yeltsin used the scheme to buy support for his forthcoming election.

Whatever the truth, in July 1996, Yeltsin was re-elected as president with a spectacular result. He had recovered from downbeat poll ratings of only 3 to 4 per cent just six months earlier.[6] Russia's wealth and power had changed hands. Around 50 per cent of Russia's assets were now controlled by just seven people – the oligarchs.

Doing business with the oligarchs

Vladimir Potanin was different from most of the other oligarchs. Roman Abramovich, Boris Berezovsky, Mikhail Fridman, and Mikhail Khodorkovsky had made their own entrepreneurial way, against all odds and from nothing. Potanin was a princeling of the communist party and had made the successful transition across to business from the party establishment. He had been well educated, groomed for the Kremlin and had been a minister. His father had been an important communist party official.

Potanin had travelled with his father and this made him more international in his approach. In the early 1990s Potanin started a bank and a trading business, called Interros, and soon "earned an enduring reputation as the *nomenklatura*'s favourite capitalist, the tycoon who had been appointed by the old elites, rather than making his own way".[7]

It was well known that Potanin had been one of the architects of the loans-for-shares scheme. Through it, he had acquired a large share of what had then seemed to me a terrible business, Norilsk Nickel, the world's largest nickel producer. It was the Soviet metals behemoth, with mining interests in the Arctic. The infrastructure and accommodation had been built by gulag labour under Stalin. Conditions were terrible. There had been little investment and it was losing money. Potanin bought it for a knock-down price. That was an extraordinary move since by early 2008 it was worth $60 billion, though considerably less by the end of that year.[8]

The other enterprise Potanin bought into was the oil and gas business Sidanco. This was what interested me. Potanin was not the only shareholder, so not only did I meet him but also some of the others involved in this consortium.

At times, it felt as though I was dealing with characters from a John le Carré story, but the plot would turn out to be a great deal more complex than that of any mere novel. Lots of people had their fingers in lots of pies in Russia; business relationships were intertwined and tangled. Some of the consortium members we met were Western, including Michael Dingman, who a few years earlier had given up his US passport to live in the Bahamas as a tax exile. Another was Joe Lewis, a man who had made a fortune in foreign currency trading, who also lived in the Bahamas. All these people were very wealthy, very powerful and, from what others told me, extremely plausible.

Sidanco seemed a good opportunity but I was cautious. I knew there were risks, not least because of uncertainty about Yeltsin's policies and hence Russia's future. When I told the BP board of the proposal to invest about $500 million to enter the Russian Federation, some members were surprised and some shocked. But they all eventually agreed. Russia was essential to our E&P strategy; the upside was enormous if we could get access to some of Russia's massive resources. And they knew that even though the Soviet Union had crumbled, success in other countries with resources in that region, such as Azerbaijan, would still need close relations with mother Russia.

However, I said: "We should consider it an outright gamble. We could lose it all."

It was good that I made that clear to the board. Within a year we had lost nearly half of our investment.

18 November 1997: We announced that BP was taking a 10 per cent stake in Sidanco for $571 million. Potanin and I signed the agreement at 10 Downing Street in London, watched by the Prime Minister, Tony Blair, and Russia's First Deputy Energy Minister, Viktor Ott. Blair described the deal as "one of the UK's biggest investments in Russia to date".[9]

I was very optimistic in public. "We believe the time is now right and, more importantly, that we have found in Sidanco a partner with a strong established position at the heart of Russia's oil industry." Privately, I was concerned about the direction that Russia was taking. Could we be confident of doing business over the long-term?

I thought Potanin and Sidanco would provide us with the right amount of political cover and help us understand the intricacies of doing business in Russia. I was wrong. Once we were in there, we were on our own. We began to learn more about Russian business, bureaucracy and politics. We soon learnt that owning 10 per cent was not enough to stop anything happening. We began to lose our assets.

A new bankruptcy law, passed in March 1998, began to lead to an unexpected redistribution of business assets across Russia. This often worked as follows. A general manager of a local subsidiary of a company would issue some short-term domestically traded debt purportedly so that he could do his business. That debt would later be bought by a friendly third party who would demand repayment at the date of maturity. The general manager would decline to redeem the debt. Then the friendly debt holder would go to the bankruptcy court and get possession of the asset. The general manager would then get a slice of the action.

Using this mechanism, businesses, often with the aid of powerful patrons in regional governments, were able to get their hands on valuable assets at a fraction of their real value.

Sidanco's assets were in lots of subsidiaries and, using these bankruptcy laws, assets began to "disappear" in the summer of 1998. It took a while for us to understand what was happening. The bankruptcy hearings would happen in remote places and we only heard about them after the event.

This might sound as though we did not have our finger on the pulse. That was partly true, but Russia was in turmoil. In August 1998 the government defaulted on its treasury obligations and the rouble collapsed. Several banks went under, triggering a major financial crisis. The country seemed to be slipping into an abyss with hyper-inflation and shortages of almost every necessity.

In the early 1990s I had experienced what I had thought was the worst of Moscow on a trip with Sir James Glover, a great soldier and non executive director of BP. We felt lucky to get rooms at the luxurious Savoy Hotel, as we discovered you could do this if you purchased a Finnair ticket. We did not use the air ticket; it just got us out of the decaying International Hotel. The silvered ornate dining room at the Savoy Hotel had a large plate-glass window onto the street and, as we began our dinner, gaunt faces of the hungry pressed against the glass to watch us eat.

Now, in the winter of 1998, the street scenes in Moscow were equally depressing. It was bitterly cold. People were hungry. The shops were empty. It was a horrible warning that Russia might be on the verge of collapse. People were so desperate that they were selling everything. At the Arbat open market you could buy precious things for next to nothing because people needed money for food.

The black market was rife. Taxi drivers did not want roubles. They would take luxury items, such as American cigarettes and European chocolate. These were more valuable than hard currency. And if they were pushed, they would accept dollars. At the apartment we used as an office, our representative, a resourceful Czech woman, kept a huge wardrobe full of barter goods: cigarettes, chocolate, tights, cosmetics and Scotch. It was like a scene out of Graham Greene's *The Third Man*.[10]

In early 1999 Sidanco began to unravel. It was not only that we were losing assets but also that operations, accounting and day-to-day office life were all going wrong. The BP people who were attached to Sidanco were at their wits' end. One day, Alekperov turned up in my office in London like a long-lost friend. He said: "You don't understand how bad these people are that you are dealing with. I will buy your interest in Sidanco."

While Alekperov tended to keep a low profile, I never underestimated him. So I knew he was not just being kind. He clearly wanted to get his hands on Sidanco. It made me realise that the company probably had better assets than we thought.

30 November 1999: The crisis came to a head over Sidanco's biggest asset. This was the oil and gas production subsidiary called Chernogorneft, located in the Tyumen region of West Siberia, responsible for three-quarters of Sidanco's oil production and the jewel in Sidanco's crown. In a court in remote Nizhnevartovsk, a city in West Siberia, Chernogorneft was declared bankrupt. A farcical "competitive" auction was then held.

The purchaser was a company called Tyumenskaya Neftyanaya Kompaniya (Tyumen Oil Company) or TNK. The major shareholder of TNK was oligarch Mikhail Fridman, who was the head of the Alfa Group.

It seemed unreal. Not only had we lost Chernogorneft, but it had been sold for what we thought was one-tenth of its value. The company's so-called "debts" could easily have been settled by BP, or one of the other investors.[11] The company could have been refinanced. A lot of people were clearly in cahoots. Now Sidanco was little more than a skeleton with hardly any assets. We were a naive foreign investor caught out by a rigged legal system. I had signed the deal in front of Blair; BP had been made to look a fool.

I was livid. We had lost more than $200 million of the money we had invested in Sidanco. Lots of people said to me: "The wise thing, John, is to cut your losses and get out."

But I knew if we allowed ourselves to get pushed out of Russia we would probably never go back. If we gave way in one place in the former

Soviet Union we could be forced to give up everywhere; we might be pushed out of Azerbaijan, too. We had to stand up and fight, using every legal means possible.

I decided not to speak to Fridman. We might not have understood the rules before, but now we were going to play TNK at its own game.

Fighting back

By this stage we had become BP Amoco and I felt we now had the power and reach to get our assets back from TNK through a broad international campaign. The first thing we had to do was to work out where TNK got the money to buy up the Sidanco debt. A lot, as we had guessed, came from Western banks, including the Ex-Im bank in the US. We reasoned that if we could cut off TNK's sources of credit we had a good chance of getting our assets back. And that is just what we did.

We made it known that we thought the Chernogorneft affair was a demonstration of corrupt business practices and that if Ex-Im were to advance further loans to TNK they would be sanctioning corruption. We asked the US Vice President, Al Gore, and Tony Blair to lend their weight to the campaign against TNK by intervening with the Russian government.

Stories that TNK was engaged in bad business practices began to feature in the Russian, British and US press. Stung by our accusation of dishonourable business practices, Fridman made numerous efforts through various channels to speak to me. I refused. Why would I speak to someone who was "stealing" BP's assets?

But eventually I did because Lord Janner called me. Greville Janner was an old friend. We were connected through his work in educating people about the Holocaust. He had recently been to Moscow and told me that I should speak to Fridman. "I have been talking to the chief rabbi in Moscow who tells me he knows Fridman. Fridman is better than the other people you were dealing with." So I agreed that I would talk to Fridman on the phone. Then we met.

Things were not as clear-cut as I had first assumed. Fridman explained to me what had happened.

It turned out that Fridman, in buying up Sidanco's assets, was pursuing what he considered his legitimate rights. There had been a private arrangement between Fridman and Potanin in 1995 around the loans-for-shares scheme; I had failed to realise how many things in Moscow rested on that event. Fridman had put up $40 million towards the purchase of Sidanco and had got one-third of the company in return.

Potanin had then used a legal loophole to buy out Fridman for $100 million. This gave Fridman a profit for his one-third share of the company but, shortly after, he saw Potanin go on to make far more money in a strategic deal with a foreign oil company, BP. We had paid $571 million for a 10 per cent share.

Fridman was furious. After the 1998 financial crash in Russia, Potanin was weakened because of his banking losses and Fridman had then decided it was time to get his own back. Initially I did not accept this version of events. However, Fridman produced a document which seemed to support his moral, if not legal, claim to Chernogorneft.

The two had clearly fallen out. The oligarchs had stood together to defeat communism but were now fighting each other. This was a glimpse of the bare-knuckle way of doing business in Russia. Fridman's battle was with Potanin and not with BP. For him, BP was just a casualty caught up in a bid to settle an old score.

When we met he was civil and charming. He was not like that with everybody. I could see the side of him which was the calculating persona with that "it's not personal, only business" stance.

Fridman was very different from Potanin. He had experienced the sort of anti-Semitic prejudices that had driven many Jews out of the Soviet Union. He had stayed and studied at the Moscow Institute of Steel and Alloys. While there, he had begun a series of entrepreneurial but illegal ventures, including buying up Moscow theatre tickets to sell on the black market. In 1987 he was one of the first to start a legal *kooperativ* and was soon involved in a number of businesses, from breeding white laboratory mice to window-washing.

Tough and hard working, he was well placed to take part in the initial privatisations and had bought some major industrial enterprises at knock-down prices.

So began a lengthy set of negotiations with the partners of TNK and Sidanco. It was like a chess game. The Russians were grandmasters. I could not afford to confuse tactics with grand strategy. Eventually we agreed to purchase an increased shareholding in Sidanco of 25 per cent, provided the company got its assets back. The owners of TNK agreed to the condition, but only if BP would pursue negotiations to buy 25 per cent of their company. This was a high-risk move. If we failed to agree a deal on TNK our shareholding in Sidanco would drop back to 10 per cent and we would probably have to get out of Russia with a consequent reduction in BP's reserves and production. Those were important factors for BP at the time; it had to show it was growing. But as important to some in BP was the feeling that we were throwing good money after bad.

Fridman was a superb negotiator. He would give you the feeling that he would rather forfeit everything than give up on a single crucial point. He was extremely focused on business. Even after many meetings, I found out very little about the man other than his love of what he called "extreme" vacations, which were more about adventure and exertion rather than rest and relaxation. He was intent on building a diversified empire, and TNK was the oil interest he wanted to grow.

I found his two partners, Victor Vekselberg of Renova and Len Blavatnik of Access Industries, just as hard to discern and equally ready to take risks. Blavatnik was born in Russia but was educated at Harvard Business School and lived mainly in the US. He subsequently bought a large petrochemicals business, Basell, the world's largest manufacturer of polyethylene, which had been a joint venture between Shell and BASF. He bought it with a significant amount of debt and added other large assets to it. The company merged and LyondellBasell Industries filed for bankruptcy in January 2009. Vekselberg was a man who liked detail; people speculated that he had been in the KGB or CIA, or both. Exceedingly wealthy, he kept out of the limelight until 2004 when he bought the Fabergé egg collection for $100 million from the family of Malcolm Forbes, the late founder and publisher of *Forbes* magazine.[12]

Why would BP decide to do business with Fridman, someone who once described himself as being viewed as a "Russian bandit"?[13]

The answer was pragmatism: we wanted to get into Russia but there were very few ways of doing that. Russia was one of the world's largest oil and gas producers with enormous resources. BP was in the oil and gas business and to me it was essential to be there. The only question in the back of my mind was whether there would be a future worth having in Russia. And that question was answered by a change of leadership in Moscow.

31 December 1999: As the world was on the verge of a new millennium, Boris Yeltsin resigned to make way for "new politicians, new faces, new intelligent, strong and energetic people". Prime Minister Vladimir Putin became acting president, and was elected shortly after.

During Yeltsin's presidency, Russia had been brought to its knees. I never had a one-on-one meeting with Yeltsin, but I was one of the few Westerners he saw frequently at bigger events. He would tell me that he liked BP because it was big and that he wanted us to do more in Russia. He was certainly no fool, but seemed to find it hard to concentrate on the matter in hand. He was unwell for much of his time and left too much space for mischievous people to fill.

Putin changed things. For a start he brought confidence. He was a trained lawyer and made it clear that he was determined to get Russian society under control. Laws were to be enforced and corruption stamped out. He said this to audiences around the world. He was a refreshing change and impressed the business people he met in London in 2000. I was one of them.

Things cannot change overnight. We knew that there would still be some corruption in Russia, but we did not want to be taken for a ride again. Sidanco was painful but not catastrophic. We had made a mistake and we did not want a repeat. We felt we had learned enough to begin discussions with Mikhail Fridman about a possible joint venture. In the meantime, I decided to explore some other options.

Considering other options

We decided to analyse all the oil companies in Russia. TNK was by no means the best. In fact, we ranked it third. Second was Sibneft and first was Yukos.

Yukos, unlike TNK, had some of the best assets in West Siberia. It had scale; it was Russia's largest oil company at the time, producing around a fifth of Russia's oil.

The man heading Yukos was another big oligarch: Mikhail Khodorkovsky. He had started out with a small private café in Moscow, moved on to the import business and started the Menatep bank. Khodorkovsky, like Potanin and Fridman, had acquired major assets from the state through the loans-for-shares scheme. At one stage he was *the* richest man in Russia.[14] After being introduced by Jacob Rothschild and some initial conversations in my office, I invited Khodorkovsky to spend the day with me at my house in Cambridge.

17 February 2002: Several large black armoured cars pulled up outside the house, and numerous burly bodyguards emerged. Khodorkovsky, like many of the oligarchs, lived in a gated compound with high walls and security lights, outside Moscow, and was paranoid about security. My house was much less grand, less protected, but nevertheless secure.

We had a pleasant lunch and discussed the possibility of BP buying a 25 per cent, plus one share, in Yukos. I did not feel that was enough. When I challenged him, he said: "You can have 25 per cent, no more and no control. If you come along with me you will be taken care of."

Bespectacled, soft-spoken Khodorkovsky could at first glance be mistaken as unassuming. But as the conversation progressed, I felt increasingly nervous.

He began to talk about getting people elected to the Duma, about how he could make sure oil companies did not pay much tax, and about how he had many influential people under his control. For me, he seemed too powerful. It is easy to say this with hindsight, but there was something untoward about his approach.

It turned out to be good judgement. In October 2003 Khodorkovsky burst on to the world's media stage as he was arrested for fraud, theft and tax evasion. He is now being detained in a Siberian prison. The company's assets were sold and in 2006 Yukos was declared bankrupt. Shortly before Khodorkovsky's arrest, in a private conversation, Putin made a passing but steely remark to me: "I have eaten more dirt than I need to from that man."

Khodorkovsky did what Putin regarded as unforgivable. He started meddling in the political arena when he was only a businessman. Putin's rule was "stay out of politics, just do business and you will be all right". Khodorkovsky crossed the line. When you do that in Russia there is no coming back.

Getting agreement with TNK

I judged that TNK was on the right side of the line. Getting to an agreement with the partners, however, was not straightforward. It was important that we both saw real mutual advantage; this was essential to overcome our earlier differences.

BP would get access to more reserves and Russian employees, and obtain a Russian profile. TNK would get our investment, technology and capability transfer and, importantly, credibility in the eyes of Western investors.

We started our discussions when the price of oil was low. I knew that putting more money into a country where we had already had our fingers burnt was high risk. I first thought of agreeing to buy a 25 per cent interest in TNK but the Sidanco incident had made me realise that would not be enough. BP would need to have a veto on all important decisions.

We knew the assets well. I had been back and forth to Moscow and out to the fields numerous times. This time there would be no rush; we would take our time and make sure we got it right. I had people poring over documents and inspecting plant and equipment; we spent more than 25,000 man hours on due diligence.

This was a huge deal – not just for BP and TNK, but for Russia and the UK. It was the largest transaction in Russian corporate history and the largest foreign direct investment in Russia.

Both Putin and Blair were involved. I had already met Putin in Moscow well before he had a significant global profile. I met him again in the UK when he was staying with Blair at Chequers in December 2001. I went down to have a one-on-one meeting with him, as did the CEO from Shell. Putin was well briefed and knew a lot about BP and about me. He was very impressive. I remember thinking to myself: regardless of what this man stands for, he is exceedingly competent.

I tried to push for 51 per cent of TNK but Putin and Fridman both told me we could not have it. I knew if we had 49 per cent we would have no power whatsoever. So in the end the only option was to go for a 50:50 deal. Putin said: "It's up to you. An equal split never works." Over the years he reminded me of this statement again and again.

The solution was a unique deal. The assets of TNK and Sidanco, along with BP's Moscow gasoline stations, were to be combined into a new company called TNK-BP. The shareholders of TNK retained 50 per cent of the shares and BP took its share up to 50 per cent in return for an investment of $8 billion. The price was only hammered out at the last moment. We had started out negotiating at $2 billion when the price of oil was low. But even if the price had stayed at $15 a barrel I knew there was plenty of upside. I suggested we pay in instalments, not because we could not afford to pay upfront, but because I felt this would further incentivise the partnership to stay together.

Overall control and board membership was balanced between TNK and BP. Fridman was to be chairman but we negotiated sufficient elements of control in our favour that made me feel comfortable. These included the right to appoint the CEO and a number of other key company officials. We also had a veto on strategy and on key personnel decisions. Russia was still a pressure cooker where the normal strains on business were amplified so we knew it was vital to tie down every detail.

I believed that in some cases our partners would protect us; in other cases we would protect them. My view was that the significance of the inter-relationship, between Russia and a foreign company of the standing and profile of BP, meant that if TNK in any way damaged the partnership it would have far-reaching repercussions, affecting foreign and other economic relationships. When the deal was announced in February 2003, one British newspaper featured a sardonic cartoon depicting Putin serving me with a cocktail. The caption was: "Shaken not stirred".[15]

23 June 2003: President Putin came to Britain on a state visit. The last time a Russian leader had been royally entertained was in 1874 when Tsar Alexander II came to see Queen Victoria. The pomp and ceremony for Putin included a state banquet at Buckingham Palace and a return banquet at Spencer House, the splendid 18th-century palace overlooking London's Green Park, both of which I attended. At Spencer House, everything had been specially flown in from Russia including, I think, the Russian waiters. But the visit was also about business.

The Russia–UK energy conference was held at Lancaster House in London. There, in front of Blair and Putin, Mikhail Fridman and I signed the historic TNK-BP deal on 26 June. TNK-BP was now the third biggest player in Russian oil and gas. BP had increased its oil reserves by almost a third and become the world's second largest private sector producer of oil and gas.

Having Blair and Putin witness the deal was important. It gave a sense of credibility, particularly as it was such a huge investment. I had not wanted either of them involved in the negotiations but had wanted them to bless the new company, as if they were its godparents.

Some months later I was invited to Moscow to attend a big reception at the Kremlin Armoury, organised by Fridman, to celebrate the TNK-BP deal. As I went into the building and up the wide stairs, I could see a massive photo of the signing at Lancaster House with Putin and Blair in the background. It had been enlarged and mounted on the wall at the top of the stairs like a huge regal tapestry. It was clear that, for everyone present, Putin was the most important figure in the picture.

Being foreign in Russia

Initially the world was sceptical. No one believed that we could make the TNK-BP deal work and certainly not all BP's shareholders viewed the deal positively. Most of them knew very little about Russia. The first meeting held with investors to introduce TNK-BP and our partners was illuminating. Our Russian partners were inexperienced at presenting to Western investors, who were ready with their probing questions and negative attitudes. And the investors were surprised by the Russians' awkwardness but they were impressed by the prospects for TNK-BP.

For a long while TNK-BP worked very well and much better than had been expected. The price of oil went up and oil production grew three times faster than originally forecast. It was the fastest-growing oil business in Russia. It deployed advanced technology. The dividends were huge. In terms of production, TNK-BP helped nudge BP ahead of Shell to the number two player in the world behind ExxonMobil. It even sold some of its more mature assets to the Chinese firm Sinopec with the blessing of the Kremlin. TNK-BP stayed out of politics and did its business well.

Russia was not a place used to living with a large foreign investment or with a large foreign company. We always knew the relationship with the Kremlin would not be smooth. At one point there was strong anti-foreign feeling in Russia. The Kremlin began planning to restrict foreign investment in the country. And a new law was proposed to prevent firms with majority ownership by foreigners from bidding for so-called "strategic assets", including certain oil and gas fields.

I was determined to have a meeting with Putin to hear from the man himself that he would respect BP's investment and property rights. Fridman arranged the meeting.

Then, out of the blue, two weeks before the planned visit to Moscow, TNK-BP was hit with a charge of back taxes of almost £420 million. This made me even more nervous. Yukos had been hit with an even bigger tax bill – a massive $27.5 billion – and, when it could not pay, its assets had been auctioned off.

21 April 2005: My meeting with Putin was a set piece with a bank of press photographers in the Alexander Hall of the Kremlin. Putin was cued up behind a door on one side of the hall and I was on the other. We were to meet in the middle to shake hands. This was to be Putin's first meeting with a foreign businessman for some time. The world's media was waiting to see if he would say something positive about the security of foreign investment. And Putin did: "We made no mistake when we supported [the creation of TNK-BP] two years ago." It was a demonstration to the world that Russia was open for business. It worked. The story was carried in newspapers around the globe.

I also had to see the Finance Minister, Alexei Kudrin, to discuss the taxes. In the conversation he mentioned that Russia was considering a new tax for oil companies on revenue rather than on profit. When I asked why they would use revenue, he responded: "It's another way of recovering stolen assets. Besides, everybody cheats when they calculate profit. Revenue is the only thing I can rely on."

It is easy to think there are no rules in Russia; if you do you will be caught out. It actually has an extraordinarily comprehensive set of laws, rules and regulations. It probably has the tightest environmental regulations in the world; so much so it is impossible to comply with them. It was the environmental laws that were used against Shell in the renegotiation of their contract for Sakhalin II.[16]

The problem is not the lack of laws but their selective application. And that is what creates this sense of lawlessness. While bureaucratic, legalistic processes are the hallmark of Russia, you never know whether someone will turn a blind eye, or whether the laws will be applied to the hilt.

You will not be trusted if you write rules and then appear to rewrite them through selective application. You cannot do that in private life, you cannot do that as a CEO – and you certainly cannot do that as a government. Companies will only invest in large numbers and at scale if the rules are clear, stable, consistently applied and transparently enforced. Those simple but very powerful concepts give companies the confidence to operate. BP has survived and prospered in Russia but not every company which has tried has succeeded. If Russia wants to continue to attract foreign companies it will have to work much harder to convince them that the rules are applied fairly and consistently.

Second only in power after the Russian state was Mikhail Fridman. Fridman controlled many things. The TNK-BP agreement was for five years. We said that for five years neither of us could sell our interests. After five years I knew that Fridman and his partners would want to renegotiate as they would be determined to expand the scope of TNK-BP and to crystallise the value of their shares. Over five years there were, from time to time, spats and disagreements. None of them was anything other than about tactics; a low-level guerrilla war carried on inside the company, often with the intention of undermining the expatriate BP staff. Overall BP prospered, but in 2008 things appeared to begin to unravel. The chief executive we appointed in 2003, Robert Dudley, had done an excellent job, achieving the highest average shareholder return (45 per cent a year) of any major Russian oil company. With media speculation as to what went on behind closed doors, he stepped aside. But that is his story and not mine.

Saying goodbye

It was always important to me to build a strong relationship with Putin, though he was a person few people got to see. He did not like to meet foreign businessmen, but he would see me. I once thought my Eastern European blood might have helped, but now I doubt it. Powerful people, like Putin and the oligarchs, engage with other people not because they have titles, or are nice, but because they could be useful to them.

To be useful you need to bring resources or help them in one way or another. It might be with advice on their economy, or it might be on how they stand on the world stage. It has to be something that no one else can give them, something that gives them the edge. People like Putin invest time in those who they think have a future. If you happen to be one of those people you will be welcome.

23 March 2007: Putin was one of the few people I was determined to say goodbye to before leaving BP. And it was important for me to introduce my successor, Tony Hayward. Relationships like the one with Putin had created a great deal of value and, if maintained, would safeguard future value. BP's initial investment in TNK had already been repaid and it was on track to make four times that investment. Time was limited

because of my accelerated departure, but Putin obliged and invited me to his dacha outside Moscow. He was very relaxed in that environment, with his dog, and we talked with less formality than usual. Perhaps the dog helped; it seemed to like me. Putin commented on BP's consistency, that we had delivered on our promises and that I had always had the same clear agenda with him. Consistency was not something he was used to.

Was any part of this story what I envisaged back in the steamy car with the hamburger in 1990? No, we could never have planned any of this.

Did the characters that instigated the privatisation ever think through what the outcome would be? How could they? Too much change, too fast, caused the country to meltdown. It was like a cultural revolution, except it produced a strange outcome. The country changed to a free market system yet retained some of the worst aspects of communism because people did not trust each other.

I doubt anyone in 1990 could have foreseen just who would rise to the top through the freewheeling, wild east, sale-of-the-century environment. But it was inevitable there would be winners and losers.

This was also to be the case in Azerbaijan, as I discovered when I went to visit Baku on Vagit Alekperov's recommendation.

9

AZERBAIJAN

Geopolitics

July 1990: I drew back the thin curtains in a grim Baku hotel room to watch the sun rise over the grey Caspian Sea. Hundreds of feet below that still water, in a stretch called the Absheron Sill, lay the promise of billions of barrels of premium oil.

Azerbaijan had been lost behind the Iron Curtain for many years. Many assumed Caspian resources had dried up because the Soviets had abandoned drilling almost completely.

I had come to find out how BP could secure a deal to extract what promised to be a sizeable prize. I had little idea then what twists and turns the venture would take. The quest to secure Azeri oil would entail extraordinary political obstacles. And I would become embroiled in the formation of a strategic East–West energy corridor; even Washington would become involved. The venture would even loosely inspire a James Bond film.[1]

In many ways the struggle to get control of Azeri oil became a repeat of the 19th-century Great Game, when Victorian Britain and Tsarist Russia had engaged in strategic rivalry for control of Central Asia. The difference was that this new Great Game involved vast resources of crude oil. There would be far more players including Western Europe, the US, post-Soviet Russia, Iran, Turkey and Georgia. And with its own independence at stake, Azerbaijan would be a protagonist rather than a kitten to be toyed with as Persia had been in the 19th century.

Azerbaijan, still a Soviet outpost, was precariously poised. In January that year President Gorbachev's army had marched into Baku, the country's capital, to suppress a national uprising and around 200 people had been killed. Times were uncertain but I knew we had to establish ourselves in Baku as quickly as possible. Following the fall of the Berlin

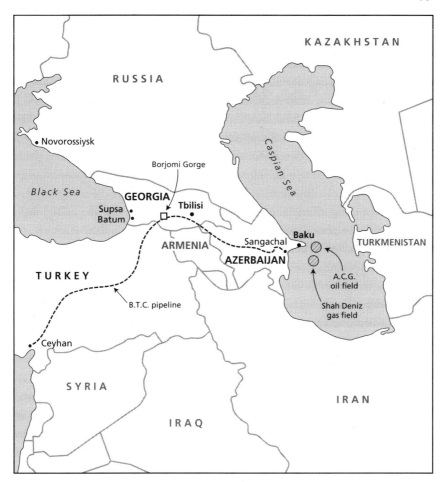

The Baku-Tbilisi-Ceyhan (BTC pipeline) was
more than an engineering feat

Wall and subsequent cracks in the Soviet Union, the area's resources
were beginning to draw interest from oil companies around the world.

Oil and gas had been seeping through the ground here since time
immemorial. Like neighbouring Iran, Azerbaijan had formed part of
Persia in earlier years. The area around the Absheron peninsula had been
the site of the everlasting fires of ancient Zoroastrian fire temples, such
as the one at Surakhany.

The first primitive oil wells were said to have been dug here as early
as the 11th century. In the 13th century Marco Polo had observed people
collecting oil from seeps, a practice reputed to date back to the time of

Alexander the Great. By 1750 there were more than 50 oil pits being worked around Baku and the product was sold for lubricants, illumination and a wonder cure for ailments such as rheumatism.[2]

By the 1870s the oil industry had taken off. Ludwig and Robert Nobel, brothers of Alfred Nobel, dynamite inventor and eponymous provider of the Nobel Prize, decided to invest. Robert had been in the area in search of walnut to manufacture rifles for the Russian government when he discovered the burgeoning industry.[3] The Baku oil venture became the basis for the family's fortunes.

The Rothschild family was another big investor. The French Rothschilds, having had their proposal of a partnership with the Nobel Brothers Petroleum Company rejected, bought the Batumi Oil Refining and Trading Company and eventually controlled, at its peak, a third of Russian oil output.[4]

At the turn of the century Baku, with its 3,000 wells and infamous gushers, was supplying half the world's oil needs and challenging Rockefeller's Standard Oil for control of Europe's kerosene markets.[5] One British journal at the time wrote: "Baku is greater than any other oil city in the world. If oil is king, Baku is its throne!"[6]

Ninety years later, I arrived to see not only decaying Baroque-style mansions from this era but also the sorry remnants of a once-great industry. The Soviet legacy was a wasteland of abandoned drilling rigs from the Second World War; nodding-donkey pumps, only a few of which were working; and the stench of oil lying in pools and soaked into the ground as a result of years of mismanagement. Neft Dashlari (Oily Rocks), the jewel of offshore Soviet exploration, was literally sinking into the sea.[7]

With countries in the Caucasus region teetering towards independence from the Soviet Union, I knew that if we were to get some business, it was likely to result more from politics than commerce. And Baku had already been centre stage in the politics of the region for more than a century.

Baku had been the breeding ground for Bolshevik revolutionaries at the turn of the 20th century. Georgian agitator Josef Vissarionovich Djugashvili was involved in rallying the oil workers in Baku and nearby Batum to strike against what he viewed as the plutocratic oil field owners.[8] This was a formative experience for the man who would later change his name to Stalin. Oil was the major reason for the occupation of Baku by British forces during the First World War. And Baku played a central role in fuelling Stalin's victorious Red Army during the Second World War.

From these glory days, oil production had plummeted to a few thousand barrels a day by 1990. It seemed that the Moscow Oil and Gas Ministry was no longer interested in the Caspian Sea, but not because there was no oil. I discovered that they had abandoned Baku because the offshore Azeri oil prospects were too technically challenging and the Soviet leadership had prioritised investment in Russia, particularly in West Siberia.

Even before Azerbaijan gained independence, its government had begun to flex its muscles and had decided that, if Moscow was not going to help it develop the oil under the Caspian, Western companies might.

Soon we were in discussion with the State Oil Company of Azerbaijan (SOCAR) and by October 1990 we had an informal agreement. BP, Norwegian state oil company Statoil, and Ramco (a small Aberdeen-based company which had got in early) had been offered the rights to develop the Azeri field, one of the giant oil fields under the Caspian Sea.

Our plans were short-lived. Within months Amoco began courting the then communist leader, President Mutalibov. By April 1991, a new contract for the Azeri field was drawn up in favour of the US company. But at the end of August 1991 Azerbaijan declared independence. Mutalibov was out.

It seemed Azeri oil was up for grabs once again.

With the collapse of the Soviet Union and the weakening of the grip of the communist party, the ethnically diverse Caucasus region was now a tinderbox. Azerbaijan and Armenia were at war over the disputed territory of Nagorno-Karabakh. Before the ceasefire was declared in 1994, Azerbaijan would see four changes of government.[9]

Neighbouring Georgia was also being torn apart by a number of smaller conflicts, including a war with Abkhazia and South Ossetia.[10] And further north, Chechnya was engaged with Russia in a bitter struggle for independence.

When we had decided on our new exploration strategy, we always knew that new places and new politics would mean new challenges. I decided we had to keep our nerve and keep talking to whoever seemed to be in charge in Baku.

We rented the first floor of a 19th-century downtown building. Past its heyday, it was exceptionally grubby but architecturally pleasing with a precarious wrought-iron balcony overlooking the street. Once cleaned, it made a half-decent office. BP staff slept four to a room at the nearby seedy Hotel Residence. On my visits I would be fortunate if I had a hotel room to myself, and even more fortunate if there was water for a shower. Food was dire, even dangerous. While waiting for the real action, we tried to make ourselves useful such as helping to set up a museum in Baku. We were well aware that other oil companies, particularly those from the US, as well as numerous undesirable middlemen, were trying equally to curry favour.

Clever moves

With time came more oil companies. They began to muscle in and we risked being pushed out. We thought of two novel moves.

The first was visibly aligning the company with the British government. In 1992, although Britain had established diplomatic relations with Azerbaijan, there was no British embassy in Baku; matters were dealt with from Moscow. So after discussions with various bodies in London, including what was then the Department of Trade & Industry, it was agreed that a "trade mission" would be sent from the UK. With spare space in our newly acquired offices, we partitioned off an area to be used by the British government representatives. A British diplomatic flag flew outside. Although BP was then a private company, it was essential for us to be closely aligned with the UK government as post-Soviet countries still found it easier to understand and accept government-to-government dealings.

The second idea was Mrs Thatcher. President Elchibey was now in power; a pleasant, charming, bookish, but ineffectual man. He loved ancient manuscripts and rose jam, which he served at meals in the presidential palace. In an effort to get him to favour BP over the other oil companies, I invited Margaret Thatcher to Baku. Even though Mrs Thatcher was no longer Prime Minister, she was still much admired in former Soviet Union countries. Her "Iron Lady" title came from an article in the Soviet army newspaper *Krasnaya Zvezda* (Red Star).[11] And, fiercely anti-communist, she was delighted to be asked. Mrs Thatcher saw oil as economically and politically important for Azerbaijan to achieve true independence in the post-Soviet era.

September 1992: Diplomatically the visit was a success. Privately there were moments when it verged on disaster. Michael Heseltine, then UK Trade Minister, joined Mrs Thatcher. I took them on a tour of some of the existing onshore oil wells and we had lunch at the Caravan-Sarai, a restored 18th-century inn built around a large courtyard for accommodating visitors travelling along trade routes in Central and Western Asia. It was swelteringly hot. The food had been left out in the sun and was diabolical, almost rotten.

Mrs Thatcher was to give a speech to some key dignitaries and business people. The rudimentary amplification system did not work. And afterwards the audience discovered black paint stripes on the rear of their suits. The chairs had been hurriedly painted to make a good impression and were still wet.

It was a shame hardly anyone could hear her speech as Mrs Thatcher had put a lot of effort into getting it right. Nick Butler, my policy adviser, had accompanied her on the plane from Hong Kong to Baku. Characteristically, she did not sleep a wink on the journey. When the plane stopped to refuel at Karachi, to their surprise, there was a guard of honour and military band on the airport apron. Not wanting to disappoint them, she quickly changed into her best blue suit and went out to take the salute.

She had spent the time on the plane amending the speech. Nick observed her produce a book of Winston Churchill's quotations from her famous handbag. She then reworked the sentiment, not the exact quotations, into her speech. And the result was impressive and inspiring, if only the audience could have heard it.

We stayed at the presidential guest house, which had been built to accommodate Brezhnev's visits. Stories were told of Chairman Brezhnev leaving impoverished Baku with lavish gifts of diamonds and carpets. Dated and ghostly, the house bore much evidence of past splendours, including a room decked out with animal furs and an indoor swimming pool, now matt vivid green, ready for a monster to emerge from its depths.

After the events of the day we stayed up until three in the morning drinking with Mrs Thatcher. What I liked about her was that she had style and was never prissy; she could be disciplined and professional but then relax and enjoy a few glasses of Scotch. Refreshingly, she called a spade a spade. Her ultimate downfall was that she thought she always knew better than anyone else.

Mrs Thatcher's visit kept us in the frame. More talks, more meetings, more waiting followed.

11 June 1993: There had been months of lobbying; oil companies were played off against each other. At last, there was a new contract, again for the Azeri field, but it was with a larger consortium including BP, Statoil and Amoco.

It was hardly worth celebrating. Within a week Elchibey was overthrown in an army coup. I was in Baku at the time and events were dramatic. Elchibey was challenged by rebel military leader Colonel Huseinov from the disputed territory of Nagorno-Karabakh. Troops were within a few miles of Baku at one point. This was the opportunity for Heydar Aliyev, the country's Soviet-era leader and a former member of the Soviet Politburo, to make his return. At one point Elchibey talked of a power-sharing agreement with Aliyev, in an attempt to avert civil war, but he soon fled the country. By mid-June Aliyev was in control.

He was in power just five days when he cancelled the contract. Every oil company would now have to talk its way back into a new deal. The risks of investing in Azerbaijan were clear. But so, too, was the size of the prize, making me even more focused. If there was going to be a deal, BP had to be the participant with the largest share.

Initial fears that Aliyev would look to his old Moscow colleagues proved to be unfounded. He had obviously decided to use key Western countries to Azerbaijan's political and economic advantage. And oil was the big lever.

Because Aliyev was huge both in size and personality, I never wanted to get on the wrong side of him. I felt I might be eliminated, incarcerated or crushed. Like people of his generation and background, he understood his position. He knew how to make an impact, how to stand, where to be, what to say and what not to get involved with. He was an extraordinarily gifted politician. He also knew how to give speeches. Or at least he thought he did.

I think Aliyev's theory of speech-making was this: since people never listen to all of your speech, you have to make it long and repetitive so that no one misses the message and everyone goes away at least remembering something. His speech themes were always the same: how Azerbaijan was going to be a great nation, how they would look after the oil money, how he would develop the nation, how they were going to be a leading nation in the world.

At one event at the Dorchester Hotel in London, he got up to say a "few words" before dinner. I had warned the restaurant not to prepare the food until he had finished. An hour later the soup arrived. His daughter was present and, with that special privilege given only to a daughter, took calls on her mobile phone throughout his whole speech.

When I went to Baku, Aliyev would often invite me to the presidential palace and entertain me to dinner. Given today's standards, it is hard to imagine just how poor and underdeveloped Azerbaijan was in the mid 1990s; even at the palace the food, while more generous in quantity, was just as tasteless as everywhere else.

Contract of the century

Covert conversations continued. At one point, we discovered different oil companies were negotiating three separate agreements for three separate oil fields.

Eventually, to share costs and reduce risks, one unified agreement emerged and after thorny negotiations there was a new deal. This was to be a single production sharing agreement (PSA) between ten foreign oil companies and the national oil company, SOCAR, for the exploitation of three already-discovered oil accumulations called Azeri, Chirag, and Guneshli, together known as ACG. This "super-giant" field, ACG, was then thought to contain more than five billion barrels of proven reserves.[12] It would turn out to be much bigger and become the ninth largest oil field in the world.[13]

Right up until the last moment, we were unsure as to whether the deal would go ahead.

20 September 1994: On the day we were due to sign, we did not know who would represent the Russian government at the ceremony, or indeed if anyone would turn up. There had been confusing signals from Moscow. We felt that they were still trying to undermine the deal.

We headed up to the Gulistan Palace, on the hillside overlooking Baku harbour, in the early afternoon. Aliyev was there along with numerous dignitaries including: Tim Eggar, UK Energy Minister; Bill White, US Energy Deputy Secretary; Thomas Young, UK Ambassador;

Richard Kauzlerich, US Ambassador; and various representatives from the international oil companies. A traditional buffet meal had been laid out for hours, and a folk-dancing display got under way. It was less than an hour before we were due to sign when Stanislav Pugach, a representative from the Russian Ministry of Fuel and Energy, arrived. Tension eased immediately. He was the signal we needed to go ahead.

We all signed.

It was the first contract made with foreign oil companies by a former Soviet Union country and it was expected to create, within five years, revenues equivalent to the country's entire gross national product. In Azerbaijan it was dubbed the "contract of the century".

I was delighted. After Azerbaijan's state oil company, BP had, by the smallest margin, the largest share, though collectively the US companies had secured more than the UK companies.[14]

The ten foreign oil companies (representing six different countries) combined in a consortium and created an operating company called Azerbaijan International Operating Company. The acronym, AIOC, was the same as that of the old Anglo-Iranian Oil Company. We hoped for the same exploration success but far better political luck.

Inevitably, jockeying for position continued. The AIOC consortium had no dominant player and suffered from management by committee. And there were lots of issues. Russia might have sent a ministry representative to the signing and AIOC might have had an agreement to develop the Azeri oil fields, but Moscow was still a cause for concern, sending some very mixed messages.

In particular, Moscow was now claiming ownership of the Caspian's rich oil reserves. It is rather common for disputes to arise over ownership of offshore exploration licences, but the landlocked Caspian Sea posed a potentially unsolvable problem.[15]

Was the world's largest inland body of water a sea or a lake? It was never resolved. If it was a sea, the boundaries would be the median line between each country; ACG would then belong to Azerbaijan. If it was a lake, each of the five new, littoral states (Russia, Kazakhstan, Turkmenistan, Iran and Azerbaijan) would be entitled to an equal share of the water and so of ACG.[16] And, indeed, Iran and the Soviet Union had an earlier agreement designating the body of water as a common lake with shared resources.

Then there was the question of how to transport the oil to market.

The local market had very limited demand, and oil sold at regulated prices below world levels. To make the project commercially viable, the oil had to get to a deep-water port with access to the global oil market.

Existing options were out of the question. The ancient wooden 19th-century Nobel pipeline to the Black Sea in Batumi, Georgia, was barely standing and a single northern pipeline ran from Russia to Azerbaijan through war-torn Chechnya.

While options for a transit pipeline began to be discussed, many in BP and other oil companies remained sceptical about the project, not only because of the scale and complexity. Within days of signing the contract of the century there had been a failed coup against Aliyev. Moscow had responded by closing its southern border with Azerbaijan, despite the fact that Lukoil, the Russian company, had a share in the consortium. And Eduard Shevardnadze, the new leader in troubled neighbouring Georgia, was flexing his muscles, too. He was looking at geopolitical opportunities offered by foreign investors in Baku.

Vision was critical. Terry Adams, a BP stalwart, became head of AIOC and did a truly remarkable job. When Terry went to Baku there was nothing. Sheer determination and entrepreneurial activity were the hallmark of those early years. In the face of seeming impossibility, he found ways to overcome many obstacles. Critically, he built trust and confidence with Aliyev.

By 1997 AIOC had managed to agree and implement an early oil project which involved a single platform on the Chirag field, connected to a small new pipeline to be built from Baku to the Black Sea at Supsa in Georgia. At the official opening ceremony on the Chirag platform in November 1997, Aliyev's delight for his nation was palpable as he wiped the first-produced oil on his face, as is the tradition.

Offshore drilling proved difficult, particularly as there were mud volcanoes to be avoided.[17] The Soviets had been defeated by sinking platforms. We now had to find new ways around other significant engineering challenges. If getting the oil out was a problem, getting equipment in was no easier. Early on we had tried to import some equipment by way of the Russian canal system. We had many problems: stolen or lost goods, enormous customs duties and water frozen for four months of the year. We decided the best option was to build everything in situ in Azerbaijan. This required a significant investment in the old

Soviet construction and fabrication yards around Baku. To save money, we reused resources already there. At one point we rebuilt Ishtar, the abandoned Soviet drilling rig, finding ever more asbestos and ever more problems. We ended up spending three times the initial budget.

I began to think we would have to pour endless amounts of money into the project. Cost overruns became an increasing problem. The Baku–Supsa pipeline for the early oil project went over budget and SOCAR demanded that AIOC bear the additional costs. The Azerbaijan side had a way of unilaterally interpreting our contract to their own advantage.

Meanwhile, the large number of partners in the AIOC consortium continued to hamper progress and jeopardise the critical timeline.

11 August 1998: BP's merger with Amoco changed everything at a stroke. We became the clear leader for the project. BP and Amoco had been the two largest owners in the consortium and combined, had 34 per cent of the equity. BP Amoco could now take the lead as the single operator and play a key role in determining the route of the main export pipeline which would be required for full production when all the fields came on stream.

I have often been asked whether Azerbaijan's oil was the key strategic driver in our buying Amoco. It was not but, fortuitously, it gave us the power we needed to get things done.

By May 1999, David Woodward, a 30-year BP veteran, had become head of BP Azerbaijan and AIOC. Under David's leadership, we installed a capable BP team to get on and deliver the project in Baku as the single operator.

Pipeline problems

The new Baku–Supsa line could cope with early oil production. It came on line in the nick of time. The northern route, through Chechnya, was blown up by rebels and was out of operation for months. But full field development, with significantly higher production rates of oil, required a new solution: a bigger export pipeline.

Geography made the choice of route difficult. Baku is about 800 miles from the Persian Gulf, 400 miles from the Black Sea and 1,000 miles from the Mediterranean.

Politics made the choice of route seem impossible. The most direct route to the Mediterranean would have been close to the southern border of Armenia, but that was out of the question because of the continuing war with Azerbaijan. Washington was in the background and determined to secure a stable East–West oil export corridor. Significant big players in the region were vying for power.

We found ourselves with a seemingly insurmountable problem. It was clear that negotiating a pipeline route would face many challenges, not least understanding and traversing complex international relations.

Three options emerged: south through Iran to the Gulf, west through Georgia to the Black Sea, or west through Georgia and Turkey to the Mediterranean.[18] By May 1999, time was marching on and a choice had to be made.

The Iran option was politically fraught.[19] AIOC included American companies, and BP, too, had assets and shareholders in the US. Deteriorating US–Iran relations had meant increasing trade sanctions and, under Clinton's administration, the US Iran and Libya Sanctions Act had deterred even non-US companies from investing in Iran.

The second option was to transport the oil by pipeline to the Black Sea and export it by tanker from there. This option involved a comparatively short pipeline of about 400 miles. There were two variants of this route, each with different politics, costs and risks: one through Russia to Novorossiysk and one through Georgia to Supsa, a similar route to the pipeline for the early oil project. These options had the advantage of being cheaper than a long pipeline to the Mediterranean. They were favoured by the Russians since they could control the ports on the Black Sea.

But any route which involved the Black Sea had a major problem. To get the oil away from Novorossiysk or Supsa would rely on yet more oil tankers crossing the Black Sea and then navigating the narrow 12-mile Bosphorus Straits to reach the Mediterranean. No one could prohibit this happening, but that was not the issue. The Straits were hazardous and the possibility of an oil spill polluting Istanbul was one risk BP was not prepared to take. The Turkish government too was understandably concerned about the ever-increasing possibility of an oil-tanker incident in the heart of Istanbul; more and more Russian tankers were moving oil through the Straits.

The third pipeline option would run for more than 1,000 miles, from the shores of the Caspian, south of Baku, through the mountains of

Georgia and eastern Turkey to the Turkish port of Ceyhan on the shores of the Mediterranean. At first this appeared to be the least attractive option. Not only was it the longest and most expensive, but it would also involve negotiations with three strong leaders of three separate countries, each with their own political agendas.

Heydar Aliyev, President of Azerbaijan, had decided that this route was a national priority since it would consolidate Azerbaijan's strategic relationship with Turkey and the West.

Süleyman Demirel, President of Turkey, viewed the pipeline as key to a wider strategy of strengthening Turkish influence in Azerbaijan and Central Asia and establishing Turkey as a key transit country for oil and gas.

Eduard Shevardnadze, President of Georgia, had spotted a strategic opportunity and rapidly positioned Georgia as vital to any transportation of oil in the Caucasus region. He was one of the key proponents of the Mediterranean route and saw that the construction of the pipeline through Georgian territory would guarantee the country's economic and political stability.

But the biggest player was the US.[20] Building the pipeline through Turkey was a way of supporting the independence of the new states of the South Caucuses and Central Asia. And US energy security would be improved by creating a strategic energy corridor for Caspian hydrocarbons.

Political wheeling and dealing went on. A declaration of support for the Baku–Ceyhan route had been signed in October 1998 by the US, Azerbaijan, Turkey, Georgia, Kazakhstan and Uzbekistan. And now BP and other members of the AIOC consortium were put under considerable pressure to support it.

We were caught in a pincer movement. Shevardnadze, then a powerful figure, told me that the route was "take it or leave it". The Turkish government increased pressure by instigating protests at our Istanbul office and a boycott of BP gasoline service stations across Turkey, claiming that we were blocking the Ceyhan route. The US government was determined to get its way. Our investors were alarmed at the thought of the enormous and barely profitable investment.

Internally we wrestled with how we could justify the capital cost, which we estimated at $3.2 billion. It was an enormous sum, especially as oil was at a low of $10 a barrel at the time.[21] We could see that Aliyev's unswerving commitment to the Turkish route was going to lead to a stand-off and further delays which we could not risk.

BP had no alternative but to try to find a way to make the route work. And there was another big factor. We knew it was the best environmental option. That is what I announced at a conference in Istanbul. Standing in front of a window overlooking the Bosphorus, I said we would support the long route to Ceyhan particularly as it would help reduce the number of tankers in the Straits. At that moment a large tanker passed behind me and darkened the window, as if to sanctify our choice.

Finding a way through

How do you negotiate the legal and fiscal arrangements for a pipeline through multiple jurisdictions? It had been done before, but not for a project of this scale. There were no precedents and no established rules. I asked Wref Digings, a long-time BP negotiator, to take on the project and find a way to make it work. Wref and his team were on the road for the next two years.

We had to find a way to drive a project that would not only be commercially viable, but would also survive 10 years in negotiation and construction, and have a lifespan of 40 years.

18 November 1999: The first step was an intergovernmental agreement (IGA) that was signed by the leaders of Azerbaijan, Georgia, Turkey, Turkmenistan[22] and Kazakhstan at the OSCE[23] summit in Istanbul under the watchful eye of President Clinton. This took on the status of an international treaty designed to align the parties around the objective of building the pipeline, which was now named the Baku-Tbilisi-Ceyhan (BTC) pipeline.

The agreement did not cover how the pipeline would be financed. It did, however, cover issues such as security, freedom of transit, and property rights. And because these were in a treaty, investors were confident that they would not be unilaterally and adversely altered.

The next step was to create separate host government agreements with each of the nations to attach to the IGA.

Turkey was the first stop. Working through BOTAŞ, the Turkish state-owned pipeline operating company, was difficult. Senior management were politically appointed and they wanted to avoid mistakes rather than get the project done.[24] Turkey's view of the project costs differed significantly from ours. Turkey estimated the cost would be around $2.4 billion, whereas our estimate was closer to $3.2 billion.

There came a moment of truth. During a presentation by BOTAŞ Valekh Aleskerov, chief negotiator for Azerbaijan, challenged Turkey's estimates. After a heated exchange, he got up from the negotiating table, walked to the flip chart and, with a black marker pen, wrote: "The Turkish government guarantees a fixed price for Baku–Ceyhan pipeline at $2.4 billion." He then pointed the marker at the Turkish ambassador and asked him either to sign, or to stop insisting that the cost would be $2.4 billion. The Turkish ambassador signed and the foundation for the Turkish government guarantee was laid.

After a nine-month negotiation with the Turkish authorities, they agreed to build the Turkish section of the line for $1.4 billion, but baulked at guaranteeing the costs of the Azerbaijan and Georgia sections, which they did not control.[25] That agreement was the key to getting the pipeline built, since it showed that the pipeline could be constructed at reasonable cost.

Negotiations with Georgia for the next piece of the treaty framework proved to be complicated and frustrating. Shevardnadze would not budge from his unrealistic opening negotiating position, which made the pipeline uncommercial.

Despite Shevardnadze's tough stance, there was something quite like-able about the Georgians. Their country was being torn apart by ethnic rivalry and undermined by Russia. On top of this, it was in a state of economic meltdown. However, when we arrived at Tbilisi airport, we would always be greeted with a traditional "Georgian Table" spread with fruit, and sweet and savoury local specialities. The hotels in Tbilisi were still dreadful. And there was a sense that, at any moment, people might take the law into their own hands. At one corporate function, my security guard said to me: "Do you realise that 95 per cent of the men in this room are carrying guns under their jackets?"

As the pipeline talks dragged on, people in London started telling me: "This is a bad decision and the project will end in tears." My response was: "I don't think so. We just have to get everyone locked in."

The US government was continuing to put enormous pressure on us to get all the agreements in place. Eventually Aliyev intervened to break the deadlock with Shevardnadze. Once the Georgian agreement was secure,[26] the Azerbaijani agreement, the final element in the legal framework, was quickly resolved.

October 2000: This was decision time for the AIOC companies. The third step was to form the pipeline company. The bulk of companies in the original consortium joined BP in the investor group, but Exxon, Pennzoil and Lukoil, for different reasons, decided not to participate. Exxon thought the pipeline simply too expensive and the environmental benefits of taking tankers out of the Bosphorus overstated.

The debate about the pipeline route continued among the oil companies involved. Some companies still favoured a two-stage solution, which involved first building a big pipeline to the Black Sea, and then making a subsequent decision on whether to proceed with the southern leg to Ceyhan on the Mediterranean coast. But the Azerbaijanis and the Turks were adamant that they wanted the pipeline to Ceyhan to be built in one stage and so locked that in by insisting that construction started simultaneously at several points along the route.

Keeping the project on track

Many issues threatened to derail the project and one was the Borjomi Gorge.

Borjomi, a famous spa town in Georgia, is the source of green-bottled Borjomi mineral water, drunk all over the former Soviet Union. The partly forested gorge is very beautiful and through it was to pass the pipeline. We realised the area was environmentally fragile but we had been given no choice but to use this route. The pipeline had to go over the Kodiana Pass near Borjomi; the route further south through an ethnic Armenian area would not be secure and a route further north would have gone through an even more environmentally sensitive and fragile area. To get the Georgian government's approval of the environmental and social impact assessment, BP agreed to a number of changes to make the pipeline more secure. Despite months of discussion, approval was still not forthcoming. The problem was Borjomi mineral water: damage to its source and damage to its brand.

I decided to pay a visit to the Borjomi Gorge, and particularly to the source of the mineral water and its bottling factory. Roads were poor, there was no sign of life in the factory and yet millions of bottles of water were somehow getting to the market. Eventually, after discussions and negotiated "compensation", all issues were resolved. Borjomi water continued to be sold.

In November 2003, Shevardnadze resigned after growing opposition ended with the bloodless rose revolution. Charismatic 35-year-old Mikheil Saakashvili walked into parliament holding up a symbolic single red rose and took control. For Georgia, with its broken economy, poverty and corruption, it was a dramatic change. For us it was a major threat to the project. David Woodward was understandably nervous and told me he had "visions of everything going up in smoke". My view was that we should keep going and I would engage with Saakashvili as soon as practically possible.

I managed to secure a meeting with Saakashvili early in 2004 in Tbilisi. It did not go well. As we had been "doing business" with Shevardnadze, the forceful Saakashvili told me, we could not be trusted. He did not want to have any further discussion.

There was a big risk we would be stranded with billions of dollars of investment and no completed pipeline. Soon after this meeting, I met Saakashvili again at the World Economic Forum in Davos. We seemed to have a better conversation. I felt I convinced him that we were not interested in taking sides, or playing politics, but wanted to do what was right for the countries involved. The project seemed secure.

Nevertheless as part of a broad reform agenda, which included changing the constitution and national anthem, Saakashvili's new government decided to scrutinise the pipeline project. One of the sticking points in getting agreement to the environmental and social impact assessment had been the security arrangements. Now the new government wanted the pipeline buried five metres deep, rather than the previously agreed one metre, and cased in a steel framework for additional protection.

Our view was that this would not enhance security and the steel cage would impede repair. But more significantly we did not have the equipment or a sufficiently large right of way to bury the pipe five metres deep. More protracted discussions followed without resolution. The upshot was a 30-day halt on the pipeline construction. Agreement to resume construction was only reached after we agreed to bury the pipeline two metres deep.

Construction work on the BTC pipeline had begun in April 2003. As a strategic crossroads between East and West, Baku had been a key staging post along the legendary Silk Road. Now it would be the starting point for a new oil route that would make history.

At 1,099 miles long, it was the second longest oil pipeline in the world, longer than the Alaska Pipeline, crossing 1,500 rivers, climbing gradients of more than 9,000 feet and crossing major faults, including the Northern Anatolian Fault. The risk of earthquake and consequent rupture of the pipeline required special engineering solutions. Work could only be undertaken in certain months of the year because of the weather. At the peak, 22,000 people were employed, and between 70 to 80 per cent were from the local areas.

The Russians continued to worry me. I felt we were particularly vulnerable in Georgia. I feared large-scale theft of equipment, attacks on working crews, or local insurrections, all designed to destabilise us and render the pipeline useless. All this meant we would have to transport the oil with the help, and therefore under the control, of Russia. There were plenty of rumours flying around about Russian plans to cause mayhem and mischief. Most of them came to nothing. We had some small problems of equipment and fuel theft but nothing significant. Meanwhile, work was under way to build a new oil terminal at Sangachal, south of Baku, and work began on the South Caucasus Pipeline (SCP) to carry gas alongside the BTC pipeline from the Shah Deniz gas field we had discovered in 1999.

By the summer of 2003 Heydar Aliyev was dying of cancer. There was no official statement, only whispers. As in the days of the Soviet Union, the "truth" was managed. The old television footage of him as a fit man was shown time and again. I got a message that he would like to see me and so flew to Baku.

As soon as I went into the receiving room, I could see that Aliyev looked thinner and weaker. As I sat next to him, I realised that his face had been made up to give him some colour. The make-up had failed to reach his ears. He talked vividly about the importance of oil for his country. He wanted to be at Ceyhan when his oil was loaded on to a tanker for Europe and the US. He would be proud to show the world that Azerbaijan had arrived. He expected me to be with him.

I was one of the last people to see him alive. He stepped down in October and died in December 2003. While many would say he was effectively a despot, few could deny that he brought stability to Azerbaijan in its traumatic post-Soviet period. He was extremely effective at keeping

Russia off his country's back. He saw oil as the way to gain true independence for the nation. Recognising that he could not achieve this alone, he had the political sense to use the international oil companies and so gain the support of the US and Europe. He left a lot to be desired, but what he did do was not all bad.

Finance and the NGOs

Behind the scenes, complex negotiations were under way on the basic commercial framework for the pipeline, the final equity shareholding in the pipeline and the capital that the partners were prepared to put at risk.[27]

The financing of the project and pipeline was particularly complex. In practice the oil companies could finance it themselves and would readily have done so to avoid delay to the construction. But we needed the involvement of international financial institutions (IFIs), such as the World Bank, and the European Bank of Reconstruction and Development (EBRD), not to get "free money", as the media said, but for many other reasons. The sovereign governments who kept stakes in the project needed finance and that could only come from the IFIs. We also needed the IFIs to underpin our property rights and we knew the IFIs would insist on the use of international standards for governance, safety and environmental protection. That would reduce the risk for the companies involved. BP had learned a lot from its experience in Colombia. We knew that to take on a project with big social and environmental impacts we needed to be ready for scrutiny. The enormous geopolitical significance of this first piece of the East–West energy corridor placed us firmly in the international spotlight. We had already been falsely accused of offering bribes in connection with the project and were under intense scrutiny from NGOs across the globe. This began to increase.

By autumn 2002 various NGOs had organised full-scale campaigns to stop the financing. So began a battle. Jim Wolfensohn, President of the World Bank, and the executive directors of the Bank came under enormous pressure not to finance the pipeline.

Different NGOs had different concerns and different ways of campaigning. Protests started at BP general meetings, outside several of our offices and at the World Bank. As I had learned, from bitter experience, we could not ignore any of them. We had to take all their concerns seriously, engage in discussion and attempt to resolve differences. Amnesty International, for example, published a report which focused on the ways the pipeline agreements, particularly the host government agreement with the Turkish government, could create a human rights-free corridor. Clearly this had never been our intention. Irene Khan, the executive director of Amnesty, was business-like and ready to engage in a constructive dialogue. We subsequently agreed to renounce unilaterally any rights under the pipeline agreements that might conflict with human rights obligations. That was the first time a multinational company had ever entered into a specific agreement to protect human rights internationally.

At the height of the NGO campaign, Jim Wolfensohn and I talked frequently. He called me one evening at my London apartment. He was very agitated: "We cannot get this through." He was worried that he could not carry his board because of the intense lobbying by various NGOs.

My response was predictable: "We need to get this done. In the end we need to say what we are doing is right. We should not be scared off by people, some of whom are making things up." What else could I say?

One of the big concerns of the environmental NGOs remained the Borjomi Gorge in Georgia. Another meeting was needed with the World Wildlife Fund and their director from Switzerland. Further discussions were had and further undertakings were agreed. Jim Wolfensohn and I were long-standing friends but the intensity of the negotiations nearly made us fall out. Eventually, the financing was agreed, but the formal financing package[28] was not signed until February 2004, by which stage over half of the BTC pipeline had been constructed. It took two full days to sign the documents as 17,000 signatures were needed. As Mike Townshend, then chief executive of BTC, said: "We could have built the pipeline out of paper."

And what of the actual pipeline? The way in which the pipeline was to be constructed and operated was changed, catalysed by the pressure from some NGOs. It was made better and we would learn how to improve it further.

Voluntary Principles

James Schlesinger, the former US Secretary for Defense, came to see me about the BTC pipeline. He brought a map of the Caspian region with him. He unrolled it in my office and my first thought was that it all looked familiar. Why was he showing it to me?

"You tell me that the pipeline is *only* going to cross three countries. There are about 100 different ethnic groups here. That is what you have to worry about." He turned out to be right. This project was not just about nations, it was about villages and tribes.

NGOs may have been highly critical and sceptical about our motives, but BTC was more than an engineering project designed to make a quick profit. Our vision was to ensure that the investment would give enduring economic benefits and that meant there had to be economic, social and environmental benefits for the ethnic groups and countries involved.

The lessons learned in Colombia were put into practice across the BTC project. And it has become a textbook example of a company "showing enlightened self-interest by collaborating in a novel way with government, international organisations, and NGOs to limit environmental damage, provide local jobs, increase transparency, and enhance the chances of sustaining both profits and peace".[29]

All the legal contracts, including the production sharing agreements and host government agreements, which ran to 12,000 pages, were published in several languages so that everybody could read them if they so wished. There were various stipulations on social and environmental safeguards. Governments and companies involved were bound by international standards.

The involvement of organisations like the World Bank and EBRD came with their own social and environmental standards, including extensive impact assessments, public consultation with communities, and the requirement to pay compensation for rights to use land. A framework of banking industry principles for addressing environmental and social risks in project financing was developed and BP, with the BTC project, became the first major test of the newly created Equator Principles.[30]

During the pipeline construction, no one was permanently relocated. Landowners were compensated according to the World Bank guidelines. More than 30,000 individual deals were struck, and some unusual claims emerged. One involved a grove of walnut trees which appeared overnight somewhere in Georgia. This type of rapid horticultural development was not unusual. I remembered instances from visits to remote parts of Papua New Guinea. There, freshly planted, immaculate gardens would spring up wherever our helicopter had landed, in the hope of compensation if the site were used for drilling.

Human rights were a big concern. We worked with the three host countries to get agreement to international human rights protocols, including the Voluntary Principles for Security and Human Rights, which we had developed with the Clinton administration after our experiences in Colombia. And we developed a partnership with Equity International, a non-profit organisation promoting respect for human rights in law enforcement.

On top of all this, I felt we needed a critical set of external eyes that would monitor our performance and point out where we could do better. So we set up the Caspian Development Advisory Panel (CDAP) to act as an independent, external advisory body to provide objective advice and criticism of what we were doing on a continuing basis.[31] CDAP was chaired by Jan Leschly, the former CEO of SmithKline Beecham, and used the same principles as TIAP, the panel set up to monitor the Tangguh gas project in Indonesia.

All our activities and project documentation were fully disclosed. A website was set up for CDAP to publish its reports, for NGOs and others to publish their observations and criticisms and for BP to publish its rebuttals.[32] The panel visited sites along the pipeline, canvassed views from NGOs and other members of civil society, and met with government leaders of the countries involved and heads of the IFIs. Four independent reports, with more than 150 recommendations, were published on the web at regular intervals.

Oil revenues

The big question is whether newly generated oil revenues will make a difference to the people of Azerbaijan.

As the leader of the BTC project, we were in the front line of the widespread and growing criticism about the consequences of oil revenues, the resource curse. For Azerbaijan there was an even bigger concern as its transition to independence and a healthy democracy was far from smooth. It was a country with a reputation for corruption.[33] Azerbaijan's economy would now be overwhelmingly dependent on oil and gas revenues. In 2004, the IMF forecast that development of the country's oil and gas fields would bring in $2 billion per year on average between 2008 and 2024.[34] In fact, with high oil prices, Azerbaijan received more than $14 billion in 2008 alone from the ACG oil field and the Shah Deniz gas field.[35] That compared to an annual GDP in 2002 of just $6 billion.

Our investments in field developments, the pipeline and infrastructure were designed to generate revenues and profits over a 30- to 40-year span. So we had a direct interest in the health of the community on a continuing basis.

I knew that in the absence of transparency and good governance, our business would bear greater costs. But I also knew from my experience that the real losers would be the ordinary people of Azerbaijan. It would have been neither morally acceptable, nor sustainable, to reap the benefits of our investment and leave others to think of them. That was part of our role in the country.

After our experience with NGOs and the government of Angola in late 2001, we saw it as vital to disclose the payments we made to the government of Azerbaijan. The government of Azerbaijan agreed to pilot the Extractive Industries Transparency Initiative (EITI). The first Azerbaijan EITI reports were published in March 2005 and now Azerbaijan is the only fully EITI compliant country.

As we discovered in Angola, transparency is only part of the story. How a country manages its oil windfall is the real issue. In 1999 President Aliyev established the Azerbaijan Oil Fund, modelled on the Norwegian Petroleum Fund. The idea of these state oil funds is that oil revenue is invested to ensure long-term benefits for the broader population. So far, so good. Azerbaijan was cited as the top reformer in the World Bank's 2008 Doing Business report, moving from 96th to 33rd in overall ease of doing business.[36]

13 July 2006: One of the great moments of my career was to be part of the official inauguration of the new Ceyhan marine export terminal and BTC pipeline. It was a hot, sunny, clear day on the coast of the Mediterranean. You could see as far as Syria. The heads of the three "pipeline countries" were there with me: Ahmet Necdet Sezer, President of Turkey; Ilham Aliyev, President of the Republic of Azerbaijan; and Mikheil Saakashvili, President of Georgia.

In my speech I commented not only on the heroic engineering achievement but also on the strategic significance: "The commissioning of the Baku-Tbilisi-Ceyhan pipeline is a significant step in the long history of the oil industry. It reintegrates significant oil supplies from the Caspian into the global market for the first time in a century."[37]

I had been to Ceyhan some years before and seen Turkish workers tending orange groves to pass the time because the smaller terminal, built originally to take oil from Iraq, was shut. Now oil from Baku would arrive at this new terminal after a ten-day journey at a rate of up to one million barrels per day.

Today Baku is a very different place from the one I visited in 1990. The city is booming, evidenced by a skyline of construction cranes. The few old mansions of 19th-century oil barons are dwarfed by glass high-rises. Russian Ladas have been replaced by German Mercedes. In the place of grim shops, smart restaurants and boutiques stand side by side. And the food is good.

Baku's prosperity belies the pessimism of those who thought the oil pipeline was doomed to failure. I was privileged to have played a lead role in a project which is an exemplar of collaboration between government, business and society to tackle the energy challenge of the 21st century.

But the country which best illustrates the energy challenge of the 21st century is for me another piece of unfinished business.

10

CHINA

Full circle

April 1979: The overriding impression was of a monochrome sea of grey-green. Chang An Avenue was filled with a mass of people seemingly all dressed in the same Mao suits, and all with the same plain haircuts. The lack of colour and uniformity in appearance was an extraordinary sight.[1]

The other unmistakable contrast to the West was the lack of vehicles. The wide streets had bicycles, a few buses and an occasional black official car. It was clear too that the Chinese people thought we looked extraordinary. People were staring at me. Few Western people had been to China by this time.

China had been closed for business under Mao Zedong. His death in 1976 brought change. Deng Xiaoping rose to power and introduced a variety of economic reforms aimed at decentralising China's economy and opening the country to international trade.

This was the start of China's "open door" or "invite-in" policy. Together with a number of oil companies, BP was invited to Beijing to discuss business. For me, the timing was fortuitous. I was based in London as a petroleum engineer and was asked to be part of one of the early BP delegations to China.

It was clearly an exciting prospect. But the purpose of the discussions was unclear. We were unsure whether we were being invited in to talk about refining, petrochemicals, or exploration and production. We arrived to find that we were cheek by jowl with other international oil companies in the Beijing Hotel, a dismal unreconstructed Russian Intourist-type hotel. There was a tense and competitive mood.

My hopes of getting to see more unusual sights in the city were dampened when I learnt that all the meetings were to be held at the hotel. We got the impression that the government offices were small, rudimentary and not well equipped. So, different oil companies were carefully segregated in various meeting rooms around the hotel.

National oil companies were starting to be established in China around this time but there was no distinction, at least to us, between government ministers and the officers of those companies.[2]

We soon learnt that China wanted to open up some offshore areas to exploration by foreign oil companies. Details were initially vague but we felt we got off to a better start and built a better rapport than the other oil companies, although quite by accident.

At the last minute, our interpreter let us down. He refused to come to Beijing. A Chinese American lawyer based in Singapore, he was worried about going to China. He had no concerns about getting into China, but he was concerned that he might not be allowed back into Singapore, because of the Prime Minister Lee Kwan Yew's anti-communist stance and relations with China.

We thought that not having an interpreter was going to be a serious problem. It turned out to be a good thing. We had to use the Chinese government's interpreter. And as we had no Chinese speaker on our side, government officials could chat among themselves freely in front of us in the room. This meant we got through the initial discussions much faster than the other oil companies and we soon built a better rapport. It also meant that, despite my earlier misgivings, we were allowed out to explore.

We had half a day to discover the palatial Forbidden City. It seemed even more impressive as we were the only people there. We stood alone in the vast square in front of the Hall of Supreme Harmony and marvelled at the scale and complexity, which was an indication of what we were to discover about this incredible country.

Our initial meetings with the Chinese were like teaching seminars. The BP delegation was on one side of the table and Chinese government officials on the other. These officials were all quite elderly, many were Russian-educated, but one had worked in the US. Sitting behind the senior officials was a cadre of young people, all eager to learn. The absence of any middle-aged people was evident; a whole generation of educated people had been lost through the Cultural Revolution.[3]

It soon became refreshingly clear that the attitude of the Chinese was quite different from that of the Russians, whom BP was also talking to at this time.

The Russians' attitude was that they knew everything. We could not tell them anything technical they did not already know. But they would be happy to take our general advice and, of course, our money. They would not allow BP near their oil fields; we had to stay in Moscow. In the event, nothing came of our discussions. Business would have to wait until many years later.

The Chinese, however, were very open and they understated what they knew about oil exploration and production. They needed the expertise of the international oil companies to explore for offshore fields and wanted to learn from us. However, we knew even then that, once they had got our knowledge, they would be ready to compete with us head-on.

Making assumptions

Over the following months, meetings continued. The Chinese were always eager to learn; they were intellectually sharp. At one meeting, joint ventures were on the agenda and, even though we had our own interpreter by now, there was some confusion.

With little exposure to international companies, the Chinese assumed that any such venture would be a bilateral arrangement. They were confused when BP mentioned that other companies could be introduced as additional partners.

The Chinese had assumed that each party in any venture would have one vote – rather like the United Nations – so involvement of more than one oil company could result in their being outvoted. We then explained about blocking votes and carrying votes and a very heated discussion followed. At the end of the session the blackboard was covered with notes, written up by the Chinese, to show they had understood our explanation. It was a lesson in not presuming that the other party understands what you are proposing.

I made numerous visits to China during this period and on one occasion we visited the Ming Tombs. Some 20 miles north of Beijing, this trip was to take a full day and we decided that it required a picnic. China Airlines came to the rescue. We discovered that we could buy an airline "Picnic Pack", complete with champagne, at the Friendship Store using foreign currency.

On another visit I was unlucky, when I had travelled via Pakistan, to lose my luggage. I had only the blazer, shirt and trousers that I was wearing. When it became clear that my luggage was not going to turn up, I had to try to buy fresh clothes in Beijing to last me the rest of the week. That might be easy today, since every brand now is available there, but it was impossible in the early 1980s. Another visit to the Friendship Store saw me in a badly fitting silk shirt and a poor copy of Western bell-bottom jeans. It was one occasion when I was pleased I was small as the clothes were only available in one small size.

Our visits generally involved at least one or more huge banquets of many courses. In the late 1970s and early '80s, the food at these banquets was traditionally ethnic with the best of everything China had to offer, including delicacies such as duck's feet and sea cucumber. Regardless of who invited whom, BP had to pick up the bill. By the mid 1980s, Western food was being introduced. The Mayor of Shanghai laid on one particular banquet to cater for all tastes. This involved alternate courses of Chinese and French food; it was most unusual to have shark's fin soup followed by *fillet mignon*.

Following our discussions, BP assumed, as did the other foreign oil companies, that China wanted to open up the Yellow Sea, the part of the Pacific Ocean between mainland China and the Korean peninsula. Early activity involved co-operative studies; there were no rights to oil or gas yet granted. BP took the lead and organised a large seismic survey on behalf of 26 different oil companies and drilled two stratigraphic wells, not to find oil but to investigate the geology.

While BP was busy with this work around the Yellow Sea, the company was offered a large house as our office and base in Shanghai. It was too good an offer to turn down. The government suggested we rent a mock Tudor mansion, which would have looked more at home in suburban Surrey than Shanghai. The Red House, so named because of its large red-tiled roof, was set behind a vast wall and had acres of well-tended garden. It was offered to BP complete with gardeners, cooks and various other staff. So we took it, despite the hefty rent.

We knew the house had some history; and understood it had been the summer villa of Victor Sassoon.[4] However, each time we tried to take a taxi there, a driver would claim not to know the address and we began to realise the history of the house was rather more shady. We later heard a rumour that the house had been used by Mao's Gang of Four as a bolt-hole shortly before they were arrested.[5]

Offshore exploration

Meanwhile, discussions continued. What none of the oil companies had realised was that while the survey activity was under way in the Yellow Sea, the Chinese were working on what licences they were *actually* prepared to offer – and these were in a very different location, in the South China Sea, more than 2,000 miles away.

In the autumn of 1981, four people from BP were asked to spend two weeks tucked away in the rooms of the Beijing Summer Palace to help the Chinese government devise a generic draft contract for the oil rights to these blocks. BP felt that the invitation was a sign of our strong relationship. We were told that other oil companies must not know we were involved. Of course, we later discovered that other oil companies were tucked away doing exactly the same thing.

John Grundon was the lead for BP and spent two weeks trawling through the contract to make sure it would stand up as an agreement between an international oil company and a national oil company. He tried to moderate the terms to our advantage. The BP team was not allowed to retain a copy of anything, but got into the habit of working through the night. The idea was to wear out the Chinese officials so they might just go to bed and leave BP to it. It worked. Out of sight of the Chinese, the BP team copied out bits of the agreement – by hand, of course, in those days – for discussion with head office.

10 May 1983: BP got the rights to five blocks in the South China Sea. We moved our office further south to Guangzhou (previously known as Canton). It was in a building which was part of a new development and is now the White Swan Hotel. But despite a large number of wells, and much activity in the South China Sea, no one found anything. BP continued to drill until we had discharged our commitment. The Chinese regarded that as important. We were as good as our word and those early exploration projects formed the foundation of a strong and long-lasting relationship.

The next time I visited China was with Sohio in the late 1980s. For many years Sohio had licensed to the Chinese a process to produce the key chemical building block of acrylic fibre, which was used mostly to make clothes. At the time around 95 per cent of the world's acrylic was made using Sohio's technology. A cynic might say why licence the technology to the Chinese because they will merely copy it? They might well have done, but they still kept buying the licences from Sohio.

Then an incident put not just our relationship but many other things in jeopardy.

Tiananmen Square

4 June 1989: Several hundred civilians were shot dead by the Chinese army during a bloody military operation to crush a democratic protest in Tiananmen Square in Beijing. Under Deng Xiaoping there had been economic and political reforms but some students and intellectuals believed these had not gone far enough. Many were hoping to prompt comparable reforms to those of Mikhail Gorbachev's under *perestroika* and *glasnost* in the Soviet Union.

The incident shocked the world and led to widespread international condemnation. By this time, BP had significant investment in China. The question was whether we should pull out. We decided not to, but to freeze all our operations. We joined in the chorus of condemnation. No one visited China for some time.

I had just returned from Cleveland full of zeal to change BP's approach, not least to exploration. I remember wondering whether BP was right; surely Tiananmen Square showed that no good could come out of a relationship with China. The incident raised a wider debate in my mind. What was the rationale for investing in any country and, as importantly, for not investing? Why stay in China but not invest in, say, Sudan? Of course, there are, from time to time, sanctions and embargoes; then the choice is already made for you. But in their absence, what is the reason to invest?

I believe it is about your ability to do profitable business sustainably. The emphasis is on "sustainably". That means you need to be convinced that the country is on a path to improve the rights and worth of its people and the quality of its laws and their consistent enforcement. A business needs to be welcomed not just by the ruling classes but also by the wider population, who need to see that the business will benefit them. And you must be able to operate in line with your values, such as honest dealing and respect for human rights, if not in the short-term, then at least in the medium-term.

Nothing is cut and dried. There are many judgements to be made. And those judgements need to be based on what you can actually achieve on the ground, not on abstract discussions in an office in New York or London.

Tiananmen Square was a wake-up call; little did I realise that the questions it raised would come back in different places and on different occasions during the rest of my time with BP. On subsequent visits to Beijing, when I drove through the Square, I remembered what it represented.

But back in 1989, BP chose to stay and, by 1991, our relations with China had improved. The Chinese government remembered that we had fulfilled all our past commitments, even in the face of inevitable failure. They wanted to continue their relationship with us and so we started investing again. It was what President Clinton would call "constructive engagement", although he, of course, was accused of being too soft on China's leadership. We developed our business, agreeing to expand our petrochemicals business significantly and to do that mostly in partnership with a state-owned enterprise called Sinopec.

Hong Kong handover

The Chinese always believed that BP was an arm of the UK Foreign Office. Some two or three years after he came to power, I was summoned to Beijing to see Chairman Jiang Zemin. By then BP had been fully privatised and I had recently become CEO. I had never met Jiang Zemin before so was not sure what to expect.

It was an extraordinary audience in the leadership's walled-off compound near the Forbidden City. The British Ambassador, Sir Leonard Appleyard, and I had to mount a flight of red-carpeted stairs to reach the waiting Chairman Jiang. He greeted us and started to speak but, when he paused, the interpreter said nothing. I was perplexed as his accent made it seem as if he were speaking Chinese. There were a few awkward seconds until I realised that Jiang was, in fact, speaking English.

After discussing BP's business, Jiang turned to politics. I was told that if BP wanted to do anything more in China, the UK government had to speed up their preparations to leave Hong Kong.

Immersing myself in Kazakhstan traditional customs and hospitality included wearing the local costume. Almaty, 1990.

Margaret Thatcher made the difference in Baku. September 1992. (BP)

The official inauguration of the BTC pipeline with (l to r): Ahmet Necdet Sezer, President of Turkey; Mikheil Saakashvili, President of Georgia; Ilham Aliyev, President of the Republic of Azerbaijan; and Recep Tayyip Erdoğan, Prime Minister of Turkey. Ceyhan, July 2006. (BP)

First attempt to get into Russia: signing the Sidanco deal with oligarch Vladimir Potanin, watched by Prime Minister Tony Blair and Viktor Ott, Russia's First Deputy Energy Minister. London, November 1997. (BP)

Second attempt: signing the TNK–BP deal with oligarch Mikhail Fridman, witnessed by Prime Minister Tony Blair and President Putin as 'godparents'. London, June 2003. (BP)

'Shaken not stirred' – The *Daily Telegraph* featured this cartoon shortly after the announcement of the TNK-BP deal. 15 February 2003 (© 2003 Jonty Clark).

My mother with David Simon, on board the BP plane. (Author's collection)

Receiving an honorary doctorate from the University of Leuven, Belgium, one of the world's oldest universities. (Author's collection)

Receiving my knighthood. July 1998. (BP)

In Moscow with our Russian security guards with Tony Hayward (second from the right). (Author's collection)

With other oil chiefs (l to r): Jeroen van der Veer, chairman and CEO of Shell; Abdullah Bin Hamad Al-Attiyah, Oil Minister of Qatar; and Rex Tillerson, chairman and CEO of ExxonMobil. (Government of Qatar)

Governor Schwarzenegger and Prime Minister Tony Blair were two of the influential people on the platform with me at Long Beach. California, July 2006. (Author's collection)

When Nelson Mandela visited BP, I sensed a collective emotion that I had never before experienced. November 2000. (Author's collection)

The joke seems to be on me (l to r): Rams Ramashia, regional president of BP Sub-Saharan Africa, and Archbishop Desmond Tutu. (BP)

My mother was my most important counsellor and my unconditional supporter. (Author's collection)

With Patti Bellinger, BP head of diversity, in Italy. (Author's collection)

My introduction to the House of Lords, with David Simon (far right), Rodney Chase (fourth from right) and writer and painter Fleur Cowles (fourth from left) who became my 'surrogate mother' after my mother died. July 2001. (BP)

Venice – my favourite place. (Author's collection)

Left: A view of the annual regatta on the Grand Canal, taken by me, from in front of my apartment. (Author's collection)

The basis for the handover of Hong Kong back to China had been agreed in December 1984 under the Prime Minister, Margaret Thatcher.[6] Under a joint declaration, Hong Kong would become an "island of capitalism" within a communist state as part of China which would then be "one country with two systems". But Jiang, it seemed, was unhappy about the pace of progress in resolving some of the outstanding issues.

So not for the first time BP was being used as a political football. In 1979 Nigeria nationalised BP's oil interests on the basis of a trumped-up charge regarding South Africa, in an attempt to influence British policy towards the newly named Zimbabwe (formerly Southern Rhodesia). But now it was a different era; BP was a public company and we should not be solving the UK government's problems or even be their message carrier. During my entire tenure as CEO I kept firmly to that position. So, Sir Leonard took the message back to the UK, time moved on, the Hong Kong problem was resolved, and we carried on with business.

30 June 1997: Along with heads of other British companies with investments in Hong Kong, I was invited to the handover ceremony. Hong Kong had been under British control for more than 150 years and now it was time to hand the reins back to China.

As the outdoor ceremonies started, it began to rain. Our small umbrellas offered little cover from the monsoon deluge. Later the British press said the skies were crying for Hong Kong. The Chinese reported that the rain had come to wash away the "final vestiges of colonialism".

By the time I reached the convention centre for the formal banquet, I was soaked to the skin. The tiny towels offered to guests were of little use. Like most of the 4,000 guests, I sat through the formal dinner in a sodden suit to watch the midnight proceedings as the Union Jack was lowered and the red flag of the People's Republic of China was raised.

Emotions ran high as the final jewel in the crown of the British Empire was handed over to the world's emerging superpower. I reminded myself that change and progress are inevitable. Britain had little choice but to hand over Hong Kong and it was time to move on.[7] I expect many people were thinking the same. However, some were sceptical as to whether China would stand by its commitments. My sense was that because of China's increasing scale and need for global trade, we had to trust that global comment and opinion would bind the Chinese to their promises.

It is the same for the relationship between a government and a foreign company. When a government makes a contract with an international company, it can alter its terms and the governing laws with ease, with no immediate comeback. That is, of course, until it wants to do business with other companies. Trust is broken and the ability to do business in the future is impaired.

More than a decade on, Hong Kong has not been knocked back by its change in control and China has surged ahead.

Making tough decisions

After the handover of Hong Kong it seemed as if BP's standing in China was waning. All the important things we had done were old news. Our American and German competitors seemed to be doing much better. Then one day I received a message from Premier Zhu Rongji. I had built a relationship with him through my interest in business education; he was honorary dean of the School of Economics and Management at Tsinghua University, a leading Chinese business school. Zhu Rongji told me that China had decided to seek outside investors in one of its national oil companies. They wanted to float 10 per cent of the shares in their biggest oil company, PetroChina. They needed help in underwriting its initial public offering (IPO). An IPO had been tried once before and it had failed. They did not want that to happen again. I agreed to see what we could do. I knew the IPO was important to China as it would give them credibility on the international markets and help expose a large Chinese state-owned enterprise to international competition.

Initially we were asked to put in a couple of billion dollars. I said it was too much. I agreed that we would be one of their biggest investors, but for a more realistic amount – and that there would be conditions.

March 2000: We decided to take a 2.2 per cent stake in PetroChina for an investment of $578 million. We were the only international company that was prepared to do this. Some countries and organisations still shunned China, and others simply did not trust them. Many believed China would change the rules at the drop of a hat if it suited them. Investments might become worthless. I had a different view. So in addition to the investment, we negotiated participation in two joint ventures, one to market gas in the Shanghai area and another to build retail sites in southern China.

Suddenly we found ourselves in the middle of a great storm of criticism. We had invested in PetroChina and they had operations in Tibet and their parent company had operations in Sudan.[8] The spectre of the earlier decision to continue business after Tiananmen Square rose up again.

When I first went into China with BP in 1978, no one could foresee how the open door policy would change the country. Just as no one could foresee what would happen after Tiananmen Square, or after the handover of Hong Kong. Business leaders have to make decisions to invest not only based on the facts of the day, but also on a judgement on the direction of change. And they need to assess whether their presence will help bring about the *right* direction of change. That is what BP did in Azerbaijan, aided by institutions like the World Bank and EITI.

China is bigger and far more complex than Azerbaijan. But on balance, I decided that the investment in PetroChina was appropriate and in line with the decision we had already made to be in China anyway. We were committed to China and this move would help develop our business.

September 2000: I took the same position when we were asked to make an investment in Sinopec, China's largest integrated petroleum and petrochemicals company and second largest state-owned enterprise. We agreed to invest up to $400 million. This also helped us take a further strategic step in China as we agreed to expand our existing business significantly with Sinopec and develop ideas for some international E&P ventures.

The investments in PetroChina and Sinopec had propelled us into an important position. At a board meeting of the Tsinghua business school, Premier Zhu Rongji had publicly welcomed me as the CEO of China's strategic partner. Just as we had thought that these investments would further our aims in China, so the Chinese government thought that our position would help them reach their goals. After the board meeting, the Premier asked to see me privately. He explained that China wanted to build a very long and large pipeline from the Tarim basin in the far west of the country to reach Shanghai, the so-called East–West gas pipeline. He wanted BP to be their sole partner in order to add credibility to the project and to pay for half of it; he assured me that we would make an attractive return.

I went back and we looked at the proposition; our view was that it could never be an appropriate investment for a public company.

I returned to break the news. He was very disappointed and our relationship cooled. It was only after other Western companies declined to participate, too, that our relationship was restored. The pipeline was a piece of public infrastructure that could only be owned by a government.

The investments in PetroChina and Sinopec proved to be outstanding. In time the companies were doing very well so we were able to sell our shareholdings at a substantial profit. In 2004 we sold our stakes in both companies for around two and a half times what we had paid for them.

19 May 2004: As I stood outside BP's head office in St James's Square in London, waiting to greet Premier Wen Jiabao, I was struck by the extraordinary symmetry in what was about to unfold.

Twenty-six years earlier I had stood outside the Beijing Hotel and marvelled at the mass of people all dressed in their identical Mao suits. China had just emerged from behind closed doors to seek a place on the world stage. We had gone to China in search of oil and gas. Now China had found its position at centre stage and that country's leader was coming to visit us in search of oil and gas.

It was very unusual for a Chinese premier to visit a commercial enterprise, and even more unusual for him to visit a foreign oil and gas company. Wen Jiabao's visit was a demonstration of the strength and significance of BP's relationship with China and its partnership with several Chinese companies. We used the occasion to announce agreements on a variety of investments, to the tune of $1 billion.

A geologist and engineer by profession, Wen debated with me China's growing need for oil and how they might obtain increasingly secure supplies of more of it. He asked me to comment on the progress of China's strategy of going abroad to get hold of oil and gas reserves; China's domestic supplies were dwindling much faster than demand was increasing.

Using carefully chosen words, I said that I thought their strategy was "wanting".

"You are doing business on too small a scale for China's needs. Some supplies should come from investments in exploration and production overseas. But this activity should be focused into a few big opportunities."

It seemed to me that China was doing the reverse and collecting a set of postage stamps. And I said so. "You should continue to build close relationships with the big players. Some supplies should come from the global markets. The only practical way of getting enough secure supplies for China is to support the markets that trade oil internationally."

I was clear that self-sufficiency in oil was neither a desirable nor practical goal. Autarky was to be avoided. Care was needed when attempting to acquire overseas companies, I explained.

The following year, one of the Chinese oil companies, CNOOC, would try to take over Unocal, the ninth largest US oil company. It would fail and that company was eventually acquired by Chevron. I suspect the failure had as much to do with the decision-making within CNOOC as it had with political activity in the US. It certainly chilled China's desire to acquire Western companies.

In 2004 Wen Jiabao's reaction to my advice, needless to say, was inscrutable. As Madeleine Albright, former US Secretary of State, said: "China is in its own category – too big to ignore, too repressive to embrace, difficult to influence and very, very proud."[9]

But one thing led to another. If we had managed to create TNK-BP in Russia against all the odds why could we not create a similar vehicle with China? What about Sinopec-BP?

17 March 2005: At the board meeting in Beijing, a city now clogged with cars, luxury hotels and shops with Western designer goods, the agenda included a proposal to create a large joint venture with Sinopec.

During the meeting I wondered whether Chinese government officials might actually be listening in; you were never sure whether hotel rooms were bugged. It seemed to me that it would be a good thing for them to hear our debate. We got the go-ahead to start discussions with Sinopec to look at setting up a joint venture. It was an exciting possibility.

Initially all seemed to be going well. On visits back and forth, I got to know Sinopec chairman Chen Tonghai. Like Potanin in Russia, Chen was a princeling; his father had been a communist party official. Qualified as both a petroleum engineer and an economist, Chen had worked in a Sinopec Group company, got involved in politics and then become head of Sinopec. He began to make his mark both in China and on the international energy stage. He was a chain smoker and I found him rather nervous; he always seemed on edge.

We had lengthy discussions on assets, structure and governance, and a BP team was set up to work on the project. They did a substantial amount of work. We seemed to be a fair way down the road and it all looked promising. But then things began to slow down on the Chinese side.

I was well used to the deliberate pace of decision-making in China so initially I was not overly worried. However, I soon realised that the discussions with Sinopec were not just slow; by mid 2006, they had stopped completely. Despite what I felt had been a tacit agreement with Chen, nothing happened. He would not return my calls.

I talked to several senior ministers and eventually spoke with Wen Jiabao, who still agreed the deal should go ahead. But I could not break the deadlock. It was taking far too much time and clearly was not going anywhere, so I dropped it.

It was not until after I had left BP that I understood why things had stalled.

In June 2007 Chen Tonghai resigned; the official version was that it was for personal reasons. At the time I thought this sounded a cover-up. Six months later the Chinese authorities revealed that Chen took what they described as "huge bribes, and abused his position to benefit his mistress". He had been arrested as he tried to flee the country and was put in prison.

BP must have got too close to something. I am not sure exactly what and will probably never find out. Chen was clearly at the centre of the honeypot. Perhaps he was worried we might uncover something and so he just stonewalled.

In July 2009 Chen Tonghai was given a suspended death sentence after being convicted of taking $28.8 million (£17.5 million) in bribes during his eight years at Sinopec.[10] It was believed to be China's largest ever bribery case.[11] Much of this was in cash, which was reportedly stashed in various secret places in his house, including under roof tiles, in a toilet cistern and in a fish tank.

World stage

When Wen Jiabao visited BP's offices, China had yet to become as much of a concern to so many as it has today. Since 2004, China has continued its astonishing growth and now rivals the US in its energy consumption and greenhouse gas emissions. Its rapid growth and vast scale represent a potential challenge to the existing world order.[12]

China requires huge energy resources merely to fuel its industrial growth. As more and more of its 1.3 billion people come out of poverty and move from rural to urban areas, they will demand more energy for heat, light and mobility. And by 2045, even with the government's one child policy, the population could be as high as 1.5 billion.[13]

As China "goes out" to satisfy its need for energy – and to satisfy its thirst for oil in particular – it is becoming increasingly involved in countries shunned by Western governments and hence by Western energy companies.

In recent years, one third of China's oil imports have come from Africa.[14] China's economic and political motives sometimes differ from those of Europe and the US. Those differences can weaken the incentives to force better governance on oil-exporting countries in the region. I expect that this tension will be there for some time. China will need to pursue a very different strategy to balance its status as a responsible global player with its short-term needs for energy.

Hosting the 2008 Olympic Games brought the air quality of China's cities to the attention of the world as Beijing struggled to clean up its polluted environment. It is estimated that as many as 75 per cent of China's cities suffer from poor air quality. Linfen City in Shanxi Province tops the list of the most polluted cities in the world with more than three million people living in permanent choking smog.[15]

Home to one fifth of the world's population, China emitted 7.5 gigatons of greenhouse gases in 2007, making it the world's top emitter.[16] However, I am in no doubt that China is concerned about the environment. I have sat through many meetings where the risks related to climate change were accepted by both the leadership and the scientific and engineering community.

The government is now taking action to address its environmental problems by setting tough targets to improve energy efficiency in domestic markets. But I suspect that tactics and preservation of negotiating advantage will still get in the way of an international agreement on meaningful targets for reducing greenhouse gas emissions.

Fareed Zakaria talks of "the rise of the rest", the dramatic improvement in economic fortunes enjoyed by developing countries such as Brazil, Russia, India and China over the past two decades as they are integrated into the global economic system.[17]

In 1981, half of the world's population lived below the World Bank's poverty line. By 2005 that figure had been reduced to a quarter.[18] China alone lifted more than 400 million people out of poverty after it decided to open up its markets in 1978.[19]

Enhanced international flows of people, finance, goods and services have improved the economic condition of many parts of the world and thereby reduced conflict. These flows have been driven mainly by business. Mutually aligned objectives, a common purpose, a common approach – these are what help to build and define relationships.

Put people in a room without a reason and they are unlikely to get to know each other. Put them in a room with a problem to solve and, in working together, they will get to know each other and will harness their respective strengths and weaknesses. I saw this in the meeting rooms in the Beijing Hotel in the late 1970s. Doing business helps bring people with diverse interests and different backgrounds together. This helps reduce suspicion and build trust.

When China sat alone, during its darkest days of communism, the isolation from the West did nothing to help its economy or its people. Deng Xiaoping recognised that development, progress and prosperity could only be achieved through integration with other nations. In the 1970s international companies, like BP, went in to do business and make money. In so doing they helped the Chinese catch up. Now the Chinese are using that knowledge and those skills to go out and compete with us in the world.

BP was once one of the "Seven Sisters" which controlled the production of the world's oil and determined the fate of oil-producing nations. Now PetroChina and Sinopec are part of a new group of state-owned companies, some of which control access to markets for oil products and others of which control the vast majority of the world's oil reserves.[20] In one way or another, these companies increasingly call the shots.

Their development, in some ways, mirrors that of BP, which in its early years could rely on the power and support of the UK government to help in its pursuit of business. And just as some nations found that the heavy hand of the British was unacceptable, so too are there signs that the Chinese are less welcome than they used to be – although in these straitened times money always counts. These Chinese oil companies have come a long way. They have learned a great deal and their competence grows daily; they will go beyond being simply procurers of international oil supplies to become competitive integrated oil and gas companies.

And just as China's relationship with BP went full circle, so have attitudes to free markets. In the 1970s the Chinese and the Western economic systems were poles apart and now they are drawing together. To date this has happened because China has moved closer to the Western model. Following the 2008–09 financial crisis, Western politicians are looking to re-regulate some areas of the market. So it seems that both sides are still trying to find the right balance between freedom and regulation. While it is clear that China could benefit from less state involvement in its markets, it is possible that the West could benefit from a little more.

11

UK

Triumphs

15 November 2000: When Nelson Mandela walked into BP's head-quarters, I sensed a collective emotion I had never before – and never since – experienced.

Mandela came to the BP office because I had invited him to London to give the first of a series of BP sponsored lectures at the British Museum on the broad topic of "Civilisation". He asked specifically if he could visit our offices and talk to the staff before giving the lecture.

We had a few moments in private in my office. As we emerged to head back down to the atrium, people were in every corridor. They wanted to touch Mandela, shake his hand, or say something to him. There was a roar of spontaneous and heartfelt applause.

People hung on to his every word. He was inspirational. With a wry glance at me, he appeared to incite the staff to revolution when he said: "The people must always be in charge; don't let the bosses tell you what to do."

That statement was even more remarkable to a few in the audience who, when they were younger in 1978, had been issued with disciplinary warnings for criticising BP's involvement in breaking sanctions against Ian Smith's Southern Rhodesia. They had been handing out leaflets to staff entering the very same building in which we were now entertaining Mandela. The warnings were withdrawn by the company when the protestors got the issue raised in the House of Commons. One of those protestors was now my policy adviser, Nick Butler.

Mandela's visit was one of the highpoints of the first year in the new millennium. BP was roaring ahead. We had a clear agenda and we were making our mark, differentiating ourselves from the other companies in our sector and the broader business community. Our financial performance was strong.

I won the UK's "Most Admired Leader" award four times in a row.[1] BP also won the "Most Admired Company" award in 2002, creating a double first. I would always view media comments with some scepticism but I did not ignore these awards because they were based on the views of my peers.

The mergers with Amoco and other companies had changed the spirit of the organisation. We knew we were not born big but we had taken ourselves from being a small player to a significant one. The atmosphere felt good, too. We tried to make the corporate environment less polluted by small-minded politics and less hierarchical. We never really totally achieved that goal; I doubt that it would be possible. However, for a period of time, the organisation did feel different; people did not change into corporate automatons when they came through the doors of the office. People were more open and managers were more accessible. The spirit of the organisation was marked by a great sense of purpose. We wanted to be a profitable, competitive business but we also wanted to make a difference to the world. Our attitude to corporate social responsibility, our investment in society, and our deep concern for the environment were paying off. BP had become a very different type of company. And I felt we now needed to articulate that difference through our brand.

New brand and new identity

The company I joined in 1969 was called British Petroleum, BP for short, and had been owned in part by the British government. By the end of the 20th century, we were no longer "British", more a multinational; we were no longer just "Petroleum", because we were now investing in gas and alternative energies; and we were, in fact, called BP Amoco. In addition, the symbolic trademark BP shield looked very dated and smacked of an imperial past.[2]

I had seen what the power of branding and effective marketing could do for a company when I was on the board of directors of Intel. Dennis Carter, vice president of marketing in the 1990s, changed Intel's brand from that of a mere component supplier to one of the world's most widely recognised consumer brands. This was achieved through the hugely successful Intel Inside campaign.[3] I found that so remarkable that, in an article in 1997, I said: "People don't ask whether BP is inside. Maybe some day they will."[4]

In 1999, we began to think about new ideas for the BP brand and identity. Brand is far more than just a new logo; it is deep and embodies the purpose and quality of a company. The identity, on the other hand, is simply a consistent signal by which people recognise a company. We engaged Landor Associates and Ogilvy & Mather, both part of the WPP Group, a communications services company, to address two specific issues. First, we wanted a new name and identity to help unify the culture of four previously independent companies: BP, Amoco, ARCO and Burmah Castrol. Second, we wanted a brand that represented what we were – and that was more than oil or petroleum.

I had started a debate about the perception of the industry with a speech at a conference in 1996 shortly after I became CEO.[5] The image of the industry was that it was old-fashioned and dirty, and still secretive and manipulative. That was not the reality. We wanted our image to reflect what we believed BP now stood for. It was to be a competitively profitable force for good, which valued top-class safe operational performance, innovation, progress and environmental leadership.

Landor recommended we keep the name BP, not as an abbreviation of British Petroleum, but as a name in its own right. Recommendations for a new identity to capture the essence of our new brand were then developed.

The meeting to assess the final options for the identity which would take the company into the new millennium was held in the dining room of a Palladian villa just outside Venice. I say "Palladian" but it was one of Palladio's students who undertook the design. Nevertheless, it was a splendid house with lovely gardens, which I was renting for a holiday with my mother. The weather was glorious, sunny but not humid. It turned out to be my mother's last full summer.

Significant work had been undertaken by this stage, including consumer research. We were down to two final logo designs.

The first logo represented progress. It was a group of five arrows, rather like paper planes flying into the future, very eye-catching in green and yellow. The second symbolised the sun as the source of energy and represented BP's goal to provide a broader range of energies and not just petroleum. It was also in green and yellow. The initial design for this idea was a sunflower which was then developed into a helios (named after the sun god of ancient Greece).

I had to choose between the two. I picked the helios. It was the bolder option but was not chosen lightly. On a practical level, the helios was one physical entity. I thought there was a risk that the five individual planes might come apart; I did not want BP planes dropping from the sky. On an emotional level, the helios seemed more welcoming and less threatening. Later Ogilvy & Mather developed the line: *beyond petroleum*. I thought it very creative and full of impact. But at the same time I felt that it would be a stretch to make it stick.

The new helios logo and the line *beyond petroleum* expressed the new identity of the company. They gave a strong message that BP was intent on becoming a new type of global energy enterprise. We meant to tell people that we were ready to do more than they would expect when it came to confronting difficult issues, such as the conflict between energy and environmental needs.

Before we launched, in July 2000, we wondered whether the advertising would be taken literally. Was BP getting out of petroleum? Coca-Cola had used many clever images over the years but people still knew it was just a fizzy drink for humans and not for polar bears. People never actually thought that Intel had BunnyPeople[6] hopping around their offices. And years before, Exxon had encouraged people to put a tiger in their tank.

As it turned out, not everyone did understand the new identity, but few could ignore it. They either loved it or hated it.

We underestimated the way in which *beyond petroleum* got converted in some places, mostly in the UK, into a literal statement. Some NGOs thought that our advertising, combined with our new logo, promised too much and we were simply "greenwashing" a dark truth that we were still in the fossil fuel business. Others simply criticised us for using the campaign to distract attention away from our "business as usual" of oil.

A different view was taken by those who saw BP as a "prescient model of credible corporate social responsibility".[7] And some companies wanted to create the same sort of image. Ogilvy & Mather had no end of organisations contacting them asking: "Can you do for us what you did for BP? We want to be that type of company. We want to say our brand is about the future and not the past."

Journalists loved to hate the new identity; they could make a parody of *beyond petroleum*, write great headlines and generally make fun. And we did not help ourselves; we were too timid in our support of the new identity.

Beyond petroleum was never intended to be a new name for the company but represented our purpose and intention. It was not about saying we could do away with petroleum. I was convinced, and remain convinced, that the industry had to start thinking differently about new sources of energy for the future.

Beyond petroleum was a great concept. It created the beginnings of a broad debate about energy and the environment.[8] Now the vision for a low carbon world is becoming clearer. The world is irreversibly on the route to change its energy mix and the way it consumes energy.

I should not have worried about whether the new image would stick. The controversy and the campaigns raised awareness of the BP brand from 4 per cent in 2000 to a high of 67 per cent in 2007. The campaigns won numerous advertising industry awards.[9]

In hindsight though, we made a huge mistake in rebranding the Amoco gasoline stations in the US. We changed them all to BP. We thought that a strong brand required all our products to be sold under the same brand. We were looking for simplicity.[10]

We should have left the Amoco stations as Amoco. With the familiar torch logo, it was a strong brand and had strong customer allegiance. In fact we should have used the Amoco brand, rather than BP, at all the US gasoline stations.

When we purchased the ARCO stations in California, we recognised that that brand was very different and distinctive. We left it well alone and, not surprisingly, those ARCO stations kept their market share. Later we kept the Aral brand in Germany; it has remained one of the most recognised brands there.

We went too far with the integration of Amoco in terms of branding and yet in other areas, as I was to learn, we did not go far enough. I will come to that later.

New people

We had a new brand, and now we needed a new approach to people – in particular, how we made individuals from diverse backgrounds feel included in the company.

As BP continued to expand, it became clear that the era of white British male domination of the company had to end. We were now competing on the global stage. We needed to recruit from the diverse universe of talent.

Exxon had decided to deny health-care benefits to newly hired same-sex couples[11] and it prompted the question: what were we going to do? We realised that we did not have a way of answering the question. We needed to decide how to make diversity work for BP and how BP could work for diversity.

The business imperative fitted with my personal views which began to develop in my childhood years in Iran. To me background, religion, ethnic origins, nationality, politics or sexual orientation were never important. I am half-Hungarian, half-British. My mother was half-Jewish and she was brought up as a Catholic. I was brought up as an Anglican but, like my mother in her later life, never felt comfortable with organised religion or religious labels, perhaps because they were so often the cause of division and discrimination. I also never liked partisan politics, although as I have got older I have come to recognise the value and necessity of the political process. That is why I sit in the House of Lords as a cross-bencher.

I decided BP had to take a leadership role in diversity and inclusion. First, we had to ensure that we used, in so far as we could, one definition of merit. That would allow us to level the playing field. So we defined what we meant by merit and put the top 450 people through an assessment process to make sure we really did have the best people at the top.

Second, we changed the way we recruited and developed people so that wherever we were in the world we were attracting the best ones – both women and men. In the past our selection panels had not been diverse; white males were likely to recruit and promote in their own image. Now we insisted on diverse memberships. We started to recruit in every country where we operated, not just to get local talent but to access an international cadre of people to run our business across the world.

Third, we looked at working practices to ensure that the culture matched the inclusive business we were trying to build. We decided to offer equal benefits to couples in same-sex relationships and more flexible working practices for people to have a more balanced family life. We began to question why we should accept conformity. We appointed women to positions such as head of global shipping and head of security in the Middle East. That would have been inconceivable a year earlier.

And finally, and perhaps most controversially, we set targets. These targets were not going to detract from merit: that is, giving a job to the best-qualified person. If we were going to achieve a very different mix of employees globally, for example, in terms of women and African Americans, then we needed targets to drive that change – on the basis that what gets measured gets done.

I was determined we were going to hold managers to these targets. Not everyone liked the idea. People came up to me and said: "You know women can't really do this level of job." Others: "You know these gay people; it is really difficult to have them in Arab countries." Or: "Why do we have to change, can't we just carry on?"

When you change the rules, people feel threatened because they are taken out of their comfort zone. You have to help them through it. But if you hold merit as your important yardstick, it is very difficult for them to fight against it.

Rodney Chase, then deputy CEO, said to me: "If you're really serious about this, we need to appoint a very senior person to drive it." So Patti Bellinger arrived. Multi-lingual and multi-skilled, Patti had been head-hunted from Bristol-Myers Squibb where she was head of culture and diversity. She set about telling us where the barriers were and began to show managers how to eliminate them.

19 June 2002: I gave the keynote speech at the Women in Leadership conference in Berlin. I explained the strategic logic of diversity and inclusion: "The people we have form our human capital. To me that is a more important corporate asset than all the plant and equipment, all the oil fields and pipelines. If we can get a disproportionate share of the most talented people in the world, we have a chance of holding a competitive edge."[12]

I said that BP was committed to diversity and to the inclusion of individuals – men and women, regardless of background, religion, ethnic origin, nationality or sexual orientation. We would now employ the best people, everywhere, on the single criterion of merit. Few people had any idea what I was going to say. It felt as if I had lit the fuse and stood back.

The British media coverage was unfortunate, adopting a sense of clumsy lumbering literalism. BP apparently was "beyond prejudice". The *Guardian*, in a story headlined "Diversity drive at BP targets gay staff", claimed that: "Gays and lesbians are being targeted for recruitment by Britain's biggest company, BP, as part of a drive to ditch traditional business prejudices."[13] We were not going to "ditch" anything but, with Patti's help, we began to engage people and the culture at BP really did begin to change.

We may have never had a woman CEO but in our senior leadership group of 600 people, the percentage of women rose from less than 10 per cent to more than 20 per cent. And the same was true for the proportions of non-Americans and non-British origins. Local nationals also began to run operations in countries like Egypt, Venezuela, Trinidad, and Colombia.

Internally, people began to understand the logic. They began to see that diversity and inclusion is about merit and that no one should be excluded because of unrelated factors. I believe that not only because it is right but also because it is good business. And this created a very different culture in the organisation.

New shape

We now had a strong new unifying identity for the four organisations we had brought together. And we still wanted and needed to grow. What is a good shape for a business one day is not necessarily the right shape for the future. As competitive positions changed, we were continually looking for opportunities to adapt and grow. And we identified an extraordinary opportunity that fitted our strategy.

16 July 2001: We announced a multi-billion-dollar deal with E.ON, Germany's largest power and gas company. We swapped our holding in Ruhrgas, a German gas distributor, for Veba, E.ON's oil business. Veba owned Germany's biggest fuel retail brand, Aral, with 560 gasoline service stations. The deal was done in two stages with the second stage taking place in January 2002.[14]

We had wanted to dispose of our Ruhrgas interest for some time, but not at any price. BP's ownership of 25 per cent of Ruhrgas had brought us significant value; it had come to BP as a valueless part of Gelsenberg, a refining and marketing business in Germany bought after the Second World War. Ruhrgas was primarily about selling gas made from coal, so-called town gas. Later, when natural gas was imported from Russia, Ruhrgas was the company that distributed it and so became very valuable.

Eventually, Gelsenberg became worthless because its refineries were no longer competitive.

We did not have a controlling interest in Ruhrgas. Its other shares were held by several of our competitors. No one controlled the company except the management, who were able to do what they wanted. We often had disagreements.

The deal allowed us to achieve two strategic aims: to achieve market leadership in downstream oil at the heart of Europe and to realise excellent value for our stake in Ruhrgas. E.ON, on the other hand, wanted to leave downstream oil and deepen its gas interests; it had its sights on buying the whole of Ruhrgas from all the other shareholders and indeed went on to do just that, changing the way the utility industry in Europe worked. The deal suited both parties.

In December 2005, we sold BP's petrochemicals business, Innovene, to Ineos Group, a privately owned UK chemicals company, for $9 billion. This was a good move; since then it has been hard to make decent returns in the petrochemicals sector.

But not everything worked out that smoothly and tidily. There had been one big opportunity that I had my eye on. I felt it offered significant synergies since the industry was having a tough time finding new reserves and it was clear that the value of existing reserves would increase dramatically over time.

That big opportunity was a merger with Shell.

3 June 2004: I attended a private off-the-record discussion between a small group of international business people and politicians at a hotel on the shores of Lake Como in Italy. Keen observers might have spotted two figures strolling beside the lake in the sun one morning after coffee. Shell CEO Jeroen van der Veer and I had taken the opportunity not just to enjoy the splendid scenery but to talk about the future.

Initially we were both cagey. However, as we opened up and the conversation progressed, we both recognised there might be some merit in exploring the possibility of merging. We both agreed that we should "deeply consider" the possibility of a merger.

I returned to London and got a BP team to start looking at how a merger might take place. We had to work on this independently; we could not discuss it with Shell. Much had changed since I avoided the prospect of a "merger" with them in 1996. That would have been much more a case of Shell taking over BP. Now BP was on a more equal footing with Shell. And, fortuitously, Shell's share price had been hit following a scandal about its reporting of its oil and gas reserves.[15]

With the price of oil at around $40 a barrel there was widespread talk about further consolidation in the industry. The media speculated on "the mother of all mergers".[16] But people discounted this prospect because they thought that the US competition authorities would never allow such a deal. What they did not know was that we had a plan to deal with this.

The plan was to dispose of the whole of BP's downstream refining and marketing operation in one go. The timing would have been perfect. There was an irrational exuberance about this sector and I believed that BP's operation would perform better as an independent company. Van der Veer used a phrase that I think everyone in BP would have subscribed to: "more upstream, profitable downstream". Our plan would have fitted that strategy well.

We estimated that a merger could create synergies of around $9 billion a year in three to five years' time. It also would have been a significant boost to the oil industry outside the US. It all seemed so obviously right to me and the executive team; but it did not to certain individual BP board members. I insisted we put the merger proposal formally before the board at its next meeting.

21 September 2005: The board was to convene in Williamsburg, Virginia. On the plane journey there I knew the answer, even before the meeting started. This would not be like the Berlin board meeting in 1996 when people were prepared to listen to the rationale for a merger strategy, even though many had thought "everything was already going so well".

This time there had been discussions between board members before the meeting. The sentiment was "why rock the boat?" The Shell merger was not discussed at the board. It was not going to be done and that was that.

There is no certainty that the deal could have been done anyway. But we never got to that point. There is a time and place to do things. Mergers and acquisitions are made or broken by their timing. They can deliver great value, but timed incorrectly they can be the ruin of a business.

In the end we did not rock the boat; we missed it. And the reason we missed the boat? My time was running out. The board was now actively thinking about who would replace me; for them, nothing could get in the way of that. As it turned out, plenty of things did.

12

US

Disasters

February 2002: "I think it might be best to discourage the article."

The *Financial Times* had indicated that they wanted to run a substantial article on BP. I was pleased initially but Nick Butler, my policy adviser, was concerned that this would be a personal profile and would be ill-advised. He wrote me a detailed note:

> Dear John
>   ... The worst thing would be an article which focused entirely on you because that would inevitably provoke jealousy among your colleagues and conflict with the board.
>   Given the way the press works, and the general resentment of success, an article focused entirely on your achievements would set you up and be quoted against you whenever something went wrong in the future ...

Roddy Kennedy, the chief press officer, saw it differently. His advice was that, if I did not co-operate, the *Financial Times* would write about me anyway and it could be negative. So, somewhat reluctantly, I went ahead.

July 2002: The piece turned out to be a hagiography; I was embarrassed. The unprecedented three-part series had a photo of me standing in front of the BP helios logo and the title: "Sun King of the oil industry".

The article began with a reference to the recent corporate scandals and their perpetrators, including Ken Lay of Enron and Bernie Ebbers of World-Com, and said: "... there is one titan who so far remains untoppled. John Browne, the 54-year-old head of BP and one of the world's most powerful executives, seems to have no enemies, and few critics or detractors.

"Fellow executives have voted him British manager of the year for the third year running, and despite recent market turmoil he can still claim to have delivered the goods to his shareholders . . ."[1]

People thought I would be pleased but I felt very uncomfortable. Nick had been right. He usually was. No good would come of it.

Everything that I did was going to be measured against the Sun King article. It was inevitable that the title would stick. Journalists would be queuing up to "topple" me or write about how I was "losing my shine". All that went wrong with the company would ever after be personalised.

It was an error of judgement to do the *Financial Times* interview. It started a trend. It set me up as an arrogant target.

The first sign came some months later in November 2002. I had been trained to "under promise and over deliver". But I knew that sometimes you need to set a very stretching objective to drive a big change. I was over ambitious in setting short-term production targets for the company.

Even when we were failing to hit them, I did not move them down far enough or fast enough. I had to reduce the targets three times in two months and took some heavy criticism. As it turned out the targets were not that wrong; they were reached but only after a much longer time period than I had specified.

Not reaching production targets was bad but not as important as the saddest and probably the worst day in my working life at BP, some three years later.

Texas City tragedy

23 March 2005: "There has been an explosion at the Texas City refinery." My blood ran cold.

The call came through when I was in California at an Intel board meeting. And, like any report on a disaster which is unfolding, the message was unclear.

My advisers told me not to go; I would only confuse things and by the time I arrived it would be dark. As more information came through, and I learnt of the fatalities, I knew I had to fly to Texas immediately.

I landed late that evening and was met and briefed at the airport; the enormity of what had happened was stark. I barely slept that night. I went straight to the refinery next morning and had already decided what I would do. Lawyers had told me not to say anything. But I made a decision to say that I deeply regretted the accident and that BP took responsibility for what happened at its sites. Those words were said from the bottom of my heart. They would be interpreted and reinterpreted in the following years.

I believe I did the right thing in going to Texas City that day. I did what anyone ought to do in the face of such a human tragedy. It was not the time or place to ask questions, but it was the time to be there, to comfort people and to offer support. I talked to many of the workforce individually. People were shocked, unsure of what to do. Emotions were confused.

Fifteen people were dead and more than 170 were injured. It was one of the most serious workplace disasters in the US for 20 years. My memory of that day is searing. It was an appalling tragedy.

Initially, some BP people in London underestimated the tragedy. As the press people said at the time, it was America and a long way away. I never doubted the seriousness. And after the start of the various inquiries into the tragedy, the reality dawned on everyone. This was a very big issue.

For years we had been trying to improve the safety in BP. Injuries, accidents and fatalities were all on a significant downward trend.[2] Safety was a top priority and it was something which had our full attention. Now people who had been working on a BP site were injured or dead. How would this affect their families and loved ones? How could this tragedy have happened? I had thought that we took safety more seriously than almost anyone else. We needed to find out what really had happened, the root cause, to make sure a tragedy like this never happened again.

We conducted our own internal inquiries. But they were not enough. So we agreed with the recommendation of the US Chemical Safety and Hazard Investigation Board that we should appoint an independent panel to look at safety across all five of our US refineries. I asked James Baker, the distinguished former US Secretary of the Treasury, former US Secretary of State and former White House Chief of Staff, to chair the panel. James Baker is independent and tough-minded and my brief to him was that the panel should produce a report that would contain not just lessons for BP but for the entire industry. Importantly, the report was to be straightforward and James Baker agreed that the "chips would fall where they would fall". I voluntarily submitted BP to a thorough and testing scrutiny of practices at our US refineries. We needed an independent panel to help us understand what had happened at the Texas City refinery on that terrible day, and why, so that we could learn how to prevent such a tragedy from ever happening again.

The Baker Panel Report was published in January 2007 and made painful reading. Why tragedies like Texas City occur is never clear-cut. They result from the cumulative effect of a whole series of things. The Baker Panel's conclusion was that the Texas City explosion was a process safety accident which could have been prevented.

BP had an aspiration of "no accidents, no harm to people". But the Panel's view was that we had not done enough to make process safety a core value at Texas City, or the other four US refineries.

We had emphasised that individuals had to be safe as they went about their daily work – "personal safety". That led to dramatic improvements. But we had not emphasised that processes and equipment had to be safe under all circumstances and operated in a safe way at all times – "process safety". I remembered the cause of the Piper Alpha tragedy in the North Sea – platforms sitting on top of pipelines that might explode in rare, but possible, circumstances. I also remembered the strenuous efforts we had made to learn from this tragedy and the subsequent awards and accolades we had been given.[3] At the Texas City refinery, we had mistakenly interpreted improving personal injury rates as an indication of acceptable process safety performance.

It was not the first process safety incident at Texas City. There had been a serious incident in the previous year. Texas City was one of the refineries that had been part of Amoco for more than 70 years. It had a proud and long history. Its workforce felt that they were the heart and soul of the refinery. But I had a sense that they felt put upon; relations were not good between management and the rank and file. Changes of local leadership did little to improve the situation. I suspect that some of these issues got in the way of fully integrating Texas City with the rest of BP. Integration might have changed nothing but it also might have changed everything.

The Baker Panel believed that there were issues with the quality of management, clarity in who was to do what and, importantly, with the relationship with the workforce. They said that we "had not established a positive, trusting, and open environment with effective lines of communication between management and the workforce".

The Panel's view was that our decentralised management system and our entrepreneurial culture delegated substantial discretion to the US refinery management without clearly defining process safety expectations, responsibilities and accountabilities. We did not make the executive managers and the refining line managers fully accountable for process safety management.

BP accepted the findings of the report. We acknowledged that we had a lot of work to do so as to learn and improve. There were questions in some people's minds as to whether the accident happened because of our size and reach. I do not believe so. Big companies can operate at a distance but they need to pay careful attention to the quality of the management and have a very clear understanding of people's roles and responsibilities. We had proved we could do this in other countries such as Azerbaijan, Russia and China, and, indeed, in other parts of the US. The media said the accident happened because BP was cutting costs. That was the easy-to-understand, single point explanation. It was not true and the Panel said that "it had found no evidence of deliberate cuts to safety funding".[4]

Industry observers agreed with the Panel's view that the deficiencies in process safety culture and management were not limited to BP. However, the tragedy happened at BP. Anything good we had done before no longer mattered. My instruction immediately after the accident was to settle everything as quickly as possible, particularly to settle the claims of the families whose loved ones were dead or injured. But once lawyers became involved everything slowed down. And the ensuing plaintiff bar litigation further damaged the reputation of the company since it went on for such a long time.

My deepest regret is that we might have avoided that accident.

Platform problems

Plant and equipment matter little compared to people but, a few months after Texas City, another incident occurred in the US and this time it was centred in the Gulf of Mexico. We had a problem with a new platform, Thunder Horse. And this resulted from the complexity of its engineering.

I had been involved with significant advances in engineering, starting with the work we did in Alaska and the North Sea and progressing to the 1,000-mile-long BTC pipeline from Baku to Ceyhan. And now in the ultra-deep waters of the Gulf of Mexico we were involved in a project which the engineers regarded "as more difficult than going to the moon".

The Thunder Horse field was to be developed with a floating platform encompassing a drilling rig, production facilities and accommodation for staff. The platform was the biggest and most advanced of its type in the world – 50 per cent larger than the second largest. It featured more than 100 industry firsts. In July 2005, we expected that it would shortly begin to process 250,000 barrels of oil and 200 million cubic feet of gas per day, from some of the deepest wells in the Gulf of Mexico.[5]

Thunder Horse was not just any platform. It was to be our flagship.

11 July 2005: In the car, on my way to a formal dinner at the Greenwich Maritime Museum to celebrate the 90th anniversary of BP's marine business, BP Shipping, I got a call from Tony Hayward, then chief executive of the E&P division and responsible for Thunder Horse. "We've got a problem in the Gulf of Mexico. I don't fully understand what's happened. It looks like Hurricane Dennis has hit Thunder Horse. The platform is listing. I need to alert everyone including the marine team."

No one was hurt. Thunder Horse had been evacuated in anticipation of the hurricane's approach. I was relieved. Then a thought flashed through my mind of a sinking $5 billion.

Tony told me that the teams were only just beginning to return offshore as the weather slowly improved. There was nothing anyone could do, especially from London.

This was the marine department's big night. Bob Malone, who headed it up and was responsible for US relationships, had to make the keynote speech at the event. I told Tony he could speak to the marine team but said: "I don't want you to speak to Bob because you don't need him. He needs to be in control here and I'll tell him after he has done his speech." So I went to the dinner and said nothing to Bob until close to the end. Then reality kicked in.

We awoke the next day to see the Thunder Horse platform on the front page of many newspapers. The aerial photographs of this huge beast on its side, with its red legs askew and surrounded by deep blue sea, were spectacular. Even with the photographs as clear evidence, we could not believe it. Thunder Horse had been designed to withstand the force of the largest hurricanes. How could this have happened?

The platform was listing by about twenty degrees. Work quickly got under way to right it and to establish what had caused the problem. Within a week we had the platform level. But it was clear there had been some damage and that start-up was unlikely to be in 2005. The delay would affect BP's production output but I was confident that it was a short-term problem. We discovered that a defective control system had caused the platform to tip over. When the crew had shut the platform down and gone ashore, as the hurricane was about to hit, ballast tanks on one side of the platform had incorrectly been instructed to fill with water.

Now, we had to implement an array of checks and repairs. All of the equipment on the seabed, more than 6,000 feet below the surface, had to be replaced; the delay in production had made it too brittle to be used. One thing led to another. The platform seemed to be beset by problem after problem. By the beginning of 2006 it began to look like start-up would be delayed for a very long time.

Every exploration and production project has challenges, particularly where leading-edge technology is deployed. BP had problems in the 1980s with what was then a state-of-the-art £1 billion platform for the Magnus oil field, in the North Sea. There was a chance it might have sunk. It was on the brink of a failure which would have damaged the company irreparably.

The Thunder Horse problem was a big disappointment but, because BP was now a large and robust enterprise, it did not lead to a company-threatening crisis. It was, however, great material for the media. As I read the coverage I was reminded of Nick Butler's warning in 2002; too big a personal profile for a CEO makes everything personal. The event prompted questions about many things including my management style and whether the event was a sign of a systemic failure of control right across BP. It was not about any of these things. It was about complexity and the fact that we had underestimated the overall risk when combining so many individual novel pieces of technology.

Thunder Horse showed us once more that you could not hide your problems and challenges. The engineering issues in Alaska in the 1970s or the near miss with Magnus in the 1980s were resolved in private. But with Thunder Horse we had to solve our problems in the glare of the world's media. Transparency was here to stay.

In the end Thunder Horse did not start up until June 2008, after I had left BP, and it then began ramping up production. It is now a spectacular success, producing more oil per day than any other field in the US apart from Prudhoe Bay.

Thunder Horse was a remarkable project but it seemed simply to add to the list of problems for BP in the US, a list which I never anticipated would grow even longer in the following 12 months.

But bad news usually comes in threes.

Oil spills

2 March 2006: "We've found a leak."

I took the call in my office. "Where?"

"Gathering Centre 2, within the field, before it enters the line. We don't think it's much."

My immediate response: "Overreact."

"We've only just discovered it. An operator smelt it first and then saw the stain coming through the snow."

Oil seeping through the snow in Alaska could only mean one thing. A leak had been happening for some time and it was serious. Twenty-nine years of testing, improved processes, leak-detection systems and alarms. Yet it had happened.

There were many questions. How long had the spill been occurring without us detecting it? Why did our system not detect a leak of this magnitude? How could we clean up quickly? How could we ensure it never happened again?

Within a few days of discovery, the leak became obvious: a quarter-inch hole, caused by corrosion, at the bottom of the pipeline. Such a tiny hole but so disastrous. Thousands of gallons of crude oil had been spilled on to the fragile tundra in the western area of Prudhoe Bay.[6]

This was completely unacceptable. It was bad not only for the environment but also for the company's reputation. I could see problems brewing.

We went into overdrive. I had one of our very best people, a former executive assistant of mine and now a senior manager, David Peattie, go over to run the clean-up operation and to look at what had gone wrong. We had inspected the line regularly, so why had the corrosion accelerated so rapidly? To ensure there was no further risk of leaks, we aggressively inspected and repaired every defect found. I insisted that we replace the whole of that particular gathering system, a three-mile section of the pipeline within the field.

By August I was assured that everything had been tested and measured and that lessons were learned. The US Department of Justice (DOJ) was carrying out an investigation of the spill and we were co-operating fully. I went across to Alaska, with the head of our US operation, and inspected the work.

I was so confident that we had successfully dealt with the problem that we even invited the press to Prudhoe Bay. I wanted them to see for themselves that we had everything under control – and of course to demonstrate BP's ability to manage confidently in light of the events at Texas City and Thunder Horse.

I left Alaska feeling we had reacted swiftly to the crisis, but bitterly disappointed that the incident had happened in the first place. I was aware that more work had to be done but I felt sufficiently reassured to take a much-delayed vacation. I headed to my apartment in Venice for a short break.

6 August 2006: I had barely unpacked when the phone rang. They had found further corrosion. Again it was in the gathering system but this time at the eastern end and only five barrels of oil had leaked. I had said "overreact" the first time. And this time they had taken my instruction literally. Our man in the US was recommending we shut down the Prudhoe Bay oil field.

When you are producing oil, you live in a glasshouse and people watch your every action. I had always erred on the side of caution but shutting down the whole oil field seemed a little extreme. But, I was in Venice and not in Alaska, and with only a few facts, it was a recommendation I could not ignore. In effect, the train was already in motion.

It was the first ever shutdown of the US's biggest oil field. It took out around 8 per cent of the nation's domestic oil production. And such was the scale of Prudhoe Bay, it began to affect oil prices worldwide. I knew the repercussions would be massive. This could be an international crisis.

I was advised not to go to Alaska; I was told that I "would only make it worse".

I did not think things could get much worse. I knew that Thunder Horse had already been wrongly linked to the Texas City explosion.

They were totally unrelated, with completely different causes. And now the problems in Alaska would also be linked for good measure.

Everyone wanted an easy-to-grasp story, not analysis. Emotions were running high. Scientific and engineering arguments are difficult to put over and are never going to be of interest. "Changing oil/water ratio and flow rates" would never make the front page. "BP out of control" would.

Disaster inquiries try and find the root cause, discovered when you have exhausted all the questions beginning with "why . . .?" When you get the answer, there is a danger in forgetting that you have been looking into a rear-view mirror and reinterpreting past events with today's information. It makes it seem as if mistakes should have been foreseen. It is never that simple and is often "retrospective fallacy".[7]

Could BP have anticipated the corrosion which caused the two spills? Our team believed that our Alaskan monitoring and repair methods were the best applicable technology. They probably were just that for a long period of time. But then something began to change. It was the change that caught us out.

Only afterwards could we ask: We used corrosion inhibitors so why had they not worked? Was it because of the increase in the amount of water in the production fluids? Or was it because of a decline in production so the slower flow created an environment more conducive to the incubation of bacteria which cause corrosion?

I clearly had relied too heavily on the technical explanation of why the first leak had taken place. I should not have been so reassured. I should have asked for more testing. But more than that, I wish someone had challenged me and been brave enough to say: "We need to ask more disagreeable questions."

As a leader it is hard to find that delicate balance between confidence, humility and arrogance. You need confidence to make decisions to keep moving the business forward. Too much humility can lead to the loudest voice prevailing. Yet arrogance may cause you to make a decision before considering the range of possibilities.

Succession stakes

I have never believed that because someone reaches a particular age they should be forced to step down from a role. A formal fixed retirement age implies that suddenly, at the stroke of midnight, when you reach a certain age, you are no longer able to do your job or to contribute to society.

In April 2006 I gave a speech, "Beyond Retirement", at the Young Foundation in the restored Wilton's Music Hall, in the East End of London. The hall had been used as a set in the movie of *The Phantom of the Opera*. In my speech, I said: "A truly civilised society is one in which people have genuine choices unfettered by their origins, their colour or their age."[8]

We had accepted that it was wrong to say: "You're a woman, there's no job for you." Or to say: "You're black or Irish or Jewish, you can't work here." But too many people still seemed to think that it was acceptable to say: "You've reached the age of 60. We don't want you any more."

Then, I was perhaps ahead of accepted thinking. Now, because of hard times, the question is different: will anyone ever be able to retire from work? But that speech in 2006 caused some internal controversy. Some believed I had used the speech as a crude ploy to extend my tenure. I thought that demonstrated a touching, if somewhat undue sensitivity to everything I said.

I was 58 in the summer of 2006 and believed that BP should scrap the mandatory retirement age for executive directors for the simple reason that we were about to do this for everyone else.

25 July 2006: BP announced that I would retire in December 2008. I would be 60 in February 2008 and would see the company through to its centenary year before stepping down. We did not announce my successor at that point, but five people were in the race: Iain Conn, Robert Dudley, Tony Hayward, Andy Inglis and John Manzoni.[9]

They had all been my executive assistants, otherwise known as "Turtles", named after the Teenage Mutant Ninja Turtles because of their speed and ability to appear whenever they were needed. It was not a name I gave them; it was just something that caught on.

I had already started looking for my successor the day I took the helm in 1995. Those who I thought had potential became executive assistants. I coached and groomed them, something I particularly enjoyed. There were two of them at any one time; one would stay in the UK and one would travel with me. During my time as CEO I had a total of 18 executive assistants and they kept a running "Turtle Bible", which was their accumulated wisdom and advice for their successors. It was regarded as "too much information for the boss", so I never officially saw it. The bits I did read were funny and irreverent.

Every year the board discussed my succession with me and there were discussions in the margins of many meetings. I once calculated that I had made 15 presentations on my succession and held at least treble that number with the chairman of the board. Gradually the number of people in the frame reduced to the five listed. I always believed the board should have more than one choice; it is not up to a CEO to select his successor. And a wise board is unlikely to pick someone just like the existing CEO. Change and new eyes on old problems are important to keep competitive advantage. While the role of the CEO is clearly defined, it is the incumbent that influences the style and priorities. And those are based on accumulated experience.

When I took over as CEO, my predecessor, David Simon, became executive chairman and hence my day-to-day boss. I found this mostly useful and sometimes very trying. But on balance it was a good arrangement. Our backgrounds were so different; he was from the people-intensive downstream and I from the capital-intensive upstream; he had mostly European experience and I mostly North American. I had already worked with him, following Bob Horton's departure, on cost-cutting and getting BP back on an even keel.

As a new CEO I was enthusiastic to change things and to grow the company. David was a moderating force; he counselled me that the spirit of the organisation would be protected and investors' confidence maintained if I played a long game. And he reminded me that, however hard you try, there are different aspirations and attitudes in different countries as there are between the upstream and downstream. It was an effective partnership. I had a seasoned boss and had inherited a top team of people all of whom had been my peers; they never held back with their opinions.

But, of course, a new incumbent may occasionally think that the "old boy" is out of touch. History and continuity have value. It is a shame that prevailing thought in corporate governance denies most companies the opportunity to make the best of them.

By late 2006, it became increasingly clear to me that it was time to leave. Succession races should not be prolonged and anyway BP needed a new leader. However, my emotional self prevailed over reason. I did not know how to leave; I always thought that there was just one more thing to do. I now can see that this is a more widespread and difficult problem than many recognise.

And frail human emotion would trump the rational in events which I could little imagine would next unfold.

13

LONDON

Betrayal

If I had paid him off I might have managed my exit better.

Whether it was an extraordinary quirk of fate, or planned with precision, I will never know. But the arrival of a carefully crafted email from a former boyfriend in December 2006 could not have come at a worse time.

I had spent my whole working life dealing with probabilities – after all, that is what oil exploration is about. Yet the coming together of disparate professional and personal strands in a perfect storm was so improbable that I could never have foreseen it. If someone had planned this series of disasters to come together for effect it could not have been done better.

The life that I had successfully kept behind closed doors was threatening to become public. My former boyfriend had written before asking for money but this email appeared to me to be a veiled threat. I ignored it.

I was at The King's School Ely when I realised I was gay. That was Britain in 1960 and homosexuality was illegal. Men went to prison. It was wrong; that was drilled into you at school. Boys were expelled. No one talked about it; individuals would just disappear, leaving hushed whispers. While I was at Cambridge the law changed. But I was still terrified – terrified of being found out. And this fear would stay with me all my adult life.

It had taken ten years for the UK government to accept the recommendations of the Wolfenden Report,[1] published in 1957. It would take many more years for homosexuality to be deemed acceptable, particularly in the corporate world.

I was certain that if people in BP had known I was gay it would have been the end of my career. Looking back, I now realise many people in BP knew. It is hard to see yourself as others see you. But I suppose it was the company's best-kept secret.

For me, it was a dark secret that I shared with few people, not even with my mother. On the rare occasions I tried to broach the subject, she would not listen. When I asked my mother to come with me to Stanford, just after my father had died, I could never have realised that any idea of coming out would be put on the back burner until after her death. I would have to lead a double life. I would not have long-standing relationships; there would be only occasional clandestine liaisons. My mother was always there.

My mother was broad-minded but had her limits, influenced very much by her experiences through one of the darkest periods of history. She believed strongly that no one should ever be discriminated against on any grounds. But her experiences also gave her an inherent wariness of trusting people. The idea that you might be found out, that someone might betray you, or someone might take away your loved ones, for any reason, was a deep-rooted fear. It had happened to her and she had seen the cruelty meted out by the Nazis. "Don't trust people with your secrets" – that was what she told me from an early age. And that wariness became part of me.

My mother died on 9 July 2000. Somehow I never thought she ever would. She had such a zest for life. The shock was enormous. She had been my most important counsellor and my unconditional supporter. Ever since my father died I had looked after her and she had looked after me. I had got used to it. I think that I was making up for lost time because of boarding school.

When she died it felt like part of me had disappeared. I was not just lonely in that I had no companion, I was also alone.

I was close to my father, but my mother and I had a special bond. When she used to put me on the plane in Iran to go back to boarding school in England, she would say: "I am pushing my life away and I am just waiting for the moment you return."

Now she was gone.

Few people knew my mother's background. She never talked about it and neither did I. In the last few weeks of her life, however, with the guilt of a survivor, she found comfort in talking to a friend, Claus Moser. He had escaped from Berlin in the early 1930s and became an extraordinary contributor to society and civilisation in the UK.

Her funeral was small and private, but some months later I held a memorial service in celebration of her life at the Farm Street Catholic Church in London. A small number of close friends were to give eulogies. They included: Judy Moody-Stuart, the wife of the then chairman of Shell; Ian Matheson, my housemaster at the senior school of The King's School Ely; Daniel Yergin, who, with his wife and family, was a close friend of my mother; and Claus Moser. The night before the service I gave a dinner for all those who were to take part and who had helped. We talked of my mother and the great moments we had celebrated with her. Claus told me that he was still preparing his remarks for the next day. He did not know whether to talk of my mother's history. She had been so silent about it. Yet it was part of her life, a door which she had sought to close, but could never be completely shut. I went to bed that night unsure of what he would say. It was not in my hands to decide.

The next day was bright and cold, a rather beautiful London autumn day. The 500 people in the Farm Street Church were quiet throughout the ceremony. I was sitting by myself in the front towards the side. As Claus began to tell my mother's story it seemed to me that there was a collective gasp behind me. Most people there had no inkling of her history. The church became absolutely still, totally silent, as the listeners were riveted by the story of what my mother had endured.

My mother had told me that her mother was Jewish and her father was a Catholic. She grew up with her six siblings as part of Oradea's Catholic community. They might have escaped the Nazis but they were betrayed. In the spring of 1944 her whole family had to leave their home to live in a packed ghetto. Then, along with more than 30,000 Jews from Oradea, they were sent on freight trains to Auschwitz. On arrival, my mother was selected for Auschwitz III, the work camp, to be used as a slave labourer in a munitions factory. Some of her other family members were selected for Auschwitz II (Birkenau), the extermination camp.[2] Only she and a few members of the family survived.

I felt relieved that the burden of knowledge had been lifted from my shoulders. My mother had wanted to keep her story secret, to bury it in the past, just to be able to go on. She never regarded it as part of her life. But now the horrors which she, her family and her friends went through; the memory of the survivors like her who had been stripped of their human dignity; and the remembrance of those who had been brutally murdered were all part of the story of her life.

I was only 32 when my father died. I was too young to know how my relationship with him would have developed and too young to understand what I was going to miss. When my mother died I was 52 and I understood the loss; it was months before I could even talk about her.

Concerned friends gave me books to try to help me through. I learnt the obvious. There were people in the same position, other people who also felt they were "adult orphans". I was alone but I was not unique.

I have no doubt that my loneliness weakened me. I became increasingly aware of the all-consuming action of being at the helm of BP and the emptiness of my private life. In different circumstances I would have spent many years building relationships and I might have found a partner with whom to share my life. That had not happened, so I absorbed myself in my work and talked of BP as my "family". But, in 2002, deep loneliness led me to search for a boyfriend.

I became involved with a young Canadian. After nine months he moved in with me. Only very close friends knew I had this relationship and I did not want them to know that we had met through an escort agency. That was to be our secret. He and I agreed that if anyone ever asked how we met, we would say while running in Battersea Park. After nearly four years with him I almost believed it myself.

Things did not work out. After we parted, I supported him financially. I do not think that I was unkind; I did everything I could to help him. But after a while I stopped; I was not prepared to go on supporting him for ever.

Perhaps I should have responded to his email but I had nothing to say. I still would not pay for his silence, even knowing all I do now. Would I have answered him if I had not been so preoccupied? Might the outcome have been different? I can never allow myself to think like that. Things were what they were.

When I did not respond, my former boyfriend sold his story to the press. I later wondered whether he had, in fact, already done so before writing to me.

Breaking news

Friday, 5 January 2007: I was staying with friends in Barbados during the New Year vacation when Roddy Kennedy, BP's chief press officer, phoned to break the news. A British newspaper had called BP to say they were going to run a story about my private life, about a young Canadian, about how I had met him and what we had done together. It would appear on the following Sunday. The newspaper asked for a comment within hours.

I had been found out; I panicked. What was in my mind is hard to say: confusion, anger, but most of all a sense of betrayal and affront. Someone I had trusted was using stories about me for their advantage. Some of it was deeply private and some of it simply not true.

With hindsight I should have left the situation alone and let the newspaper publish the story. But I was desperate to protect my privacy and my secrets. I decided, after consulting my friends, to try to stop the newspaper from going ahead with the story. I would find and brief top lawyers and take out an injunction. That was my first mistake.

My second mistake was to persist with the "Battersea Park" cover story of how we had met. It was one thing to use it to push aside the casual questioning of friends; it was quite another to use it as an explanation to your lawyers and in court papers. I was ashamed and embarrassed, and had yet to confront the secret I had hidden in a dark corner all my life. I had never openly admitted to strangers that I was gay and now I was talking to a lawyer whom I did not know, on a long-distance phone call, with my Barbados host in earshot. When asked how I met my former boyfriend, I used the "Battersea Park" story. I just could not bring myself to tell the truth.

The newspaper was prevented from publishing the story on Sunday, 7 January, but the legal machine then started behind the scenes. I flew back from Barbados, via Trinidad, where I had to do some business. I did it without blinking; I was in denial.

I knew that the statement to my lawyer contained an inaccuracy. I should have corrected it as soon as I got back to the UK but I was focused on professional matters, particularly the freshly published findings of the Baker Panel on the Texas City incident. I had to concentrate on how I would manage the impending press conference.

Friday, 12 January: I began to focus. It was clear to me that I could no longer continue as CEO of BP. I spoke to the chairman who was keen to move things on very quickly as he judged the combination of the Baker Panel report and my personal story as a "perfect storm". The board, however, agreed that I should stay on until the summer and we announced my successor. The race was over. Tony Hayward would take over from me at the end of July.

Wednesday, 16 January: We made the findings of the Baker Report public and held a very difficult press conference. It was emotionally draining. It brought back the memories of the tragedy with the terrible scene and inconsolable anguish on the day of my visit, after the explosion in March 2005. My private legal case and my inaccurate statement to my lawyers boiled up in my mind.

Friday, 19 January: I came to my senses. I knew that I had to correct my witness statement. I did, but it was too late; by then my former boyfriend was making further allegations.

Publicly I kept control of myself. The guarded behaviour I had learned as a child meant I was able to maintain a "stiff upper lip" right to the end. I had to continue to lead BP and that meant no one needed to know about my personal problems. I knew people who had been through far worse. My role models were those who managed to stay composed and not be pulled down by the undercurrents – and, at the time, Tony Blair was one of them. He managed to continue with his day-to-day business while under enormous pressure, mainly because of British involvement in the Iraq War.

In my private life, events were bubbling up. It was like watching a bad film in slow motion. I had begun to guess what the ending might be and no longer wanted to watch, yet I was compelled to sit through until the very end.

I lost the case against the newspaper, which meant they could publish the story. I never met the judge. My future was being decided on paper.

I decided to go to the Court of Appeal, although I knew my chances were slim.

Friday, 30 March: I made all the plans to resign with a press release drafted and internal arrangements made. But there was a problem. How could I explain why I was resigning when my case was still pending and had to remain confidential until the judgement was published? I stayed. The bad film was getting worse.

I lost the appeal and tried to go to the House of Lords but was told there was no case. Now everything moved very quickly.

Resignation

Tuesday, 1 May, noon: The court ruling was made public. I resigned. I decided it was no longer appropriate for BP for me to stay. My former boyfriend's story was in every paper, on every news channel and on the internet. It had the perfect ingredients to get a business story on to any front page – power, sex and lies. My private life was broadcast around the world.

Replaying all this now, I wish I had not been with BP on that day. The events would have been less newsworthy. It would have been better for the company.

My first decision was that I was not going to run away or go into hiding. I was going to continue to conduct my life in the way I thought fit because I had the right to do so. I felt, and still do feel, very strongly about that.

I knew the press would be all over me and that I would have to face up to them. At around 5.00 pm, I walked out of the main entrance of BP's office in St James's Square. The press were swarming; they pushed and shoved me in the short distance it took to reach my car. They door-stepped me as I returned to my apartment, and chased me on motorbikes when I left. It was intrusive and unpleasant.

Two days after my resignation I was due to give a speech in Brussels. It was the second in the Amartya Sen Lecture Series on Sustainable Development,[3] before an invited audience of diplomats, European officials and academics. My office made a number of hasty calls. The answer came back: "No question. Lord Browne must still come and give the lecture."

Every member of that packed audience knew what had happened. They knew that any question about my resignation or personal life was inappropriate and off limits.

Despite this, one journalist stood up boldly and asked: "Lord Browne, are you looking forward to going to jail? You lied. You must answer. This is a matter of public interest." The packed audience booed him. He was put down swiftly.

The audience's support was of tremendous comfort. No, I was not worried about going to jail. What I did was wrong but at least I had not lied under oath. I had not committed perjury but I had made a false witness statement. I had lied about how I met a man. That was a very serious error of judgement, for which I had publicly apologised.

Mr Justice Eady, the High Court Judge who had handled my case, said that my punishment was to be to my reputation. He was right. I might have been "most admired" for years but all that was overshadowed because of a momentary slip. Friends and colleagues knew that this was not how I would have normally behaved, but to explain then why I had made that error seemed futile.

Within days I was overwhelmed by the caring reaction of friends and colleagues. I was deeply touched when a large number of them wrote to the national newspapers to express their support. I received more than 4,000 personal emails and letters of support and answered almost every one where there was an address. Many were from business colleagues, and some from friends who simply wanted to reach out to help. Some were from people I had never met who wanted to sympathise by sharing their own personal tragedies. Journalists, who were friends, wrote personal notes. One added: "I will have to write to you in a professional capacity to ask you for an interview. Please make sure you refuse."

I soon discovered who my friends really were and realised that I was enormously privileged; I had a lot of friends. Many said that if they had found themselves in similar circumstances they would have done the same thing. That does not justify what I did; I know that too well.

I also saw the very few who would cross to the other side of the street as they saw me coming; I was no longer useful to them.

Younger people might ask why there was so much drama around this event and why I did not simply come out and say I was gay 10 or 20 years ago. They are right to ask the obvious question but the answer is less straightforward. It is about past events, which fed my fears; about my unusual family circumstances, which shaped my lifestyle; and about my own human weakness.

My work with BP had consumed more than 40 years of my life. After I resigned, that part of my life had been severed. It felt as if it was no longer anything to do with me, or I with it.

For some time I looked at my career with BP with distaste and dissatisfaction. It was hard to take a balanced view of the era that had occupied more of my life than any other.

BP had begun with my father and had involved my mother. BP went back as far as Iran, when I was ten. And it encompassed deep friendships with many people who were my "family".

It had been an extraordinary journey. I had joined a national institution. I had been with the company through privatisation and political, technological and scientific change. When I became CEO in 1995 we were described as "middleweight". BP went on to reshape the oil industry, be at the forefront of global investment, achieve many firsts and change views on the environment and corporate social responsibility (CSR). When I left in 2007, it was nearly five times bigger[4] and an international force that could open doors around the world.

And this success was not just confined to the company and its employees. It ensured the future of many people around the world, not least in the UK. Many people benefited. I once worked out that BP accounted for about £1 out of every £6 received in dividends by UK pension funds.[5] Those dividends trebled between 1995 and 2007.

There is no doubt that I became obsessed with BP and its challenges. When determination and enthusiasm turn into obsession, you lose your balance. I have always thought that it is important to be able to step right back to gain a better perspective. I used to think I was able to do that, but actually it became more and more difficult over time.

Why did I stay on as CEO of BP for so long? First, there always seemed to be something I wanted to follow through, something I wanted to finish, some problem to solve. That is what a lot of people in similar positions think, but it is a bad reason for staying. There is never a moment when there is not a business action to finish, something to put right or a deal to be done. Someone else, in another era, will get to do those things.

Second, because when I had looked around I could see nothing which was as exciting or as valued. At least that is what I thought. I had believed BP defined my life completely. But with time and distance, I can now see that it gave me opportunities to develop different and new capabilities and shape my breadth of interests. My journey with the company had taken me to exciting places, enabled me to witness good and bad events, and allowed me to change some things for the better, meet extraordinary people and learn about far more than just the oil industry.

Many of my interests have been spawned by my travels. Opera started in the front parlour in Chesterton Road, Cambridge in 1956. Art, photography and music began in that hot summer of 1973 in New York, and wine in San Francisco shortly after.

I began to collect pre-Columbian artefacts from Colombia and Ecuador because someone sparked my interest on a visit to Colombia in 1989. My collection encouraged me to buy books on the subject and learn more. And I expect this knowledge helped my appointment as a trustee of the British Museum. There, over almost ten years I served with remarkable people, one of whom was the archaeologist Colin Renfrew. He lectured me on the evils of illegal excavation. And so I stopped collecting pre-Columbian objects, just in case.

Now, every time I walk into my library, I go past two full-sized reproductions of terracotta soldiers which I bought on a visit to the buried army of the first Emperor in Xian, China. They remind me of my private journeys to China: the visits to the Great Wall before it became so accessible; and the opening of the Shanghai Museum in 1996 with its superb collection of ceramics. That inspired me to start collecting ceramics from around the world.

While a trustee of the British Museum, I met the wonderful Anthony Griffiths, its keeper of prints and drawings, who ignited my passion for Venetian printed works, now one of my most exciting collections.

It was through BP that I got involved with the Tate Gallery. BP, under Bob Horton, had supported the Tate and its outstanding director, Nick Serota, since 1990. I was particularly interested in contemporary works. I started collecting Hockney in New York because he reflected a life – at least in my fantasy at the time – I would like to have led. My contemporary art collection expanded. And now I am chairman of the Tate.

Other pursuits come and go. Some have stayed. All started with meeting someone of interest who had a passion for his or her subject. These, and my continuing interest in engineering, science, energy, climate change and business, created the basis for the change to a new life.

I had thought BP was the vehicle for me to champion change. I now see that change is a way of thinking and that you can champion change in any walk of life.

After I had resigned, I gave up smoking cigars. It was a start. Now many things are different: what I value, what I think is important, what I think the world needs and how I can contribute.

Today, there are yet more places to go, more people to meet and more conversations to be had. And, most of all, there is more learning to come. As Joseph Needham, the great historian of Chinese science, often said: "The dogs bark but the caravan moves on."[6]

14

VENICE

Lessons

20 August 2009: The end of this journey brings me to Venice, a place that makes me happier than anywhere else, a place to reflect and think.

Venice, *La Serenissima*, creates a curious mix of calm and inspiration. If people are prepared to listen, I believe the stones themselves speak to you. But I did not appreciate that for some time.

My first visit was with my parents in 1965. For a young boy, Venice had little appeal. It seemed no more than a city of faded glories. Even in the following summer, when I visited Venice on a pre-university "grand tour" with friends in an old red post office van, the city was just a sightseeing stop en route to Greece, through former Yugoslavia.

Now it seems strange that I used not to like Venice. I saw the individual buildings and did not understand the city as one entity. I was too young and inexperienced to see that in "Venice more than anywhere else, the whole is greater than the sum of the parts. However majestic the churches, however magnificent the *palazzi*, however dazzling the pictures, the ultimate masterpiece remains Venice itself."[1]

It was a weekend visit, after Stanford, when I first saw the city in that entirety. I began to see that the history and culture of Venice could help me appreciate the present, and look to the future.

Venice was built from nothing. The marshy lagoon, then a malarial wasteland, offered a remote refuge for mainlanders under attack from barbarians who pillaged and burned their way down the coast. Venice formally began at the stroke of noon on 25 March, AD 421, when a consul visiting from Padua established a trading post on the islands of the Rialto.[2] From these humble origins, Venice rose to become a thriving mercantile sea power which lasted, as a republic, for almost a thousand years.

The date of this great city's demise was as precise as that of its foundation. On 12 May 1797, the Great Council voted to hand the city to Napoleon. Lodovico Manin, the 118th Doge of Venice, came out of that final council meeting and returned to his apartment with dignity. He did not attempt to flee like many of his fellow nobles. He removed his ducal corno and white linen cap, handed them to his valet and said: *"Tolè questa no la dopero più"* (Take it, I shall not be needing it again).[3] And that was the end of what had once been the richest and most powerful republic in the civilised world.

Several years ago, my deep interest in Venice led me to buy an apartment which overlooks the Grand Canal. I stay there over the summer for as many weeks as possible. In the early morning the city awakes slowly and few people are on the streets. The Rialto market is nearby and there is bustle and commerce as restaurateurs and *casalinghe* (housewives) buy their fish, fruit and vegetables.

You can get a coffee and watch scenes unchanged for many years. "What news on the Rialto?"[4] was not a question asking for gossip; the Rialto was the great commercial exchange at the very heart of the republic. As trade expanded, people came from around the world "to swap currencies, to invest funds, to rent ships, to talk diplomacy and war, to take passage, to learn the news from the East, to buy and to sell".[5] As early as the 13th century, Venetian bankers were located here.[6] In time, Venice became governed by complex laws and when there were problems the government intervened.[7]

Venice was never perfect but it provides a great pool of ideas, good and bad, from which we can still learn about business, human frailty and governance – and it is the ideal place to reflect, to "study the present in the light of the past for purposes of the future".[8]

The lessons we learn, of course, derive from experiences which were had in a certain time and in a certain place; whether that learning will apply to a future time and place is unclear. Karl Popper said that all science is provisional; I believe that, at least as far as business is concerned, all learning is provisional. I have learned from my own successes and failures. The failures are entirely mine but the successes are built on the shoulders of giants, of those who went before me.

My learning provided me with a framework within which to address dilemmas and to solve practical problems which I faced as I developed oil, gas and energy businesses around the world. That framework is about the role of leaders, about the importance of purpose, about the relationship between business and government and about openness. What I experienced kept changing my view; I expect and hope that will continue, since learning must never stop.

Leaders

I keep reflecting on what I have learned. It is that so much of what is actually delivered and enacted depends on having the right leadership in the right place at the right time. The world yearns for clear and trusted leadership; it is in short supply. Yet we need leaders in every place and in every walk of life to meet the grand challenges of our era: mitigating the expected effects of climate change, changing the way we use energy, improving people's wellbeing, and bringing more than one billion people out of extreme poverty. This takes not only leaders on the world stage but also great leaders in local communities, who understand the fears and hopes of their neighbours.

We need to create more leaders; I believe that can be done. Leaders must, in my experience, first prove themselves as good managers.

Managers have to organise so that actions can be delegated and co-ordinated, so that people and financial resources can be deployed efficiently. They need to build a plan, set targets, measure performance and take actions if those targets are not met. Managers make sure that the people they employ are competent, continuously educated and trained and placed in the right jobs. They communicate with and listen to their teams, coach them and encourage them. All of that is about management. It is a function that I fulfilled for all of my time as CEO of BP. At least four times a year I would review the performance of each part of the company against their targets and I would ensure that corrective measures were undertaken. Costs, revenues and the quality of future prospects all had to be competitive. I visited operations, customers and governments on a routine basis; there was never a substitute for knowing what was going on. But all this had to be done in such a way as not to undermine the authority of the managers who were empowered to run the different parts of the company.

Leaders must never forget how to be managers but they must be far more than managers; good managers are not necessarily good leaders.

Leaders "must contemplate the particular in terms of the general, and touch abstract and concrete in the same flight of thought".[9] Leaders must not reject abstract thought in business in favour of purely concrete actions. Both are needed, not least to develop a rigorous strategy to fulfil the purpose of a company. Let me suggest four areas for leaders to focus on: setting direction, bringing people with them, establishing boundaries to actions, and creating powerful constituencies.

First, leaders must be very clear about what they want to achieve, how they will go about getting there and the risks involved. They need to define their path and themselves, not in contrast or comparison to others, but as who they really are. They have to understand, accept and harness the personal risks associated in taking a specific direction by having the right degree of self-confidence but not arrogance. Being a leader is more risky than most people imagine since an effective leader takes full responsibility for the consequences of his or her decisions. Perhaps this explains why we have such a lack of leadership in both business and politics globally.

When I became CEO in 1995 I knew BP needed scale and reach to survive. We had to merge or we would have become an acquisition target. We chose to merge and, in the end, rose to become a leading player in the industry. We incorporated those thoughts in a strategy for the board. The board meeting at the Four Seasons Hotel in Berlin in 1996 was a turning point for the company: in strategy, the board saw the future and understood what it would take to get there.

Once you are clear on your direction, you must make sure that you are not sidetracked. You can only fight strategic battles. I saw that when we first got involved in Russia and lost Sidanco. We had to win that asset back, otherwise it would have started a domino effect and we would have been chased out of other places in the former Soviet Union.

Second, leaders cannot just set a direction; they need to capture the loyalty and energies of people to get them to come along with them. To achieve this, they need to inspire people and understand their concerns and anxieties. They need to explain the direction to be taken and show that they understand how things get done. Since people are subject to the pressures of the urgent driving out the important, a leader has to explain and reinforce that direction – what I call "the plot" – time and again. This is one of the great duties of leadership. You must understand the direction you want people to take so well that you can describe it on a postcard. Then it is clear and only then can it be made clear to everyone else.

You cannot do everything yourself. Leaders and organisations are strengthened, not weakened, by empowering others. You have to enable people to challenge you. That is, in my experience, very difficult to achieve especially when people are jockeying for position – even your position. My friend Peter Hennessy, the great historian, reminds me that the role of the British Civil Service was to "speak truth unto power". That is the culture leaders must foster.

Fine-tuning to find the balance between the right amount of space to give people, and the rules to hold them back, is not easy. But if you can get it right, as we did with the re-organisation of BP in the early 1990s, it can create an entrepreneurial spirit which is hard to restrain.

You must be morally responsible for the consequences of every decision you make and never pass the buck. This is what inspires loyalty and credibility. It is the implicit contract between a leader and those she or he is leading. Leaders are not gods, they are not perfect, but they do have to accept responsibility as I had to in my final years with Texas City and the Alaskan oil spills. Only a weak leader blames his or her team.

Third, leaders have to deploy and then work consistently to rules and within boundaries. As importantly, they must be capable of actively influencing, shaping, and changing externally imposed boundaries where and when necessary.

And that is what I did in our operations in Azerbaijan and Indonesia. BP had painful experiences with security and human rights in Colombia. We were determined not to repeat our mistakes in other similarly difficult countries. We worked out how we could apply the UN Declaration of Human Rights to our activities and so got involved with the UK Foreign Office, the US Department of State, NGOs and our industry colleagues to develop what became the Voluntary Principles on Security and Human Rights. These we subsequently applied in the BTC pipeline project and at the Tangguh field in Indonesia.

Fourth, leaders cannot go it alone. You have to win people round to your way of thinking. I did this with climate change in 1997 and started a ripple which became a wave of realisation that crashed through the oil industry.

I was never afraid to ask other leaders for support when I knew they could be more effective than me. You have to do this; it is not a sign of weakness but a sign of strength. Prime Minister Tony Blair took the leadership role with the EITI, President Clinton lent his weight to the BTC pipeline and Margaret Thatcher made the difference in Baku.

You also need to deploy institutions when you can see that there is a clear win-win. We used the World Bank to help fund the BTC pipeline, not because we wanted "cheap money" but because we knew the bank would insist on applying tough international standards, to protect human rights and the environment, on the governmental borrowers.

Using all the support you can muster – leaders, NGOs, and government bodies – you can protect your brand and keep a licence to operate. You need to be prepared to go toe-to-toe with tyrants, as much as with elected leaders. They will challenge you, but you in turn need to challenge them so that your relationship does not corrupt your important values. This, I believe, I achieved in places like Angola and China.

Purpose

During all my time with BP, there was a debate on the wider purpose of business. Shortly after I joined, the *New York Times* published an article by the economist Milton Friedman in which he famously said: "... there is one and only one social responsibility of business – to use its resources and engage in activities designed to increase its profits".[10]

Increasing short-term profits is often thought to be the same as creating "shareholder value".[11] For my part, I started my tenure as CEO thinking that "10 years was merely 40 quarters"; or in other words, if you took care of the quarters, the years would look after themselves. That view was hardly surprising; I had just taken over from David Simon and helped him pull BP rapidly out of a hole. But I began to understand that this way of thinking erodes a commitment to the longer term. After all, shareholder value is not about returns and growth rates alone; it is also about how long a company can keep growing.

The "how long" means a business must invest in the societies from which it derives its profits to ensure that its customers continue to be there and that governments continue to renew its licence to operate. A business must be useful to society and be seen as such. This approach to investment has commonly been called corporate social responsibility (CSR).

I firmly believe that a business needs a greater purpose than just making profits.[12] CSR must be integrated into its daily thinking and activities over a sustained period. In BP's case that greater purpose became to fulfil basic human needs: to provide heat, light and mobility and to go *beyond petroleum*.

It is clear, from their actions, that some businesses and CEOs think that there is a no greater purpose than profit-making. The actions of some players in the financial sector, as an example, have resulted in recent disastrous consequences. The wreckage will lead to plenty of regulation but, in the end, it is the tone set by boards of directors that will remind executives to make sure that what they are doing is sustainably useful to society as a whole.

When I became CEO in 1995 my purpose was: to give the company scale and reach; to handle the issue of climate change; to make the company include a diversity of people; and to learn from the harsh experiences in Colombia and make CSR part of our strategy.

How well did I do against these objectives? First, BP got scale and reach, got access to some of the best and lasting oil and gas developments in the world, and invented the "Supermajor". Second, BP got a seat at the table to discuss what to do about climate change, and then did something about it. Third, BP became much more diverse and welcomed that diversity. And fourth, it not only made good profits but also made the sustainable development of society, in every country in which it was active, an integral part of its strategy and day-to-day business. I saw that having a greater purpose in business gives employees greater motivation and keeps them from "losing the plot".

Role

Over 40 years, I have seen the relationship between business and government change and I came to recognise that both working together is the best way to tackle the pressing issues of the day. I was reminded recently of a conversation I had many years ago. I had just returned to London, after living in the US in the late 1980s; my colleague Bryan Sanderson was running BP's petrochemical business and was a staunch supporter of the British Labour Party. Bryan was more than surprised when I told him that my experience had made me dislike politics and that I did not want to get involved; indeed, my mother, as a result of her own experiences, had repeatedly told me not to. My opinion has evolved.

I have never liked partisan politics because my views do not fit an easy partisan or ideological analysis. I have, however, come to see more value in the political process, the necessity of politics for advancing human progress. I saw some great qualities in many politicians and I have come to understand both the pressures on them and the complexity of the relationship between business and government in many countries – well beyond the lobbying and the corruption assumed by the media.

Government's role is to set the rules so that markets can evolve, and to intervene when markets fail. In my view, a government constructs a box bounded by rules. Inside that box, business can find its own way, innovating, competing and sometimes failing. The smaller the box, the less the competition and innovation; the larger the box, the greater the chances that markets will fail because the rules are not specific enough.

This requires careful balancing. I well remember that before Reagan and Thatcher the "box" was too small; the government in the UK, for example, seemed to have been involved in anything and everything. It was a monumental political struggle to make the box bigger. Then things changed. The free market became more lightly regulated, and increasingly so over the following 30 years.

Business has to perform in the box. Businesses understand better than governments how to deliver products and services efficiently and sustainably. Businesses have a role in advising governments on how to set rules, but it is not an exclusive role. NGOs and civil society have an equal say. That is what I realised when we were working in Alaska and later when we were building the BTC pipeline through three different countries.

Governments need to listen with an open mind and not be swayed by threats made by vested interests. The transition to a low carbon economy will require new sets of rules to produce a level playing field between different types of energy sources, carbon-free and hydrocarbon. And that will require great leadership. Rules must be set such that the cost of putting carbon into the atmosphere is borne by fossil fuels. Vested interests will object strongly and with threats.

In my early days with BP, its legacy was business that had been built on the back of the power of the British government. That started to change. I began to learn that business has to be based on mutual advantage between parties; otherwise business cannot be sustained over the long-term. I learnt my first real lesson when I was group treasurer. The sale of the Forties units in the North Sea nearly ended in failure; it appeared as if we were taking too much advantage of the UK government and no one can get away with such a one-sided deal.

There is no point in doing a piece of business that gives one party an unfair advantage. Consistently taking advantage drives people into the arms of others who are more willing to share what is on the table.

Openness

Today there is much talk about transparency. I knew, even before I started work at BP, that the behaviour of business was despised and mistrusted. I believe that such feelings mostly result from people's thinking that companies have something to hide.

The challenge for a leader is to determine the right level of trans-parency or openness in order to build rather than to undermine trust in a world of suspicious media and single issue NGOs. Some things should be kept confidential; for example, information on individuals or com-mercial discussions that are not yet fully developed. But the bias should be towards being as open as possible, certainly when it comes to actions that affect the lives of individuals.

Within any company there is a natural desire to project the best of all possible worlds but openness requires a different mindset. It requires businesses to communicate the good and bad as they happen. In this way, I found that openness builds trust and confidence in business dealings. That was evident as the independent panels, which were set up to monitor BP's developments at Tangguh in Indonesia and along the BTC pipeline, began to engage in dialogue and produce their reports.

And, indeed, within many governments there is a similar desire to keep all things confidential. BP got into trouble when it could not explain what it was paying to the Angolan government and what they were doing with the money. So we helped to create a whole new set of rules to encourage transparency: The Extractive Industries Transparency Initiative (EITI). The early signs are that EITI is helping to improve governance in some countries.

Learning and change

You should never accept the status quo unconditionally. I always wanted to question, to challenge, to press forward. But success and scale tend to make companies more cautious, and BP was no exception.

ICI was once a great British company, under the colourful leadership of John Harvey-Jones, but it became complacent. It passed up opportunities to get out of sectors such as heavy petrochemicals, and to strengthen its investment in other sectors such as pharmaceuticals. Now ICI no longer exists.[13]

You have to embrace change. As Rodney Chase pointed out to me in 1997, if society is changing then business has to change or it will simply be left behind. Many companies fail to capture opportunities or to survive significant change. Concern for the environment and investment in alternative energy were essential for BP to remain sustainable in the long-term.

If you give up on new ways of thinking or new technologies you will close down your future. You must embrace technology as a way of seeing that future. My first business experience with technology was an understanding of the power of computers to solve complex problems. I learnt about that before most people when I was at Cambridge. I took that learning with me to Alaska and then around the world.

Leaders must move with the times and the competition in order to survive. You have to watch and be mindful of competitors. You can copy what fits, as we did with Shell's exploration strategy in the early 1990s. At one time Shell was our paragon and paradigm. But the nature of competition changes. By 2004 Shell was a much weaker organisation; we might have merged with them. And around the world, other companies, such as Sinopec in China, were gathering strength and presented new opportunities for alliances. Nothing is frozen in time.

Along the way many people shared their wisdom and ideas with me. Andy Grove once told me that you "should never be too busy to learn". It was what they had tried to teach me at Cambridge. You have to listen to many different views to learn and then make a considered judgement. That was what I did before the Stanford speech in 1997. I sought views from an international cross-section of scientists, business people and NGOs. I was trying to understand climate change before coming to the view which I eventually shared with the broader audience.

Back to the Rialto

If you stroll at a leisurely pace, it takes about 15 minutes from my apartment to walk through narrow alleys, across *piazzas*, alongside canals, past my favourite church, *Santa Maria dei Miracoli*, to reach a small guildhouse, *Scuola di San Giorgio degli Schiavoni*. The *scuala* was built as the guildhall for the Dalmatians (Slavs) and was both a place of worship and a "kind of seaman's institute for the benefit of visiting Dalmatians".[14]

Standing outside, you might think the white marble facade unremarkable. But go inside and you will find a wonderful cycle of soft-coloured paintings by Carpaccio around the walls, full of symbolism of Dalmatian history and culture, with episodes from the life of Saint George (the patron saint of the *scuola*) and Saint Jerome (the patron saint of Dalmatia). Each time I visit, I see Carpaccio's charming attention to detail and find further meaning in his paintings.

I would never have discovered these paintings had I not ventured inside.

In business, you must never be complacent. You can never afford to look at yourself and just admire. You have to be inquisitive, never too busy, open to new experiences and restless for change. And, most of all, you have to understand the context around your business.

I see business today as a rich tapestry, part of society, weaving together people, governments, NGOs, industry and educational institutions. Think of any one of these strands as something in isolation and you will miss the point – rather like I did when I first visited Venice.

Leaders in all walks of life have to work together to tackle the grand challenges of our era. We have to continue to make progress.

If there is only one lesson we should learn from Venice: it is that if there is no "News on the Rialto" there is no business.

And no business means no progress and no future.

BRAZIL

Energy and the low carbon future

It is now more than two years since I left BP in May 2007. I have been involved with energy for the whole of my professional life. When I witnessed the raging fire at Ahvaz No. 6 well as young boy in Iran, it ignited an interest in energy that has lasted until now. Today, I am struck by how that country's relationship with the world also seems like a fire that has raged since the revolution of 1979. The world of energy has seen much change; it continues to evolve politically, with new technology, with new standards of care for the environment, with new players and new demands from customers. And I continue to be involved in energy as a partner in a New York-based investment firm, which invests solely in conventional and renewable energy enterprises. Not being CEO of BP allows me to do a variety of things; I am involved with the arts, engineering, and developing energy and climate change policies. I can now speak on a broad range of issues and not worry about sticking to the "corporate script". On the whole, I have a much freer and more enjoyable life.

I am visiting Brazil to see if there is good business to be done, in particular in renewable energy. I have visited Brazil many times before. BP had made a significant investment in E&P but none of it came to much. Now Brazil is a growing nation under President Lula and it seems to be offering serious opportunities for investment.

I find myself in a large room in a modernist house, outside Rio de Janeiro, which is open to the elements. The sun streams in with its warmth. The scent of damp leaves from the garden, the sound of screeching monkeys and croaking toucans in the trees, the exotic menu, and the stimulating discussion make for a memorable occasion.

Our host, Israel Klabin, founder of the Brazilian Foundation for

Brazil is witness to the raging destruction of the Amazon rainforest
but has vast potential to produce green energy

Sustainable Development, has strong views. He believes that we can no longer overuse and overwork our planet. We need to find a better balance for the planet and stop people doing purposeless activity. One might think Klabin had just been reading James Lovelock, a scientist, environmentalist and originator of the Gaia theory.[1] In many ways Klabin's views evoke Lovelock's apocalyptic scenario in which the earth is "about to catch a morbid fever that may last as long as 100,000 years".[2] But Klabin is a visionary in his own right and has made environmental issues his life.

During the meal, Klabin asks many questions: "The battle against climate change needs clean energy but is this battle more important than the battle against poverty or disease?

"Should developing countries be denied the access to fossil fuels which have made other countries so rich?"

And I respond with questions of my own: "How can we stop the massive deforestation around the world and, more particularly, here in Brazil?"

These tough questions pose political, economic and social dilemmas of the highest order. Climate change is only one of the problems related to our use of energy. Whether we can resolve our all-consuming dependence on energy from finite natural resources is another.

Finding answers will be crucial not only for the wellbeing of our communities but perhaps for our very survival. The answers are not clear-cut; emotion can blind rationality.

Brazil is a good example of "not clear-cut". Our serene, idyllic surroundings mask a particular reality. Brazil has immense natural beauty. It has the greatest biological diversity in the world and in its rich wildlife, new species are found almost every day. Yet it is also a place of raging destruction. The alarming shrinkage of the rainforest should concern us all. But we should not lose sight of Brazil's potential to produce green energy;[3] it is probably the world's first and only sustainable biofuels economy.[4] That should deserve at least as much attention as the vocal monkeys and toucans now cavorting outside Klabin's house.

Enjoying lunch and listening to the debate among Klabin's guests gives me an opportunity to think about my own questions: how much energy do we need; how much longer can we live with oil; what will influence the mix of energy we use; how do we build a low carbon future; what can governments do; how can we tackle climate change? The answers to these questions will shape our future.

How much energy do we need?

Energy is, and always will be, crucial to our way of life. It has played a fundamental role in shaping the human race as our ability to use energy is what sets us apart from the rest of the animal world.[5] How we find, produce and consume energy plays a key role in human progress, the shape of societies and economic growth.

We are living in what Daniel Yergin, author of *The Prize*, calls the "Hydrocarbon Age".[6] The energy we use – and have used over the last half-century – is derived from the three dominant types of hydrocarbons (fossil fuels): oil, gas and coal.

Harnessing energy from these resources has enabled "hydrocarbon man" to make rapid progress in the developed world. We communicate and travel across the globe. We have heat, light and mobility at the flick of a switch. We think none of this is remarkable; we simply take it for granted.

For many years, these fossil fuel resources appeared to have no inherent use and value to mankind. As humans *we* have made them highly useful and valuable by using our intelligence. Natural gas, for example, used to be a useless by-product of oil production. We then developed ways of transporting it cheaply and using it for cooking and heating. And, of course, there is oil. We have known about its presence on earth for thousands of years but only in the last 150 years did we find ways to harness its energy fully.[7] In this very short time, the energy revolution made possible the development of highly advanced technologies that have become ubiquitous and indispensable today: aeroplanes, automobiles, computers, mobile phones and so on.

Back in the 1990s, many people I knew were completely uninterested in the energy business. Saying you were "in the oil business" often prompted a bored look at social functions. That began to change as people became more concerned about issues emerging in the global arena: how oil was skewing world politics; how international companies were sourcing oil in countries with undesirable political regimes, such as Sudan; how oil was affecting the environment. And the big question was whether we had enough oil to last.

This is, of course, about supply *and* demand. Many people have focused attention on the supply side. But reflecting on how much oil we use is equally, if not more, important. Oil provides one third of all our energy, and about 60 per cent is used for transport fuel and the remainder in petrochemicals, agriculture and industry.

When I first started in the oil industry, the biggest markets for oil were the US, Europe and Japan. In the past decade, oil consumption has barely risen in the US and has declined in the EU and Japan.[8] During the same period, with the "rise of the rest", Chinese oil consumption has risen by a staggering 90 per cent and India's by 50 per cent.[9]

During my lifetime the world's population has so far almost trebled to seven billion people. The population continues to grow and with more people coming out of poverty, we will need perhaps as much as 45 per cent more energy, in all its forms, by 2030. India and China alone will account for half of this additional energy demand.[10]

It is not surprising that many people are concerned. And because of this concern, we have to apply our intelligence yet again to create energy from new and different sources so we can build a sustainable future.

How much longer can we live with oil?

When will oil run out? And what will we do when it runs out? As it is a finite resource, there is no question that it will peak and then decline. The proponents of "peak oil" argue that the supply of oil will not keep up with the anticipated demand. That argument was given a big boost by the popular book, *Twilight in the Desert*, by the most vocal "peakist", Matt Simmons.[11] In my copy he kindly wrote: "I suspect my report is very different from BP's official view ... " He was a master of the understatement; I still believe there is little sign that oil production will peak in the immediate future.

In the past two decades proven oil reserves have increased by around 40 per cent and proven gas reserves by around 70 per cent.[12] At expected growth rates of demand, I believe we have enough oil and gas for at least 30 years, even if no more reserves were discovered.[13]

But new and significant oil and gas fields are being discovered all the time, most recently, for example, in Brazil, the Gulf of Mexico, and offshore West Africa. And enhanced oil recovery techniques continue to extend the life of old oil fields and open up new areas in ultra-deep waters, tar sands and shales. Overall we probably have enough oil to last us for at least half another century.[14]

A similar story can be told of the future supply of coal and uranium. And the potential of renewable energy is limited only by the amount of land needed to build generating plants. On top of all this, if we used energy more efficiently, the planet's remaining natural resources would last longer. If energy-efficient working practices were adopted in Europe alone, we could save around 20 per cent of our current energy use.[15]

All this creates a compelling picture. We have a crucial period of around 50 years in which we must change, must invent and must learn to tap a much broader array of energy sources.

It is an existential challenge. However, we have the time to carry out the transition in an orderly manner. In fact, with the right policies in place I believe that *demand* for oil will peak long before we run out of supplies. I am reminded of the comment made by Sheikh Yamani, the former Saudi oil minister, during the 1970s: "The Stone Age didn't end because we ran out of stones, and the oil age will end long before the world runs out of oil."

Early signs are already there. US oil demand fell for the third year in a row in 2008,[16] and with tougher vehicle efficiency standards and the government mandating the use of biofuels, demand may be on a progressive decline. In future, as climate change policies begin to bite, demand for fossil fuels could be permanently reduced as people use a greater proportion of low carbon alternative energies: electricity generated from waste, hydropower, geothermal sources, solar facilities, wind turbines, waves and tidal movement; and transportation fuels made from sugarcane, corn and eventually from grasses.

One thing is abundantly clear: with so much choice available, the energy mix is bound to undergo major changes in the coming decades. After so many years of energy dominated by oil, gas and coal, we are likely to be heading into a brave new world: the "Low Carbon Age".

What will influence the mix of energy we use?

Which energy sources, and how much of each we will use, is driven by four competing factors: cost, technological innovation, national energy security and environmental concerns.

The first and most important is cost. At present, energy from fossil fuels is inherently cheaper than alternative renewable energy sources. However, as renewable energy technologies are increasingly deployed at scale, they are becoming cheaper. As a useful rule of thumb, renewable energy costs are falling by 20 per cent for every doubling of capacity.[17] The gap between the costs of energy sources from renewable technology and those from conventional fossil fuels is slowly closing.

Second, engineering breakthroughs will extend the bounds of what we thought possible. For example, hydrocarbons could be burnt to generate electricity without emitting carbon dioxide to the atmosphere, provided that the process of carbon capture and storage (CCS) is developed. This technology exists, but will be challenging to scale up. CCS is a process by which carbon dioxide from the burning of fossil fuels is captured and stored in deep geological formations. Achieving the transition from the high carbon to the low carbon energy mix in the immediate future is going to be very difficult unless this crucial technology is brought to fruition quickly.

Third, national security considerations will shape the choice of energy sources to be used by each country. I am reminded, again and again, just how vulnerable to interruption our supplies of energy are to political and military events: the Yom Kippur War in 1973, followed by the oil embargo by OPEC; the Iran–Iraq War; the invasion of Kuwait by Iraq; the Iraq War and, of course, 9/11. I was flying to the US on that tragic day. As the news became clear, my first concern was for the safety of BP's people in New York and Washington. My next concern was whether our refineries or oil fields would be attacked. That would have caused economic chaos.

Today, oil and gas reserves are in the hands of a small group of nations, several of which are considered politically unstable or have testy relationships with large consuming countries. Eighty per cent of the world's remaining proven oil reserves are located in three regions only: Africa, Russia and the Caspian, and the Persian Gulf. And more than 50 per cent of the world's remaining proven gas reserves exist in three countries alone: Russia, Iran and Qatar.[18]

To the US, the world's largest oil importer,[19] these statistics are alarming as they touch on the country's Achilles heel. The quest to secure energy is limiting its power on the political world stage. It has led the US to compromise on other interests, such as its commitment to democracy and freedom.[20] And the US is not alone in making these compromises.

Concerns over energy security prompt policymakers to seek independence from foreign sources of energy. In Europe, new coal-fired power stations are back on the political agenda, partly because Russia is no longer seen as a reliable supplier of gas. In the US, home-grown biofuels have been promoted by successive administrations as an alternative to Middle Eastern oil imports, even though they are considerably more expensive.

Recently, I visited the Oak Ridge National Laboratory in Tennessee. This site was established during the Second World War to carry out a single, well-defined mission: the pilot-scale production and separation of plutonium.[21] At the time, the development of a nuclear bomb was seen as vital for the nation's security. Today, it is a sprawling research centre and most of it is no longer behind closed doors. I had gone to learn more about its work on specialised energy biomass crops such as domesticated poplar trees. Oak Ridge was again working for the national security of the US.[22]

The more governments can extract themselves from the dependence on foreign sources, the more secure they feel – a belief bordering on that of autarky. In my view, the argument that energy security can only be achieved by national or regional self-sufficiency is mistaken. In my experience, real energy security can only come from open global supply markets as these ensure a diversity of sources, both domestic and international. I am reminded of Winston Churchill's statement that "security comes from diversity and diversity alone".

Fourth and last, growing concern about the local and global environment will be a major driver in determining which energy sources are deemed socially acceptable. As was clear by the time I returned to Stanford in 2007 to give a second speech on climate change, standards have changed. The oil industry used to be judged by two metrics: its contribution to energy security and the price of gasoline. We now must add a third metric: its success in reducing greenhouse gas emissions, chiefly carbon dioxide.[23]

It is very clear that how we use energy and where it comes from have to change radically. What is not so clear is how to navigate that transition. Governments have responded to this by putting in place a raft of regulatory and fiscal measures. But we can do more.

How do we build a low carbon future?

"In the long run, we are all dead."[24] Keynes may not have thought of climate change when working out how to tackle the Great Depression. Then the conventional wisdom was simply to do nothing. Leave things to market forces and market equilibrium will establish itself. Keynes thought this was foolhardy. This could mean waiting 10 or 15 years, or however long the "long run" turns out to be. In the 1930s Keynes made two points: we need government intervention and we need to do something now.

And that is what climate change needs today.

In a speech at an oil industry conference in 1996, when talking about a "magical breakthrough in the use of energy" – in essence, what we are now calling the low carbon economy – I said: "I don't underestimate the possibilities, but equally I don't underestimate the time scale involved in changing the capital base of one of the largest sectors in the world economy."

In the medium-term, we will continue to rely very heavily on fossil fuels but we need to push existing technologies to help reduce carbon. For the long-term, evolutionary technologies need to be deployed and revolutionary ones invented. In all this mix, we need government participation, not only to devise policies for the short-term but also to set the right framework for a lasting future.

This, in essence, is about getting some balances right: the balance between using existing technologies and exploring new ones; the balance between government intervention and market forces; and the balance between short-term and long-term goals. With the right mix of action we will secure a sustainable long-term future.

Doing nothing is not an option.

To achieve that future, we need to reduce emissions across the world. More precisely, we need to halve emission levels, against 2000, by 2050. This is based on the best scientific analysis to date, a study by the IPCC, suggesting that achieving this goal reduces the likelihood of adverse global warming significantly.[25]

The recent recession has proved, however, that emissions tend to fall only when economic activity slows down significantly. Sacrificing economic growth in the future to meet tough emissions targets is neither sensible nor desirable.

To halve emissions, we must limit emissions to the atmosphere to only a tenth of the amount of carbon that we do today for the same amount of economic activity. That is the same as achieving the "Industrial Revolution in a third of the time".[26] And like the Industrial Revolution and other examples of innovation, a low carbon revolution will be marked by false starts, frenzied investment and inevitable winners and losers. The same happened with the invention and creation of the canals, the railways and digital communications.

The challenges are enormous but so are the opportunities. In my experience, we must never underestimate human ingenuity and the capacity of humankind to develop and to adapt. When we start to rattle the technology cage, new possibilities emerge that were thought improbable. The first computer I used at Cambridge occupied a whole room. By the 1980s the same power could be replicated by a hand-held calculator.

When started, change creates the unexpected. Remember the prediction made by Gordon Moore of Intel in 1965? He said that the power of microprocessors would double every 18 months. He turned out to be spot on. This trend has continued for almost half a century and is not expected to slow down for some time yet. But could Moore have imagined how this would have changed our modern lives? When computers began to change the way business was conducted, people were concerned that jobs would be lost and we might have too much leisure time. Few could have predicted how the IT revolution would open up a completely new array of possibilities. In the past 40 years I have seen business patterns shift from local to global and from the manual to the cerebral. Traditional leisure time has reduced rather than increased. Advanced communications technologies now allow people to stay constantly connected and available. The BlackBerry is a perfect example.

Realising a low carbon world will not only require a revolution in low carbon electricity generating technology but also a secondary revolution in the infrastructure that supports it. Smart grids and smart meters could completely change the pattern of electricity use globally. They could enable utilities to manage supply and demand in real-time, common household appliances could communicate with the grid and consumers could sell back to the grid surplus electricity generated in their home.

The prospects and impacts of revolutionary innovations are evident but these will take time to implement. So, we must also work out how to make the transition from today to that future. Many people think of renewable energy as *the* alternative to fossil fuels. In the long run this may be the case, but not just yet. Their contribution to global energy supply is growing rapidly but from a very small base. In the transition, fossil fuels will provide the bulk of our supply. We need to use them in ways which are both cleaner and smarter. To do this we need to focus not only on carbon capture and storage (CCS) but also on all forms of making energy use more efficient. We also need to expand the safe use of nuclear power plants, use natural gas in preference to coal in power generation and make electricity the energy source of choice for as many things as possible, including ground transportation.

Nuclear power plants provided 15 per cent of the world's electricity in 2008. There are around 430 operating plants and around 50 in construction with many more planned. China and India, in particular, are pursuing ambitious expansion programmes. A nuclear power plant's carbon footprint is roughly the same as that of an equivalently sized wind farm when everything from the mining of iron and uranium to the dismantling of the plant is taken into account. Plants are expensive to build but cheap to operate; increasingly, the electricity they generate is cost competitive, except when low-cost fossil fuels are available. Industry and regulatory authorities around the world have ensured that designs evolve to be ever more safe and robust to security threats.

Natural gas is the cleanest and most efficient of the three fossil fuels in generating electricity. It is well adapted for use in power generation, making it the perfect transition fuel in our attempt to decarbonise the energy mix. In the US natural gas is being found in abundance in shale deposits and would therefore make a good and reliable substitute for coal. With the US being the world's largest electricity consumer, the substitution of natural gas for coal would have a significant impact.

The more widespread use of electricity allows another route to clean up our use of fossil fuels. Electric automobiles create no carbon emissions at the point of use, significantly improving the quality of our urban environments. One major criticism of them is that we simply shift emissions back to the point of electricity generation, where more fuel must be burned and extra capacity added. But this overlooks the fact that electric vehicle systems convert energy more efficiently than current transport fuels.[27] And combined with CCS technology, it will be much easier to reduce emissions from fossil fuels as they are centralised and controllable at the point of generation.[28]

What can governments do?

Government policymakers must not single-handedly determine the future energy mix. There are simply too many options beyond their scope of expertise. But there is an essential role for policy in guiding the low carbon transition towards its ultimate goal. Despite the 2008–09 financial crisis, I believe that the regulated free market remains the most effective delivery platform available to society. But the market will not deliver new, low carbon infrastructure at the scale and pace required unless governments take a more proactive approach.

This begins with articulating a vision for a low carbon future. By sanctifying the ultimate goals and describing the course of action to achieve them, governments can both inspire and persuade people into action. The Brazilian biofuel industry is a long-standing example of government-led innovation, albeit in a different political era.[29]

Policymakers at every level need to be involved – whether they are national leaders at an international conference or local councils outlining plans for local energy generation. At this level of policy activity, political leaders are doing rather well. Thanks to persistent campaigns by NGOs and the efforts of politicians like Tony Blair, for example in my meeting in Los Angeles with him and Governor Schwarzenegger, climate change has entered the political mainstream.

In March 2009, I was involved with the UK government's first summit on how to build businesses for a low carbon economy. The media were distracted from the important business of the day by the suit of Peter Mandelson, the Business Secretary. It had been covered with green custard in protest against the expansion of London Heathrow Airport. But the *serious* messages from that event were clear. Everyone present agreed on the importance and urgency of moving to a low carbon economy yet everyone agreed that practical delivery has so far been wanting, with too much rhetoric and consultation.

In July 2009, G8 leaders agreed to the target of halving global emissions by 2050. In the UK, an 80 per cent target for 2050 has been enshrined in law, along with interim targets and innovative five-year carbon budgets. Even the most notorious laggards in climate change have begun to be active. China has set itself ambitious energy efficiency targets, while President Obama has promised to double clean energy capacity in the US as part of his fiscal stimulus programme.[30]

Setting targets and meeting targets are very different as I discovered in BP in the 1990s when we began to use performance contracts as a way of ensuring that commitments were delivered.

Politicians now have to move beyond rhetoric and focus on practical delivery. There is a fine balance to be struck. Too little government intervention in the market, and clean energy solutions will not be developed fast enough, or not at all. Too much intervention, and competition will be crowded out, with innovation being the primary loser.

In addition to setting the right rules, the government's role must also be that of an umpire ensuring compliance by market participants. Whatever rules are laid down by governments in pursuit of their climate change targets, it is crucial that businesses can operate with confidence. Businesses interested in developing low carbon solutions must be protected against overbearing competition from fossil fuel incumbents and given enough freedom to compete among themselves. Governments occupy a unique role as market umpire and only they can set and enforce a clear framework of rules which makes the development of clean energy possible.

Making the correct policy choices begins with understanding how investments in energy are made. Those investments are often paid back over 20 or 30 years. That means that the regulations and incentives which affect them must be, above all else, certain and stable. And they must be clear, transparent and accessible to all players, not just specialists. That is crucial when tackling the vested interests of dominant fossil fuel businesses who are now seeking to corner the burgeoning clean energy markets.

In the long-term, the regulations and incentives set by the governments must, at their heart, put a price on carbon. This will provide a level playing field for carbon-free types of energy to compete with those that emit carbon. In practice it will take years to create the fully functioning carbon market that is required.

Meanwhile, knitting together a strong web of low carbon incentives and regulations should continue alongside efforts to incorporate gradually the use of tradeable carbon permits which we began to use within BP in the late 1990s. And these incentives must be designed to encourage technology innovation while not favouring specific technologies or businesses. They must level the playing field between renewables and their fossil fuel competitors.

The pursuit of low carbon energy does not come without a cost. In the US, proposals to cut emissions by 17 per cent by 2020[31] could cost the average consumer less than 50 cents per day – the price of a postage stamp.[32] That price increase is significantly less than the double digit increases of the oil price spike in 2008, reaching over $147 per barrel. Oil price spikes are likely to occur again. But the less oil we use, the less these price spikes will matter.

It also does no harm to remember *why* the cost of energy needs to increase. With all the talk of emissions targets and goals for renewable energy it is sometimes easy to lose sight of what climate change is really all about: our human existence.

How can we tackle climate change?

The impact of climate change may well be demonstrated by the Arctic ice cap retreating and thinning at a record rate. But it is more far-reaching. It is likely to affect not only our natural environment, but also our economies, geopolitics, national security and, most importantly, people.

In May 2009, former UN Secretary General Kofi Annan, in his role as President of the Global Humanitarian Forum, announced the results of a report on the effects of climate change on people across the world.[33] The report emphasised that the changing climate is not just a problem for the future but is likely to be hurting people today. The first and worst affected are the world's poorest groups, and yet they have done the least to cause the problem.

The report paints a bleak picture for the year 2030: more than 600 million people displaced, around $300 billion in annual economic losses and more than 500,000 deaths per year, as climate change turns populated areas into desert, destroys agricultural land and causes significant flooding. The areas at particular risk cover some of the poorest countries in the world; climate change could mean significant migration, resettlement and adaptation, and this will challenge both the relationship between nations and their domestic security.

Burning fossil fuels is not the only contributor to climate change.

Another big factor is deforestation. Forests are natural carbon sinks; they capture and store carbon dioxide and so are vital in maintaining the level of greenhouse gases and stabilising climate change. As much as one fifth of the world's carbon emissions are absorbed by forests in Africa, Amazonia and Asia.[34]

It is estimated that an area the size of England is cleared every year from the world's tropical forests.[35] The impact of these activities means that deforestation is responsible for around 17 per cent of global emissions, making it the third largest source of greenhouse gas emissions – larger than the entire transport sector.[36] But at the Klabin lunch the point was forcefully made that around 20 million people, many impoverished, live in the Amazon rainforest and depend on it for subsistence.[37] Curtailing their activities, which are a major cause of deforestation, will be a significant political, social and economic challenge.

As much as the issue of deforestation is important, we should not allow forest protection to be an excuse for not cutting emissions in the developed world. The two must go hand in hand to tackle climate change.

The developing world now emits more greenhouse gases than the developed world. This is caused by the combined effects of deforestation and of rapid industrialisation in China and India. These countries therefore contain by far the most material opportunities to reduce emissions and at a very low cost. For example, two-thirds of the potential reduction in global emissions could be delivered from these countries with only one-third of the total capital expenditure required to reduce all global emissions. And the capital needed is around $100 billion a year.[38] That is about the same as the world's official development aid spending. Who bears what share of these costs is an open issue, and I suspect will remain so for some time. The developing world will look to the developed world to pay. The developed world will worry about supporting those who could compete with it.

We will need new institutions and new methods to provide the capital. A good start was made with the Clean Development Mechanism (CDM) which was established by the Kyoto Treaty, allowing rich nations to pay for carbon reduction projects in poorer nations. In return, the financing countries obtain credits which can count towards complying with their own emission reduction targets at much lower costs. But the CDM, with its project-by-project focus, has proved inadequate to the task and difficult to scale up. The CDM should not be abandoned but will need to be altered and broadened.

Action needed

There remains a frustrating sense of inertia when it comes to taking action. Yet there is certainly no shortage of vision and intent among politicians. The attitude of the business community and the mindset of our societies are equally important.

Go to one of the numerous clean energy conferences around the world and you will hear policymakers, alongside business leaders and scientists, united in making the case for low carbon energy, frequently with great passion and conviction.

The biggest such gathering I attended, as a keynote speaker, was the inaugural World Future Energy Conference in Abu Dhabi in January 2008. That event, hosted by Masdar, the UAE's pioneering $15 billion clean energy initiative which I helped launch in 2006, included heads of state, renowned business leaders and a projection of Prince Charles as a hologram. The chorus of voices saying the same thing was deafening.

In June 2009, I shared a platform with former US President Bill Clinton at the World Ethanol Summit in São Paolo where I discussed the importance of making biofuels into a global industry, building on learning from the oil industry. And one piece of learning is never to ignore concerns about the environment; in this case, the impact of growing biofuels on the use of land for other activities.

And what are the sentiments in the business community? They are mixed. Some see tackling climate change as a great opportunity for new products, increased diversified sources of revenue growth, innovations, and efficiency. But when the global economy slows there is a great temptation for some businesses to say they cannot afford to tackle climate change. Some will see it as a threat to their business, as I saw with some oil companies in 1997. It is hardly surprising that one survey found "shades of green" among chief executives ranging from believers and opportunists to agnostics and sceptics.[39]

In wider society, many are ambivalent. In the US, a record proportion of citizens now say that the seriousness of the effects of climate change has been exaggerated.[40] A recent Pew Research poll found that a declining number of American citizens view global warming as a very serious problem; in October 2009 only 35 per cent agreed on the problem, down from 44 per cent in April 2008.[41] UK voters consistently rank concern about the environment as an unimportant issue, behind the state of the economy, immigration, unemployment, health care, inflation, education and defence.[42]

What do we draw from these observations? Whether we think of taking action now as staving off a disaster or merely a sensible insurance policy, the fact remains that we have to do something. Inevitably we will have to wait for the political debates to mature, not least in and among the US, the European Union, India, China and Japan, each of which is simply too important to take a free ride on the back of the rest of the world. During that time, we need to build global capability and capacity to make it possible to identify and implement actions to reduce carbon emissions, not least from increased efficiency. This should be funded through the World Bank. While long-term aspirations are essential, we should use medium-term targets for emission reductions as these will allow for learning and changes as technology develops. Investment in long-term research and development of new forms of energy and energy use must continue. Until global agreements are in place, national plans with enforceable targets, global offset mechanisms such as an improved CDM, and mechanisms to transfer relevant technology need to be put in place.

Left to its own course, climate change could eventually cause environmental degradation on such a large scale that humankind might never recover to the levels of progress which we now enjoy. That is the dark possibility lurking in the corner.

Yet admitting this possibility, it seems, will not make much difference to our actions now. Anthony Giddens talks of the paradox that abstract and future risks do not motivate people to act until the effects are felt – and by then it is too late. This is much the same as Charles Handy's frog sitting happily in the pan of water as it is slowly warmed. It feels increasingly comfortable until being eventually boiled to death.[43]

Stimulating a quick and timely transition to a low carbon economy should not be about scaring people into action, but about emphasising the great opportunity that lies ahead. Like the Industrial Revolution, the transition will occur once, requiring the effort of a few generations. The big difference to the Industrial Revolution, however, is that we can be neither ambivalent nor indifferent as to *when* it occurs.

All science is provisional but we have to balance the facts, form a view and take some action. Change will not be easy. We will have to be rational and not allow emotions to sideline us. The great task falls on us, here and now. We have to use our intelligence and address how we produce and use energy. It is a duty to ourselves and to future generations to see it through.

CHRONOLOGY

	World Population[1]	World Events	BP History	John Browne (EJPB)	Oil Price[2]
1939		1 September: Germany invades Poland starting Second World War			
1945		7 May: Germany surrenders			
1947				17 May: Captain John Browne and Paula Wesz marry in Hamburg, Germany	
1948	2.47 bn			20 February: Edmund John Philip Browne born in Hamburg	
1951		December: Prime Minister Mossadeq nationalises Iran oil industry	Anglo-Iranian Oil Company (AIOC) thrown out of Iran		
1952				Captain John Browne posted to Singapore with British Army	
1953		August: Mossadeq deposed; pro-Western Shah returned			

	World Population[1]	World Events	BP History	John Browne (EJPB)	Oil Price[2]
1954			October: Iranian Oil Participants (the consortium) returns to Iran. AIOC is the largest shareholder and renames itself British Petroleum (BP)		
1955				Captain John Browne returns to civilian life in Cambridge, UK, and is employed by Iranian Oil Services	
1956		July: Egypt nationalises Suez Canal prompting Suez crisis October/November: Hungarian Revolution			
1957				John Browne (senior) moves to Iran to work for BP, joined later by Paula Browne and nine-year-old EJPB	
1959				January: EJPB returns to UK to attend The King's School Ely prep school	
1960	3.04 bn	September: OPEC formed			
1966				July: EJPB wins scholarship to St John's College, Cambridge and is awarded BP university apprenticeship	
1968		March: ARCO and Humble Oil strike oil in Alaska			

	World Population[1]	World Events	BP History	John Browne (EJPB)	Oil Price[2]
1969			March: BP strikes oil in Alaska		
		20 July: Apollo 11 lands man on the moon		July: EJPB graduates with a First Class degree in Physics and joins BP	$2
		September: Colonel Qadhafi seizes power in Libya			
				November: EJPB arrives in Alaska	
1970	3.71 bn		January: BP takes shares in Sohio, later to rise to 55 per cent ownership		$2
			BP begins diversification strategy		
			19 October: BP announces oil strike in the North Sea		
1971				June: EJPB moves to New York	$2
			December: BP's interests in Libya are nationalised by Colonel Qadhafi		
1973		October: start of Yom Kippur War, followed by OPEC's 70 per cent increase in oil price and embargo on oil shipments to US			$4
		November: Trans Alaska Pipeline Authorization Act becomes law			$5
1974				April: EJPB moves to San Francisco	$13

	World Population[1]	World Events	BP History	John Browne (EJPB)	Oil Price[2]
1975			March: Trans Alaska Pipeline construction starts		$13
			November: First oil from North Sea officially arrives in UK		$15
1976		September: Mao Zedong dies		September: EJPB returns to work in BP's head office, London	$13
1977			June: First oil through the "Alyeska Pipeline"		$15
1978		March: Deng Xiaoping becomes China's paramount leader		EJPB moves to Calgary, Canada	
			December: BP invited to Beijing as China starts its "open door" policy		$15
1979		January: Iranian revolution. Iran's oil is nationalised	BP's association with Iran ends and in July its interests in Nigeria are nationalised. The company is now reliant on "two pipelines": Alaska and the North Sea		$16
				April: EJPB visits Beijing with BP	$19
		4 May: Margaret Thatcher becomes Prime Minister of the UK			
1980	4.45 bn			1 August: John Browne (senior) dies	
		September: Start of Iran–Iraq War		September: EJPB attends Stanford University Sloan programme	$34

	World Population[1]	World Events	BP History	John Browne (EJPB)	Oil Price[2]
1981		20 January: Ronald Reagan becomes 40th President of the US			$39
				September: EJPB returns to UK to head the E&P commercial unit, and later becomes manager of the Forties field	$35
1984				September: EJPB appointed group treasurer and chief executive of BP Finance International where he opens an internal "bank"	$29
1986		March: Mikhail Gorbachev, General Secretary of the Communist Party of the Soviet Union, introduces his policy of *perestroika*			$14
				April: EJPB resigns from BP and joins Sohio board (Cleveland) as executive vice president and chief financial officer	$13
		July: Oil prices hit a low with glut in oil production and Saudi Arabia's refusal to accept quotas			$11

	World Population[1]	World Events	BP History	John Browne (EJPB)	Oil Price[2]
1987			July: BP acquires full ownership of Sohio	EJPB stays in Cleveland as executive vice president and chief financial officer of BP America and is responsible for the company's North American E&P operation	$19
			BP begins to explore in Colombia		
		19 October: London stock market collapses, termed "Black Monday"	15 October: BP privatisation – sale of government shares and issue of new shares		
1988			February: BP buys Britoil		$15
		6 July: Piper Alpha accident			
			BP begins exploration in Gulf of Mexico		
1989		January: George H.W. Bush becomes 41st President of the US			$16
		24 March: *Exxon Valdez* catastrophe		EJPB returns to UK to become CEO of BP's worldwide E&P	
		4 June: Tiananmen Square massacre			
		November 1989: Jiang Zemin takes over as Chinese Communist Party General Secretary			$18
		9 November 1989: Berlin Wall falls			

	World Population[1]	World Events	BP History	John Browne (EJPB)	Oil Price[2]
1990	5.28 bn			Early 1990: EJPB first visits Kazakhstan and Azerbaijan	
		2 August: Iraq invades Kuwait			
		28 November: Margaret Thatcher resigns and John Major becomes Prime Minister of the UK			$30
1991				September: EJPB appointed to board of BP	$19
		December: Mikhail Gorbachev resigns. Boris Yeltsin becomes President of Russia and the Soviet Union is dissolved			$17
1992		June: "Earth Summit" in Rio de Janeiro; objectives set to encourage industrialised countries to stabilise greenhouse gas emissions	June: Bob Horton resigns and the role of BP chairman and CEO is split		$20
		September: Voucher privatisation scheme in Russia		September: EJPB invites Margaret Thatcher to Baku	
1993		20 January: Bill Clinton becomes 42nd President of the US			$17
		24 June 1993: Heydar Aliyev becomes President of Azerbaijan			

	World Population[1]	World Events	BP History	John Browne (EJPB)	Oil Price[2]
1994		Venezuela announces "field rehabilitation" projects			
			20 September: "Contract of the century" is signed in Baku for the ACG oil field		$16
1995	5.69 bn		February: Official commissioning of the Cusiana production facility in Colombia		
				10 June: EJPB appointed Group CEO of BP	$17
		August: Loans-for-shares scheme in Russia			
1996			September: BP board agrees merger strategy		$22
1997		2 May: Tony Blair becomes Prime Minister of the UK		19 May: EJPB delivers *Addressing climate change* speech at Stanford University	$19
		30 June: Britain hands Hong Kong back to China			
			18 November: BP takes 10 per cent stake in Sidanco	EJPB and Vladimir Potanin sign Sidanco deal in front of Blair and Viktor Ott, First Deputy Energy Minister of Russia	$18
		December: Kyoto Protocol adopted			$16
1998		17 March: Zhu Rongji becomes Premier of China			$12
				22 July: EJPB knighted	
		Oil hits low of $9	31 December: Completion of merger of BP and Amoco, then the largest-ever industrial merger.	EJPB becomes CEO of the combined BP Amoco	$9

	World Population[1]	World Events	BP History	John Browne (EJPB)	Oil Price[2]
1999		2 February: Hugo Chávez becomes President of Venezuela			$10
		March: Oil prices still low and pundits suggest may go as low as $5	1 April: BP Amoco announces merger with ARCO		$15
		18 November: Intergovernmental agreements signed in front of President Clinton aligning countries around the objective of building the BTC pipeline			
		30 November: Chernogorneft is declared bankrupt and is bought by TNK			
		December: Putin takes over from Yeltsin in Russia			$24

	World Population[1]	World Events	BP History	John Browne (EJPB)	Oil Price[2]
2000	6.08 bn		23 March: BP Amoco takes stake in PetroChina		$28
			18 April: BP Amoco combines with ARCO		
			7 July: BP Amoco acquires Burmah Castrol	9 July: Paula Browne dies	
			24 July: BP Amoco changes name to BP and launches helios logo and "beyond petroleum"		
			11 September: BP takes stake in Sinopec		
			October: Consortium formed to build BTC pipeline		
			15 November: Nelson Mandela visits BP's head office in London		
		December: Voluntary Principles on Security and Human Rights agreed			$25

	World Population[1]	World Events	BP History	John Browne (EJPB)	Oil Price[2]
2001		20 January: George W. Bush becomes 43rd President of the US			$24
				February: EJPB states that BP will publish payments to the Angola government and is summoned to meet President dos Santos	
			16 July: BP disposes of Ruhrgas and buys Veba oil with its Aral brand	18 July: EJPB is made a life peer	
		11 September: Terrorist attacks on the US			$23
		2 December: Enron files for bankruptcy			$16
2002				19 June: EJPB delivers *The strategic logic of diversity* speech at the Women in Leadership conference in Berlin	$23
		October: Extractive Industries Transparency Initiative (EITI) announced			
			December: A double first as BP wins "Most Admired Company" award ...	... and EJPB wins "Most Admired Leader" for 4th year running	$27

	World Population[1]	World Events	BP History	John Browne (EJPB)	Oil Price[2]
2003		16 March: Wen Jiabao becomes Premier of China			$29
		20 March: Start of the Iraq War			
			April: Construction work begins on BTC pipeline		
		June: Putin's state visit to UK	BP becomes largest ever foreign investor in Russia through the TNK-BP joint venture	EJPB and Mikhail Fridman sign TNK-BP deal in front of Blair and Putin	
		November: Shevardnadze resigns and Mikheil Saakashvili takes over as President of Georgia			
		December: Saddam Hussein captured			
2004			February: Formal financing package for BTC pipeline agreed		$31
		14 March: Putin re-elected for second term			
			19 May: Wen Jiabao visits BP's head office in London		$36
		26 December: Indian Ocean earthquake triggers one of the worst ever natural disasters			

	World Population[1]	World Events	BP History	John Browne (EJPB)	Oil Price[2]
2005		20 January: George W. Bush is sworn in for a second term as President of the US			$46
			23 March: Texas City refinery accident		
				19 June: EJPB meets Qadhafi in Libya	
		7 July: Terrorist attacks on London	11 July: Thunder Horse is hit by Hurricane Dennis		
		August: Hurricane Katrina hits New Orleans			
			November: BP launches Alternative Energy to combine all its renewable energy businesses		$51
			16 December: BP disposes of Innovene		
2006			2 March: Leak in the pipeline causes oil spill in Alaska		$55
				6 July: EJPB appointed President of The Royal Academy of Engineering	
			13 July: Official inauguration of the BTC pipeline at Ceyhan		
				26 July: BP announces that EJPB will retire in December 2008	
			7 August: A further leak in the pipeline causes small second oil spill in Alaska		$66
		4 December: Sarah Palin elected Governor of Alaska			

World Population[1]	World Events	BP History	John Browne (EJPB)	Oil Price[2]
2007		5 January: British newspaper contacts BP press office about a story it plans to run	6 January: EJPB takes out injunction	$50
		12 January: BP announces that EJPB will step down in July 2007 and Tony Hayward will become new CEO		
		16 January: Baker Report is published		
			19 January: EJPB corrects witness statement	
			26 April: EJPB delivers *Energy and the environment: 10 years on* speech at Stanford University	
	10 May: Tony Blair announces resignation and steps down on 27 June. Gordon Brown becomes Prime Minister	Tony Hayward becomes Group CEO of BP	1 May: EJPB resigns from BP	$61
			August: EJPB joins Riverstone, a private investment company specialising in energy	$68

	World Population[1]	World Events	BP History	John Browne (EJPB)	Oil Price[2]
2008				January: EJPB is keynote speaker at World Future Energy Conference in Abu Dhabi	$85
		11 July: Oil prices peak at $147 (Brent crude oil spot)			$128
		August: Beijing Olympics			$111
		15 September: Lehman Brothers files for bankruptcy. A global financial crisis gathers momentum			$96
		5 November: Barack Obama wins historic US election			$49
2009	6.76 bn	20 January: Barack Obama becomes 44th President of the US		January: EJPB appointed Chairman of the Tate Gallery, UK	$37
				March: EJPB attends UK government summit on building low carbon economy	$46
			14 April: BP celebrates the company's 100th anniversary		$50
		May: Global Humanitarian Forum predicts 600 million people will be displaced by climate change by 2030			$57
		December: UN Climate Change Conference, Copenhagen			

1. World population figures taken from the US Census Bureau International Data Base, using the total midyear population figure for the world. The figure of 2.47 bn used in 1948 is an estimate using the figure of 2.55 bn from the year 1950, when the data base first started, and a growth rate of 1.5%. www.census.gov

2. Price in nominal US dollars from historical data provided by the EIA. Price per barrel quoted before April 1974 is the official price of Saudi Light. The price in April 1974 and thereafter is the Refiner Acquisition Cost of Imported Crude Oil. The price quoted is the average price against that month and not on the specific date shown. www.eia.doe.gov

ENDNOTES

Prologue NEW YORK

1. Henry Longhurst, *Adventure in Oil: The Story of British Petroleum* (London: Sidgwick and Jackson, 1959).
2. Thomas L. Friedman, *The World is Flat: The Globalized World in the Twenty-First Century* (New York: Penguin Books, 2005).
3. Fareed Zakaria, "The Rise of the Rest", *Newsweek*, 12 May 2008.

1. IRAN

1. "The Fire Beater", *Time*, 9 February 1953.
2. Ibid.
3. No. 88 is now student accommodation for Cambridge University.
4. The Hungarian Revolution in October 1956 was arguably the most important armed rising against the USSR during the Cold War. Spontaneous demonstrations by students and workers, mainly in Budapest, were inspired in part by riots in East Germany (1953) and the Soviet troop withdrawal leading to Austrian neutrality (1955). Soviet troops sent in to Hungary to crush the rebellion were forced to withdraw as Hungarian soldiers joined the insurgents. In November 1956, stronger Soviet forces returned and put down the uprising with force. The rebels were crushed, and their leaders executed. Nearly 200,000 refugees crossed the Austrian border and Soviet troops remained stationed in Hungary until the collapse of the USSR in 1991. Erwin A. Schmidl, László Ritter, Peter Dennis, *The Hungarian Revolution 1956* (Oxford: Osprey Publishing, 2006).
5. One of the people who escaped from Hungary leaving his family behind was 20-year-old András István Gróf. He went straight to the US, arriving in 1957 as a penniless refugee. Years later I would meet "Andy Grove" at Intel.
6. During the last century, sovereignty of Transylvania passed between Hungary and Romania. My mother was from Oradea in the north, which after World War I became part of Romania. The Second Vienna Award in 1940 returned northern parts of Transylvania, including Oradea, to Hungary – an arrangement which lasted

until the end of World War II when the lands were again given to Romania in the 1947 Treaty of Paris.

7. My mother's belief in education led me to set up a charitable trust, after her death, to enable female scholars from overseas to attend Cambridge University.

8. William Golding, *Lord of the Flies* (London: Faber & Faber, 1954).

9. In BP's operation in Aden, which was a British colony until 1963, the recreation facilities for refinery staff were divided into A, B and C categories, depending on seniority. J. H. Bamberg, *The History of the British Petroleum Company, Vol 2: The Anglo-Iranian Years, 1928–1954* (Cambridge, UK: Cambridge University Press, 1994).

10. J. H. Bamberg, *The History of the British Petroleum Company, Vol 3: British Petroleum and Global Oil, 1950–1975: The Challenge of Nationalism* (Cambridge, UK: Cambridge University Press, 2000).

11. Henry Longhurst, *Adventure in Oil: The Story of British Petroleum* (London: Sidgwick and Jackson, 1959).

12. This early history of BP is well documented in other books. Ronald W. Ferrier, *The History of the British Petroleum Company, Vol 1: The Developing Years, 1901–1932* (Cambridge, UK: Cambridge Press, 1982) and J. H. Bamberg, *The History of the British Petroleum Company, Vol 2: The Anglo-Iranian Years, 1928–1954* (Cambridge, UK: Cambridge University Press, 1994).

13. Mary Boyce, *Zoroastrians: Their religious beliefs and practices* (London: Routledge, 2000).

For Zoroastrians, fire is the supreme symbol of purity, and sacred fires are maintained in fire temples. These fires represent God's light or wisdom, and are never extinguished. Zoroastrianism is one of the world's oldest monotheistic religions. Founded by the prophet Zoroaster in ancient Iran, approximately 3,500 years ago, it dominated much of the Middle East until the 7th century. It is now one of the world's smallest religions with about a quarter of a million followers worldwide.

14. Later I found out that the ruins were more likely to have been a terrace built by the Achaemenians, probably as a prototype of the large one in Persepolis.

15. A detailed account of The Great Game can be found in: Peter Hopkirk, *The Great Game: The struggle for empire in Central Asia* (New York: Kodansha America, 1994).

16. The quote is attributed to Lord Curzon, Viceroy of India. Daniel Yergin, *The Prize: The Epic Quest for Oil, Money & Power* (New York: Free Press, 2008).

17. D'Arcy paid the Shah of Persia £20,000 plus £20,000 worth of shares and 16 per cent of annual net profits. The definition of those "annual net profits" was to prove contentious. Ibid.

18. Charles Greenway, 1st Baron Greenway of Stanbridge Earls, was chairman of BP 1914–27.

19. In 1914 Winston Churchill, then First Lord of the Admiralty, instigated a move to secure a source of oil for the Royal Navy. In July he asked the House of Commons to pass the "Anglo-Persian Oil Company, Acquisition of Capital Bill", by which the British government acquired 51 per cent of the company for £2 million. Churchill was far-sighted. Just weeks after Parliament agreed to purchase the shares,

World War I began. Berry Ritchie, *Portrait in Oil: An Illustrated History of BP* (London: James and James, 1995).

20. J. H. Bamberg, *The History of the British Petroleum Company, Vol 2: The Anglo-Iranian Years, 1928–1954* (Cambridge, UK: Cambridge University Press, 1994).

21. It would not have been possible for the Anglo-Iranian Oil Company to return to Iran in its monopoly position, particularly as the British government would have been seen to be continuing to interfere with Iranian affairs. However, Anglo-Iranian Oil Company (later British Petroleum) owned the majority share of the consortium at 40 per cent. Ibid.

22. This was the expression used at the time. The practice of using more local people was referred to as "localisation".

23. Madingley Rise was the site of Cambridge University's Department of Geodesy and Geophysics run by Sir Edward Bullard (universally known as "Teddy").

2. ALASKA

1. Prudhoe Bay is 3,594 miles from Washington DC and 1,200 miles from the North Pole.

2. J. H. Bamberg, *The History of the British Petroleum Company, Vol 3: British Petroleum and Global Oil, 1950–1975: The Challenge of Nationalism* (Cambridge, UK: Cambridge University Press, 2000).

3. BP presented 70 separate applications for lease blocks of 2,560 acres, which meant that by February 1960 the company held leases or options on about 200,000 acres on the North Slope. Ibid.

4. Ibid.

5. Today, the Prudhoe Bay field is the largest field in North America and the 18th largest field discovered worldwide. More than 11.5 billion barrels had been produced from the field to date. www.bp.com

6. Introduced in 1965, the 1130 was the first IBM computer to give small business firms a versatile, economical data-processing facility for a wide variety of applications. According to IBM: "The desk-sized 1130 combined ease of operation with big computer performance and features, including high-speed arithmetic capability, stored program flexibility and a wide variety of input and output devices. Interchangeable magnetic disks provided virtually unlimited direct access storage capability." www-03.ibm.com/ibm/history/exhibits/1130/1130_intro.html

7. Cobol and Fortran are computer-programming languages both developed in the 1950s, Cobol for commercial applications and Fortran for scientific and engineering applications.

8. The CDC 6600, a mainframe computer, was considered the world's fastest computer in 1964 and remained so for five years until the introduction of the CDC 7600 in 1969. www.computerhistory.org

9. The oil industry was a male-dominated environment and I had experienced first hand how this created an unpleasant bravado culture. For example, during vacation work at a refinery in Llandarcy (now closed) I had been doused in crude oil as an

initiation rite. In the 1970s BP was starting to change and I remember the first female pipeline engineer, Frances Lewis, visiting Alaska.

10. The Organization of the Petroleum Exporting Countries (OPEC) was formed in September 1960 by five founding nations: Iran, Iraq, Kuwait, Saudi Arabia and Venezuela. Additional members have joined and now include: Qatar, Libya, UAE, Algeria, Nigeria, Ecuador and Angola.

11. The term Seven Sisters, coined by Enrico Mattei of Italian energy company ENI, referred to Exxon, Mobil, Texaco, Chevron, Gulf, Shell and BP. The French oil company, Compagnie Française des Pétroles (CFP) was a similar-sized company with similar concessions in the Middle East. For more than half a decade, these seven oil companies had made the rules, and appeared immune to the change that was the norm in other industries.
    Anthony Sampson, *The Seven Sisters: The Great Oil Companies and the World They Shaped* (New York: Viking Press, 1975).

12. Daniel Yergin, *The Prize: The Epic Quest for Oil, Money & Power* (New York: Free Press, 2008).

13. For a summary of the TAPS project challenges see James P. Roscow, *800 miles to Valdez; The Building of the Alaskan Pipeline* (Englewood Cliffs, NJ: Prentice-Hall, 1977), referenced in J. H. Bamberg, *The History of the British Petroleum Company, Vol 3: British Petroleum and Global Oil, 1950–1975: The Challenge of Nationalism* (Cambridge, UK: Cambridge University Press, 2000).

14. Alyeska Pipeline Service Company incorporated in 1970. www.alyeska-pipe.com

15. Ibid.

16. United States Energy Information Administration. www.eia.doe.gov

17. The *Exxon Valdez* is considered to be one of the most devastating environmental disasters ever to occur at sea. Exxon was fined $150 million for spilling 11 million US gallons of crude oil and contaminating about 1,300 miles of coastline. The company also agreed to pay out $900 million in civil settlements over a ten-year period. Environmentalists estimated 250,000 seabirds, 3,000 sea otters, 300 harbour seals, 250 bald eagles and 22 killer whales died because of the spill. *Exxon Valdez* Oil Spill Trustee Council. www.evostc.state.ak.us

18. I was involved in the drilling of the only ANWR well, Kaktovik, in a joint project with Chevron.

19. To be eligible for a permanent fund dividend, citizens must have been an Alaska resident for the entire calendar year preceding the date they apply for a dividend and intend to remain an Alaska resident indefinitely at the time they apply for a dividend. There are other criteria for eligibility under Alaska Statute 43.23.005 and AS 43.23.008. www.pfd.state.ak.us

20. 2008 was an exceptional year; the dividend included a one-off rebate of $1,200. In 2007 the dividend was $1,654.00 and in 2009 it was $1,305. Ibid.

3. CLEVELAND AND SCOTLAND

1. Eric Drake, Sir Eric Drake, was chairman of BP 1969–75.

2. Berry Ritchie, *Portrait in Oil: An Illustrated History of BP* (London: James and James, 1995).

3. The UK government and Bank of England together held around three-quarters of BP's shares. In the late 1960s, Burmah Oil had overstretched itself on an ambitious programme of exploration in the North Sea, investment in tankers and acquisitions. It had borrowed heavily using its 23 per cent shareholding in BP as collateral for the loans. In 1974, when share prices collapsed following the energy crisis and the defeat of Edward Heath's government, Burmah Oil was rescued from bankruptcy by the Bank of England, which in turn took the BP shares. Ibid.

4. Love Canal was named after William T. Love, who in the late 19th century had the idea for an ambitious hydroelectric project based on a new canal connecting the two levels of the Niagara River, which are separated by the Niagara Falls. A short stretch of canal was dug but never used. In the 1940s the Hooker Chemical Company lined the canal with clay and used it to bury toxic waste. Homes and a school were built on the site some years later. The leaking chemical waste caused major health problems, particularly for children. A state of emergency was declared at the site in 1978.

5. David Verey would go on to become CEO of Lazard Brothers in 1990 and chairman two years later.

6. "Lawson plugs £1 bn oil tax loophole", *The Times*, 14 September 1983.

7. Berry Ritchie, *Portrait in Oil: An Illustrated History of BP* (London: James and James, 1995).

8. Peter Walters, Sir Peter Walters, was chairman of BP 1981–90.

9. Daniel Yergin, *The Prize: The Epic Quest for Oil, Money & Power* (New York: Free Press, 2008).

10. Oil had been discovered in 1859 in western Pennsylvania and in the early days, with no other means of transport, teamsters had to haul the barrels by hand from the oil fields to the nearest railroad. Eventually the railroad would be superseded by pipelines and tankers, and although much else has changed in 150 years, those early barrels remain the basic unit of measurement in the industry today. The measurement of a standard 42 US gallon barrel is still used for pricing, regulation and tax. This is equivalent to 34.972 Imperial gallons, or approximately 159 litres. The 42-gallon barrel was borrowed from England where it was the standard-size barrel for herring. That was chosen as the standard rather than the barrel used for wine (31½ gallons) or London beer (36 gallons). Ibid.

11. Ron Chernow, *Titan: The Life of John D. Rockefeller, Sr.* (London: Vintage Books, 2004).

12. Daniel Yergin, *The Prize: The Epic Quest for Oil, Money & Power* (New York: Free Press, 2008).

13. Ida M. Tarbell, *History of the Standard Oil Company*, first published in *McClure's Magazine* in 1904 and available in Morgen Witzel (ed), *Big Business and the Muck-Rakers 1900–10* (New York: Thoemmes Press, 2002).

14. Paul Johnson, "A Second Opinion, The Prospering Fathers" in Jack Beatty (ed), *Colossus: How the Corporation Changed America* (New York: Broadway, 2001).

15. Sohio was the original Standard Oil of Ohio, one of the few Standard Oil companies that kept the Standard name. Standard Oil of Indiana changed its name in 1973 to Amoco and ARCO was formed from Atlantic Refining (a Standard Oil Company) merging with the Richfield Oil Company in 1966 to form Atlantic Richfield Company. All these businesses became part of BP.

16. BP came to own Standard Oil of Ohio (Sohio) because of Alaska. When BP found oil in Alaska it needed direct access to the US market as it had no downstream operation there. Initially BP bought Sinclair's chain of gasoline stations in New England (from ARCO, which had taken over Sinclair but had been forced to sell these stations because it became too dominant in the market) but soon decided it needed the financial and managerial resources of a larger organisation in the US. Sohio was short of reserves and a deal was done whereby BP swapped most of its Alaskan oil holdings, plus the ex-Sinclair marketing business, for an initial 25 per cent of Sohio's share capital. In the agreement this was to rise to 55 per cent when Prudhoe Bay production increased to a certain level. BP continued to operate the Alaskan oil field but Sohio managed the two companies' combined businesses in the rest of the US. The deal almost did not happen because the US Department of Justice looked set to block it as it might contravene certain antitrust laws. But Eric Drake, BP chairman and CEO, flew to Washington and resolved the problem with his usual diplomacy. The deal was completed on 1 January 1970. Berry Ritchie, *Portrait in Oil: An Illustrated History of BP* (London: James and James, 1995).

17. Bob Hope was born Leslie Townes Hope in Eltham (a borough near London), England and emigrated to Cleveland, Ohio with his family in 1907 when he was four. www.bobhope.com

18. "Straightening out Sohio", *Sunday Times*, 18 March 1986.

19. The Cuyahoga River was full of debris and oil pollution as this extract, from a 1960s magazine, shows: "No Visible Life. Some river! Chocolate-brown, oily, bubbling with subsurface gases, it oozes rather than flows. 'Anyone who falls into the Cuyahoga does not drown,' Cleveland's citizens joke grimly. 'He decays.' The Federal Water Pollution Control Administration dryly notes: 'The lower Cuyahoga has no visible life, not even low forms such as leeches and sludge worms that usually thrive on wastes.' It is also − literally − a fire hazard. A few weeks ago, the oil-slicked river burst into flames and burned with such intensity that two railroad bridges spanning it were nearly destroyed. 'What a terrible reflection on our city,' said Cleveland Mayor Carl Stokes sadly." "The Cities: the price of optimism", *Time*, 1 August 1969.

20. Mayor Ralph J. Perk, predecessor to Dennis Kucinich, accidentally set his hair on fire with a blowtorch at a ribbon−cutting ceremony in 1972.

21. "BP America's Hatchet Gentleman: Robert B. Horton, cost cutter with a soft touch", *New York Times*, 10 January 1988.

22. Berry Ritchie, *Portrait in Oil: An Illustrated History of BP* (London: James and James, 1995).

23. Isambard Kingdom Brunel was arguably the leading British engineer of the 19th century, responsible for the design of tunnels, bridges, railway lines and ships. He is

most famous for his work on the country's Great Western Railway.

24. BP press release: "BP Announces Giant Oil Discovery in the Gulf of Mexico", 2 September 2009.

25. In just 15 years, Enron grew from nowhere to become the US's seventh largest company, employing 21,000 staff in more than 40 countries. In December 2001 Enron filed for bankruptcy.

4. TRANSATLANTIC

1. Shell was the exemplar in exploration and production performance in the late 1980s but that changed in time. Shell's reputation was damaged in 2004 when it was found to have overstated its reserves.

2. Bob Horton, Sir Bob Horton, was chairman and CEO of BP 1990–92.

3. Quoted in the City Diary of the *Daily Telegraph*, 11 December 2008.

4. Lord Ashburton was chairman of BP 1992–95.

5. David Simon, Sir David Simon, was chairman of BP 1994–97; he was formerly CEO 1992–94. He left the company when he was appointed Minister for Trade and Competitiveness in Europe by the Prime Minister, Tony Blair, in 1997.

6. See John Roberts, *The Modern Firm: Organizational Design for Performance and Growth* (Oxford: Oxford University Press, 2004) and Steven Prokesch, "Unleashing the Power of Learning", *Harvard Business Review*, September–October 1997.

7. In the 1980s inefficiency and poor shareholder returns had made oil companies a target for corporate raiders, such as Carl Icahn and T. Boone Pickens.

8. Based in Chicago, Amoco was previously the Standard Oil Company of Indiana; founded in 1889 it changed its name to Amoco in 1985. Prior to the merger with BP, it was the US's fifth largest oil company.

9. Although by this time both companies were investors in Azerbaijan, I had never dealt with Larry Fuller on this but always dealt with one of his direct reports.

10. BP press release: "BP and Amoco Merge to Enter Global Top Trio of Oil Majors", 11 August 1998. This stated: "This merger is a superb alliance of equals with complementary strategic and geographical strengths, which effectively creates a new supermajor that can better serve our customers worldwide. We are uniting two portfolios of assets and people to create a group that will have the financial resource, scale and global reach to compete effectively in the 21st century. International competition in the industry is already fierce and will grow more acute as new players emerge. In such a climate the best investment opportunities will go increasingly to companies that have the size and financial strength to take on those large-scale projects that offer a truly distinctive return." www.bp.com

11. "The next shock?", *The Economist*, 4 March 1999.

12. BP press release: "BP Amoco and ARCO in $26.8 Billion Deal Agreed by Boards of Both Companies", 1 April 1999. This stated: "For BP Amoco, the strategic rationale for this deal is the immense potential it offers for future growth ... Against the background of uncertain oil prices and the increased competitive pressure across the sector, it is clear that the uniquely complementary operations of our companies

can compete more effectively together than apart to deliver our respective share-holders a superior return on their investment ... In Alaska in particular, the synergies we can achieve from combining our operations will greatly increase the competitiveness of the state in the face of uncertain oil prices and provide a strong incentive for significant investment in existing and future fields ... The addition of ARCO's international assets powerfully strengthens our global portfolio. Most significantly, it gives us a major platform for upstream growth in Asia where we will now have world-class gas reserves ready to supply Japan, Korea and other key markets when recovery comes to the region, which it undoubtedly will." www.bp.com

13. Jeremy Bulow and Carl Shapiro, "The BP Amoco/ARCO Merger: Alaskan Crude Oil" (Stanford School of Business, Nov 2002). Also published in John Kwoka Jr. & Lawrence White (eds), *The Antitrust Revolution: Economics, Competition and Policy, 4th Edition* (Oxford: Oxford University Press, 2004).

14. Ronald W. Ferrier, *The History of the British Petroleum Company, Vol 1: The Developing Years, 1901–1932* (Cambridge: Cambridge University Press, 1982). The other 3 per cent of the shares were held by Lord Strathcona, the first chairman of the company.

5. CALIFORNIA

1. BP speech: "Addressing Climate Change", Stanford University, 19 May 1997. www.bp.com

2. The sun not only warms and lights the earth but is also the world's principal source of energy. Plants and organisms harness solar radiation through the process of photosynthesis. Over time these are transformed into fuels such as peat, coal, gas and oil when they collect as sediment and are compressed by geological processes. Solar radiation is also the ultimate source of most other sources of energy. For example, it provides energy which causes water to evaporate and rise into the atmosphere as vapour, and creates potential energy for hydropower when it falls as rain in high places.

3. Francis Fukuyama, then deputy director of the US State Department Policy Planning Staff, put forward a view that, with the end of the Cold War, liberal democracy marked "the end point of mankind's ideological evolution" in an essay which appeared in the US journal *The National Interest*. This was followed by his book: Francis Fukuyama, *The End of History and the Last Man* (New York: Free Press, 1992).

4. The United Nations Conference on Environment and Development (UNCED) was informally known as the Earth Summit. It was unprecedented in terms of both its size and the scope of its concerns. Objectives to encourage countries to reduce greenhouse gases were first set at this event by the United Nations Framework Convention on Climate Change. www.un.org/geninfo/bp/enviro

5. More than 160 nations met in Kyoto, Japan in December 1997 to negotiate binding limitations on greenhouse gases for developed nations to follow through on objectives set at the United Nations Framework Convention on Climate Change of 1992. The Kyoto Protocol was adopted on 11 December 1997 and entered into

force on 16 February 2005. The major feature of the Kyoto Protocol was that it set binding targets for 37 industrialised countries (including a joint target for the entire European Union) to reduce greenhouse gases (GHG) emissions. Some countries, including the US and Australia, declined to ratify the agreement. www.unfccc.int

6. The Pew Center on Global Climate Change is a US-based non-governmental organisation, which brings together business leaders, policymakers, scientists, and other experts to find a new approach to a complex and often controversial issue. The Pew Center's approach is based on a belief that organisations can work together to protect the climate while sustaining economic growth. www.pewclimate.org

7. American Petroleum Institute (API) is the national trade association that represents all aspects of America's oil and natural gas industry. www.api.org

8. The Intergovernmental Panel on Climate Change (IPCC) was established in 1988 by the World Meteorological Organization (WMO) and by the United Nations Environment Programme (UNEP) to provide an objective source of information about the causes of climate change, its potential environmental and socio-economic consequences and the adaptation and mitigation options to respond to it. www.ipcc.ch

9. Sir John Houghton was co-chairman of the scientific assessment working group for the IPCC from 1988–2002 and lead editor for the first three IPCC reports. He had previously been director general of the UK Meteorological Office.

10. Karl Popper believed that a scientific theory cannot be proved right but must be shown to be wrong or incorrect. "The criterion of the scientific status of a theory is its falsifiability, or refutability, or testability," Karl Popper, *Conjectures and Refutations: The Growth of Scientific Knowledge* (London: Routledge & Kegan Paul, 1963).

11. The greenhouse effect was first identified by French polymath Jean-Baptiste Joseph Fourier in 1824. British scientist John Tyndall suggested in the 1860s that the ice ages could have been caused by variations in the concentration of CO_2 in the atmosphere. In 1896 the Swedish chemist Svante Arrhenius, in a remarkably comprehensive calculation, estimated that a doubling in the concentration of CO_2 in the atmosphere would increase temperatures by 5°C to 6°C. The first person to claim evidence for global warming was British meteorologist Guy Stewart Callendar in an address to the Royal Society. Data collected from 200 weather stations around the world over the period from 1880 to the 1930s supported his conclusions. But in 1938 the Fellows of the Royal Society challenged his theory and the outcome was that no more was heard of Callendar's work for some time. For a summary of the science see "The Ninth Zuckerman Lecture: The Science of Climate Change: Adapt, Mitigate or Ignore?" Sir David King. www.foundation.org.uk/events/pdf/20021031_king.pdf

12. WBCSD is a CEO-led, global association of some 200 companies dealing exclusively with business and sustainable development. The WBCSD was founded after the 1992 Earth Summit to involve business in sustainability issues. www.wbcsd.org

13. Sir Robin Nicholson was a non executive board director for BP 1987–2005. He

was chief scientific adviser in Prime Minister Margaret Thatcher's Cabinet Office from 1981–85.

14. Andrew Grove, *Only the Paranoid Survive* (New York: Doubleday, 1996).

15. I have always been of the view that a great leader needs to be a good orator and this requires constant practice. A book I have found very helpful more recently is Max Atkinson, *Lend Me Your Ears* (London: Vermillion, 2004).

16. Lord Watson was European chairman of Burson Marsteller for over ten years. He was a regular presenter on *The Money Programme* on BBC2 and *Panorama* on BBC1.

17. *Financial Times*, 20 May 1997.

18. *Washington Post*, 23 May 1997.

19. The Global Climate Coalition was eventually wound up in 2001.

20. www.us-cap.org

21. Fred Krupp co-authored with Miriam Horn, *Earth: the Sequel* (New York: W. W. Norton, 2008).

22. The IPCC's Fourth Assessment Report suggests that transport is responsible for 13.1 per cent of emissions. www.ipcc.ch

23. One example of work with customers was with Arriva, the UK bus company, on a new and more efficient combination of lubricants and fuel. The fuel included water to cool down the burning temperatures, reducing emissions and increasing miles per gallon.

24. UK cap and trade policies were informed by the US SO_2 and NOX trading schemes. California's AB32 is now informing federal US and Australia cap and trade initiatives.

25. www.gov.ca.gov

26. Other regions had also begun to implement comprehensive programmes of regulatory and market mechanisms. The European Union Emissions Trading Scheme (EU ETS) was a positive step but in practice the first phase of the scheme (2005–07) encountered many difficulties. The UK Emissions trading scheme had already been running for three years with a number of UK organisations volunteering to gain experience at trading prior to the introduction of the EU ETS. http://ec.europa.eu/environment/climat/emission

   Some US states had also begun to implement programmes, such as Regional Greenhouse Gas Initiative (RGGI) where ten Northeastern and Mid-Atlantic states agreed to cap and then reduce CO_2 emissions from the power sector by 10 per cent by 2018. www.rggi.org

27. BP speech: "Energy and the Environment, 10 Years on", 26 April 2007. www.bp.com

28. S. Solomon, D. Qin, M. Manning, Z. Chen, M. Marquis, K. B. Averyt, M. Tignor and H. L. Miller (eds), *The IPCC, 2007: Summary for Policymakers, in: Climate Change 2007: The Physical Science Basis. Contribution of Working Group I to the Fourth Assessment Report of the Intergovernmental Panel on Climate Change* (Cambridge, UK, and New York: Cambridge University Press).

29. The Stern Review was published in October 2006 to provide a report to government on the nature of the economic challenges of climate change and how they can be

met, both in the UK and globally, and was led by Lord Stern, the then head of the government economic service and former World Bank chief economist. The report stated that to address the climate challenge we need: "international frameworks that support the achievement of shared goals. It requires a partnership between the public and private sector, working with civil society and with individuals."

6. COLOMBIA

1. According to the BP website: "Production peaked in December 1999 at 434,000 barrels a day. At December 2007, BP's gross oil production stood at 148,000 barrels of oil per day, representing 25 per cent of Colombia's total production." www.bp.com

2. This violence has deeper roots as since the 19th century, despite the country's commitment to democracy, Colombia suffered two bitter civil wars. The most recent and continuing conflict, *La Violencia*, claimed 300,000 lives during the late 1940s and 1950s.

3. As a revolutionary, political leader and battlefield general, Simón Bolívar was one of the key figures in Latin America's struggle for independence in the 19th century. Known as *el liberator*, his political legacy continues to influence South American ideals and culture today, for example with Hugo Chávez's Bolivarian Revolution in Venezuela. John Lynch, *Simón Bolívar: A Life* (New Haven, CT: Yale University Press, 2006).

4. The legend of El Dorado (the Golden Man) may have come from the story that Colombia's Muisca Indians, who dwelt in the highlands of the Andes, near present-day Bogotá, used fine gold dust to anoint the naked bodies of their kings. The ritual was completed with the king's washing in Lake Guatavita and the casting of gold and jewels into the waters as offerings. Unlike much of the Aztec, Maya and Inca treasures, which the Spaniards melted down and shipped home in the form of ingots, many ancient gold objects of the Muisca Indians survived. This may have resulted from the country's rugged terrain and the dispersion of objects over a wider area in many different tribal groupings. The Muisca Indians also buried their treasures in tombs that escaped detection until recent times. Bogotá's Museo del Oro (Gold Museum) alone has some 26,000 ancient gold pieces, many bought from *guaqueros* (professional tomb robbers). Peter Lourie, *Sweat of the Sun, Tears of the Moon* (New York: Atheneum, 1991).

5. In July 2006 BP settled a land rights issue with a Colombian farmers group, setting up an environmental and social improvement trust fund with no admission of liability.

6. The pipeline continues to be sabotaged today.

7. Various independent bodies have also investigated this murder and found "no evidence to suggest that BP was involved in the murder of Arrigui". Professor Jenny Pearce, "Beyond The Perimeter Fence: Oil and Armed Conflict in Casanare, Colombia" (London: London School of Economics, June 2004).

8. Ken Saro-Wiwa was a member of the Ogoni people, an ethnic minority, and was

executed along with eight others on 10 November 1995, by the Nigerian government. He had campaigned for increased autonomy of the Ogoni people, a fairer share of the proceeds of oil revenues and remediation of environmental damage by oil companies to Ogoni land in the Niger Delta. On 8 June 2009, Shell agreed to settle a court case related to allegations in connection with the Nigerian military government's execution of Ken Saro-Wiwa and others in 1995, making a humanitarian gesture to set up a trust fund to benefit the Ogoni people. At the same time the plaintiffs dismissed all claims made in the litigation against Shell. The trust fund will support initiatives in education, skills development, agriculture, small enterprise development and adult literacy. Shell denied the allegations and reiterated that it had attempted to persuade the government of the day to grant clemency. www.shell.com

9. One of the best books on pre-Columbian art, which covers archaeological sites and covers the primary cultures of the South American continent, is Alan Lapiner's *Pre-Columbian Art of South America* (New York: Harry N. Abrams, 1976).

10. In December 2008, Siemens agreed to pay €1bn ($1.36bn) in fines to US and German authorities after prosecutors and the company's internal investigation found some €1.3bn of suspected payments by managers to officials around the world to win contracts. In Washington, a US district court accepted Siemens' settlements of charges that it violated the Foreign Corrupt Practices Act through a lack of internal controls and bookkeeping violations. "Siemens to pay €1bn fines to close bribery scandal", *Financial Times*, 15 December 2008.

11. Fiscalía General de la Nación, Unidad Nacional de Derechos Humanos, Fiscalía Regional Delegada, Bogota mimeo, 10 January 1998.

12. A top rebel leader admitted that his men bombed Colombia's largest oil pipeline in October 1998, killing at least 70 people. In a video statement, Nicolas Rodriguez, head of the 5,000-strong ELN, described the attack on the OCENSA pipeline as a "grave error" and vowed to punish those responsible. The blast and ensuing inferno virtually wiped the village of Machuca off the map and led to one of the worst losses of civilian lives during Colombia's long-running guerrilla war. "Colombia rebel admits oil pipeline bombing mistake", Reuters, 12 November 1998.

13. "What We Stand For" was developed into a Code of Conduct and a statement of Group Values in BP's Management Framework. This was subsequently updated into BP's "Green Book" to conform with the Sarbanes–Oxley legislation and to tighten certain processes such as how reserves were recognised in BP's accounts.

14. BP Colombia employs more than 480 people and 98.5 per cent are native Colombians. www.bp.com

15. Details of the many elements of BP's programme are on the company's Colombia website. www.bp.com/Colombia

16. Examples of independent reports are: N. Galvez, G. Verdugo & P. Torrente, "Study to Identify the Needs for Justice and the Feasibility of an Alternative Justice Program in the Department of Casanare" (Corporación Excelencia en la Justicia, Bogotá, 2001) and A. Gaviria, J. G. Zapata & A. González, "Assessment of the Economic

and Social Impact from Oil-related Activities in the Department of Casanare 1985–2000" (Fedesarrollo, Bogotá, 2001).

17. A. Gaviria, J. G. Zapata & A. González, "Assessment of the Economic and Social Impact from Oil-related Activities in the Department of Casanare 1985–2000" (Fedesarrollo, Bogotá, 2001).

18. N. Galvez, G. Verdugo & P. Torrente, "Study to Identify the Needs for Justice and the Feasibility of an Alternative Justice Program in the Department of Casanare" (Corporación Excelencia en la Justicia, Bogotá, 2001).

19. On 10 December 1948 the General Assembly of the United Nations adopted and proclaimed the Universal Declaration of Human Rights, the full text of which can be found on the UN website. Following this historic act the assembly called upon all Member countries to publicise the text of the declaration and "to cause it to be disseminated, displayed, read and expounded principally in schools and other educational institutions, without distinction based on the political status of countries or territories". www.un.org/Overview/rights

20. The Voluntary Principles on Security and Human Rights were agreed in December 2000 by the US and UK governments; NGOs, including Amnesty International and Human Rights Watch; and several extractive industry companies, including BP.

21. Other studies, such as M. Warner, E. G. Larralde and R. Sullivan, "Business Partners for Development Case Study 10: Oil Production and Long Term Regional Development" (London: Business Partners for Development, 2003) have also shown the benefits of BP's approach to corporate citizenship in Casanare.

22. Members of TIAP included Lord Hannay, Reverend Herman Saud and Ambassador Sabam Siagian. Copies of TIAP reports, in English and or Bahasa (Indonesian), and BP responses can be found on the BP website. www.bp.com

7. ANGOLA TO LIBYA

1. The United Nations estimated that in 1999 as many as 15 million landmines were scattered across Angola with about 23,000 amputees (one out of every 470 people in the country). "Impetus towards a mine free world", 29 April 1999. www.un.org/ecosocdev/geninfo/afrec/vol12no4/mines.htm

2. At the start of the conflict there were other factions, in particular the FNLA (National Liberation Front of Angola). FNLA was anti-communist, also supported by the US, but its importance declined as UNITA fast became the main anti-MPLA opposition movement under Savimbi.

3. BP ERM report on Angola, November 1997, and quoted in the Global Witness Report, "A Crude Awakening: The Role of the Oil and Banking Industries in Angola's Civil War and the Plunder of State Assets", 1 December 1999. www.globalwitness.org

4. When it first entered Transparency International's Corruption Perceptions Index in 2000, Angola ranked 85th out of 90 countries, making it one of the most corrupt countries in the world at that time. www.transparency.org

5. Extract from a letter from the BP chairman to Lord Avebury in response to concerns regarding BP's payment of signature bonuses to the Angolan government. Letter reprinted in the Global Witness report, "A Crude Awakening: The Role of the Oil and Banking Industries in Angola's Civil War and the Plunder of State Assets", 1 December 1999. www.globalwitness.org

6. Ibid.

7. All limited companies in England and Wales have to register at Companies House and then file company information, including annual accounts, under the UK Companies Act and related legislation. The information is not only stored but is also available to the public.

8. Global Witness then issued a press release, "Campaign Success: BP Makes Move for Transparency in Angola", 12 February 2001. www.globalwitness.org

9. Extract from letter from Sonangol to BP, quoted in "Some Transparency, No Accountability, Human Rights Watch", 12 January 2004. www.hrw.org

10. "Interview Lee Raymond, ExxonMobil: The Oil Chief Makes No Apology for His Company's Dominance – or for His 'Political Incorrectness'", *Financial Times*, 12 March 2002.

11. According to the EITI: "3.5 billion people live in countries rich in oil, gas and minerals. With good governance the exploitation of these resources can generate large revenues to foster growth and reduce poverty. However when governance is weak, it may result in poverty, corruption, and conflict. The Extractive Industries Transparency Initiative (EITI) aims to strengthen governance by improving transparency and accountability in the extractives sector." The EITI sets a global standard for companies to publish what they pay and for governments to disclose what they receive. http://eitransparency.org

12. In 2008 Angola's daily oil production was 1,875,000 barrels. BP Statistical Review 2009. www.bp.com

13. In 2008 Nigeria was Africa's largest producing nation at 2,170,000 barrels a day. Algeria was the second largest at 1,993,000 barrels a day. Ibid.

14. Each year, since 1990, the United Nations Development Programme (UNDP) Human Development Report has published the human development index (HDI) which looks beyond GDP to a broader definition of wellbeing. The HDI provides a composite measure of three dimensions of human development: living a long and healthy life (measured by life expectancy), being educated (measured by adult literacy and enrolment at the primary, secondary and tertiary level) and having a decent standard of living (measured by purchasing power parity and income). The 2009 report provides the 2007 HDI rank and value. http://hdr.undp.org

15. Interview by the author with Jonas Moberg, head of the secretariat, EITI.

16. The figure is based on the Oil Diagnostic monitoring system, which was set up by the IMF in 2000. "Some Transparency, No Accountability", report by Human Rights Watch, January 2004. www.hrw.org

17. The Mo Ibrahim Foundation, founded by a British Sudanese-born businessman and philanthropist, provides an annual index which reports progress on Africa's 53 countries. Four criteria measure progress: safety and the rule of law; participation

and human rights; sustainable economic opportunity; and human development. The 2009 Ibrahim Index of African Governance, based on statistics from 2007–08, showed Angola as the third most improved country. www.moibrahimfoundation.org

18. Quoted directly from www.bp.com

19. Out of 180 countries ranked by the 2008 Corruption Perceptions Index, the seven oil nations in the bottom third were Nigeria (121st), Libya (126th), Iran (141st), Kazakhstan (145th), Russia (147th), Venezuela (158th) and Iraq (178th). The other three in the top ten were United Arab Emirates (35th), Kuwait (65th) and Saudi Arabia (80th). Reserve levels taken from BP's 2009 Statistical Review.

20. Dutch Disease is a term thought to have been first coined by *The Economist* to describe the decline in the Netherlands' manufacturing sector following its oil and gas discoveries in the 1960s. "Dutch Disease", *The Economist*, 26 November 1977.

21. Nigeria's economy heavily depends on the oil and gas sector, which contributes 99 per cent of export revenues and 85 per cent of government revenues. World Bank, Nigeria Country Brief. http://web.worldbank.org

22. "Tackling the natural resource curse: an illustration from Nigeria", IMF survey, 15 March 2004.

23. J. H. Bamberg, *The History of the British Petroleum Company, Vol 3: British Petroleum and Global Oil, 1950–1975: The Challenge of Nationalism* (Cambridge: Cambridge University Press, 2000).

24. Nigeria, like many other oil-producing nations, began to assert control over supplies in the early 1970s. Participation discussions led to the Nigerian government taking a 35 per cent participation in BP's oil concession in 1973. In 1974 this was raised to 55 per cent. Eventually it would rise to 100 per cent when General Obasanjo nationalised all BP's interests overnight on 31 July 1979. Berry Ritchie, *Portrait in Oil: An Illustrated History of BP* (London: James and James, 1995).

25. The Niger Delta in southern Nigeria is the most densely populated region of Africa's most populous country. It is a heaving melting pot of 30 million people, from 40-plus ethnic groups, speaking more than 200 different languages. In the 1950s the area was riven by ethnic conflict, a civil war and separatist aspirations prior to Nigeria's independence from Britain. The area's complex problems were compounded when oil was discovered in the 1950s. Revenue from the oil could have helped the country to prosper from independence, but has instead been used by corrupt politicians and businessmen to enrich themselves at the expense of their people. By the 1990s, the Niger Delta was characterised by lawlessness, armed gangs, and kidnappings, with an illicit trade in stolen oil helping to fuel the daily violence. On top of this are superimposed ethnic conflicts and continued separatist demands, led most recently by the Movement for the Emancipation of the Niger Deltas (MEND). In 1995, the Nigerian government took drastic action: Ken Saro-Wiwa, a member of the Ogoni people, an ethnic minority, was executed along with eight others after campaigning for greater autonomy for the Ogoni people, a fairer share of the proceeds of oil revenues and remediation of environmental damage by oil companies to Ogoni land in the Niger Delta. See note 8, chapter 6.

26. BP's investment in Algeria was increased by addition of the Amoco-heritage In Amenas gas project and the ARCO-heritage enhanced oil recovery project at Rhourde El Baguel, near Hassi Messaoud.

27. Scarlet ibis (*Eudocimus ruber*) favour the wetlands of Venezuela. Their characteristic red colouring comes from their diet of shrimps, crabs and other crustaceans which are rich in carotene.

28. See note 3, chapter 6.

29. In 2006 Rafael Ramirez, Venezuela's energy minister and head of PDVSA, caused a political storm by telling state oil workers to back President Hugo Chávez or leave their jobs.

30. Libya was ahead of Saudi Arabia and Kuwait. BP Statistical Review of the World Oil Industry 1970, quoted in J. H. Bamberg, *The History of the British Petroleum Company, Vol 3: British Petroleum and Global Oil, 1950–1975: The Challenge of Nationalism* (Cambridge: Cambridge University Press, 2000).

31. Ibid.

32. Algeria was very different from Libya. Europeans had lived and worked as part of the Algerian community rather than as expatriates, as they had done in Libya. And even when the French left Algeria in 1962, it was still influenced by European thinking and culture, with Europeans still doing business in the country.

8. MOSCOW

1. Chevron CEO, Kenneth Derr, also did not want to help fund the new soccer stadium in Astana and reputedly turned his back on President Nazarbayev when he was asked. Nazarbayev "was suitably flabbergasted and insulted". Steve Levine, *The Oil and the Glory: The Pursuit of Empire and Fortune on the Caspian Sea* (New York: Random House, 2007).

2. Despite losing an estimated $5.2 billion during the 2008–09 economic downturn, Alekperov remains the world's 57th richest person with an estimated fortune of $7.8 billion. "The World's Billionaires", *Forbes*, 11 March 2009. www.forbes.com

3. An interesting interview with Boris Jordan, conducted on 10 March 2000, describes the speed of the process of voucher privatisation. "When we were hired, we were asked to implement a legal process that was developed by a group of both American and Russian advisors to the Russian government. Harvard University was involved with this. Jeffrey Sachs and a group of Russian advisors were involved as well and put together a legal structure and a legal framework for the privatization of Russian assets. The problem lay in the fact that these were largely lawyers and theoreticians who did a fantastic job putting the framework together, but to put that into practice, none of them had the experience." http://www.pbs.org/wgbh/commandingheights/shared/minitext/int_borisjordan.html

4. Chrystia Freeland, *Sale of the Century: The Inside Story of the Second Russian Revolution* (London: Little, Brown and Company, 2000). As the head of the Moscow bureau for the *Financial Times* in the 1990s, Chrystia Freeland was well placed to observe what happened during this period and describes the turbulent political backdrop to

the voucher privatisation scheme and subsequent auctioning of companies.

5. Chrystia Freeland's book is one of the best that covers the loans-for-shares episode, and indeed she interviewed me because of my involvement with some of the key players. Ibid.

6. David Hoffman, *The Oligarchs: Wealth & Power in the New Russia* (New York: Public Affairs, 2001).

7. Chrystia Freeland, *Sale of the Century: The Inside Story of the Second Russian Revolution* (London: Little, Brown and Company, 2000).

8. "The meaning of Norilsk", *The Economist*, 13 March 2008.

9. BP press release: "BP Makes Major Strategic Move into Russia", 18 November 1997. www.bp.com

10. Graham Greene's *The Third Man* was written as a screenplay for a film. The action is set in Vienna, after the Second World War when the city was divided into separate zones and the black market was rife.

11. George Soros and Boris Jordan (through his business Sputnik) were also investors in Sidanco.

12. *St Petersburg Times*, 25 February 2005.

13. "BP: from hate to love in Russia", *Sunday Times*, 5 October 2003. www.timesonline.co.uk

14. "The oligarch who came in from the cold", *Forbes*, 18 March 2002. www.forbes.com

15. *Daily Telegraph*, 15 February 2003.

16. In April 2007, after pressure from tax authorities and environmental bodies, Shell sold a stake in the Sakhalin II project to Gazprom, the controlling stake of which is owned by the Russian state. Gazprom now holds 50 per cent plus one share and Shell holds 27.5 per cent in the Sakhalin II project. Shell press release: "Gazprom Enters Sakhalin II Project", 18 April 2007. www.shell.com

9. AZERBAIJAN

1. *The World is Not Enough*, MGM, 1999.

2. Robert W. Tolf, *The Russian Rockefellers: The Saga of the Nobel Family and the Russian Oil Industry* (Stanford: Hoover Institution Publication, 1976).

3. Daniel Yergin, *The Prize: The Epic Quest for Oil, Money & Power* (New York: Free Press, 2008).

4. Niall Ferguson, *The House of Rothschild: The World's Banker, 1849–1999. Volume 2* (London: Penguin Books, 2000).

5. Daniel Yergin, *The Prize: The Epic Quest for Oil, Money & Power* (New York: Free Press, 2008).

6. James Dodds Henry, *Baku: An Eventful History* (London: Constable, 1905).

7. Neft Dashlari was a complex of oil rigs, production facilities and living quarters for workers along a maze of roads stretching out into the Caspian Sea built by the Soviets in the late 1940s. Almost a full town on the sea, by 1990 parts of it were underwater and many of its 600 wells were inoperative or inaccessible.

8. Simon Sebag Montefiore, *Young Stalin* (London: Weidenfeld & Nicolson, 2007).

9. The ceasefire has held since 1994 with Nagorno-Karabakh in ethnic Armenian hands and more than a million people displaced in the two countries. Discussions between the presidents of Armenia and Azerbaijan to resolve the continuing conflict in Moscow in July 2009 ended without a breakthrough. "Armenia, Azerbaijan still apart on Karabakh", Reuters, 19 July 2009.

10. This conflict would erupt again in August 2008 and end with Russia recognising the independence of Abkhazia and South Ossetia. However tension in the area remains high. "Russia raises combat readiness in South Ossetia", *Financial Times*, 5 August 2009.

11. Chris Ogden, *Maggie: An Intimate Portrait of a Woman in Power* (London: Simon and Schuster, 1990).

12. BP estimated the field to contain over five billion barrels. The International Energy Agency (IEA) World Energy Outlook 2008 cites ACG as a "super-giant", a term which they apply in the report to any field holding more than five billion barrels of initial reserves.

13. According to Cambridge Energy Research Associates, ACG produces 850,000 barrels per day, making it the third biggest-producing field in operation. "World's Largest Oil Fields and Top Oil Producing Nations", 18 August 2009.

14. The original participants were SOCAR (20 per cent, Azerbaijan); BP (17.127 per cent, UK); Amoco (17.01 per cent, US); Lukoil (10 per cent, Russia); Pennzoil (9.82 per cent, US); Unocal (9.52 per cent, US); Statoil (8.563 per cent, Norway); McDermott (2.45 per cent, US); Ramco (2.08 per cent, UK); TPAO (1.75 per cent, Turkey), Delta-Namir (1.68 per cent, Saudi Arabia). Over time the participants changed as various partners sold their shares, including SOCAR's sale of 10 per cent of the equity, mainly to Exxon; and Ramco and McDermott's decision to sell out. Holdings also changed through mergers, notably as a result of the merger between BP and Amoco, the merger between Chevron and Unocal, and the merger between Devon and Pennzoil.

15. For BP, the uncertainty over ownership of the Caspian Sea manifested itself on at least two occasions. In 1999, BP had to cease marine-survey activities in the Alov contract area in the southern Azerbaijan sector when its vessel was threatened by the Iranian coast guard. And in the case of the ACG fields, Turkmenistan disputed Azerbaijan's ownership, on the grounds that the median line between the two countries should be measured from the base not the tip of the Absheron peninsula. A number of times it dispatched planes to fly by the ACG platforms as a reminder of the Turkmen claim.

16. The dispute is not fully resolved, despite separate bilateral agreement between Russia and Azerbaijan, Russia and Kazakhstan, and Kazakhstan and Azerbaijan. "Energy overshadows Caspian border disputes", *United Press International*, 5 August 2009.

17. Mud volcanoes are formed by some of the same geological processes which create oil and gas deposits. Like magmatic volcanoes, pent-up geological gases expel sedimentary deposits from beneath the Earth's surface in molten form, sometimes accompanied by flames hundreds of feet high. Unlike their magmatic cousins,

however, the rock exits at an ambient or cool temperature and creates less enduring structures on the surface. As many as half of the world's mud volcanoes are located in eastern Azerbaijan and the Caspian Sea.

18. There were other transportation proposals in circulation. The strangest was probably a proposal that the consortium buy 120 airships to shuttle the oil by air from Baku to Ceyhan. Another proposal, discussed in the press, was to route a pipeline through Armenia. The idea was that a peace pipeline could replace conflict with a shared interest in peace and stability. But the conflict with Armenia was too fresh and raw, and the topography too mountainous, for this idea to be politically or commercially viable.

19. One idea discussed and rejected was whether there could be a swap arrangement with Iran. In Iran the bulk of oil production was in the south near the Gulf, but the bulk of consumption was in the north, which includes Tehran with its population of over ten million. One obvious option would have been to supply Azeri oil to Iran in the north in return for Iranian oil in the south for export, which would cut transportation costs for both parties. There would have been difficulty in agreeing fair value since the quality of the crudes varied, with heavy and sour Iranian crude being swapped for light and sweet Azeri oil, and it was not clear whether Iranian swaps could accommodate a million barrels of oil per day. There were other challenges to do with enforceability and political acceptability.

20. The US government provided a constant source of diplomatic intervention which was often crucial in keeping the project on track. In the early 1990s the US formulated a policy to support the independence of Azerbaijan and the other former Soviet states, promote strong links to Turkey and the West and secure an alternative source of hydrocarbons by supporting multiple oil and gas pipelines. Since pipelines to the north through Russia already existed, and the US opposed any pipelines to the south through Iran, this meant particular US support for new pipelines running East–West. The US was active and effective in pursuing this agenda, with a working group at the National Security Council, liaison officers at the White House, a series of senior US officials with special responsibility for Caspian energy, and other officials in the Clinton and Bush administrations prepared to invest time and influence to support various projects.

21. In the end the total pipeline cost turned out to be nearly $4 billion, partly due to inflation and partly due to change in scope as the project progressed. www.bp.com

22. Turkmenistan was involved as, at the same meeting, a framework for a gas pipeline from Turkmenistan to Turkey through Azerbaijan was agreed. The same pipeline would later take Azeri gas – it became known as the South Caucasus or the Shah Deniz pipeline after Azerbaijan's major gas field.

23. Organization for Security and Co-operation in Europe. www.osce.org

24. In 2000 Ahmet Necdet Sezer was elected president of Turkey, which made things somewhat easier as he was solid and a good constitutional lawyer. Then there was a further major change in the regime in 2003 when the Ecevit government was replaced by that of Prime Minister Erdogan. Turkish institutions, including BOTAŞ, took six months to adjust and this affected continuity on the project.

25. BOTAŞ, the state-owned construction company, agreed to build the Turkish section under a lump-sum turnkey contract for $1.4 bn, with the Turkish government bearing the risk, covered by a $300 million collateralised guarantee from the Turkish Treasury to cover any cost overruns.

26. Specifically, of the 20 cents per barrel available for the pipeline tariff in Azerbaijan and Georgia, Georgia got 12 cents rising to 14 cents in 2010, even though the pipeline is twice as long in Azerbaijan as in Georgia.

27. The final equity shares in BTC were BP (30.1 per cent), SOCAR (25 per cent), Chevron (8.9 per cent), Statoil (8.71 per cent), TPAO (6.53 per cent), ENI (5 per cent), Total (5 per cent), Itochu (3.4 per cent), Inpex (2.5 per cent), Conoco (2.5 per cent), Amerada Hess (2.36 per cent). www.bp.com

28. About 30 per cent of the investment was provided in the form of equity and 70 per cent, or $2.6 billion, in the form of financing raised from third parties, including IFC and EBRD, seven export credit agencies, a syndicate of 15 commercial banks and loans from four partners (BP, Total, Statoil, Conoco).

29. Jill Shankleman, "Oil, Profits and Peace: Does Business Have a Role in Peace-making?" (US Institute of Peace Press, 2007).

30. The Equator Principles are a set of principles to be used by the financial industry to manage social and environmental issues in project financing. They were developed by a group of private sector banks and were launched in June 2003. The banks chose to model the Equator Principles on the environmental standards of the World Bank and the social policies of the International Finance Corporation (IFC). They have become the *de facto* standard for banks and investors on how to assess major development projects around the world.

31. A recent independent report by Massachusetts Institute of Technology (MIT) on the Lessons Learned from the CDAP external evaluation of the BTC project concluded that the use of an independent body was a striking success and of considerable value to the BTC project, BP generally, and to the people and states of Azerbaijan, Georgia and Turkey. In addition to the four independent reports published by the panel containing more than 150 recommendations, a number of innovative and important initiatives emerged from the panel's work. The conclusion was that the selection of independent panellists, the interactive and iterative processes, the capable secretariat, and using lessons learnt from the Tangguh Independent Advisory Panel (TIAP) all helped CDAP to perform an effective role. Richard Locke, John Van Maanen, and Eleanor Westney, "Caspian Development Advisory Panel: Lessons Learned" (MIT Sloan School of Management, April 2007).

32. www.caspiandevelopmentandexport.com

33. Azerbaijan is repeatedly cited by Transparency International as one of the most corrupt countries in the world. In 2008 Azerbaijan was ranked 158th (jointly with Angola) out of 180 countries on its corruption perceptions index. www.transparency.org

34. International Monetary Fund – "Managing Oil Wealth: The Case of Azerbaijan" (2004).

35. Azerbaijan State Oil Fund reported 2008 revenues of 11.6 billion manats (AZN)

from the sale of oil. (Using an exchange rate of 1.25 USD to the manat, this is $14.5 billion.) www.oilfund.az/en

36. www.doingbusiness.org

37. BP press release: "BTC Celebrates Full Commissioning", 13 July 2006. www.bp.com

10. CHINA

1. In time I could see that the Mao suits were not in fact identical. There were discernible differences; better fabric or tailoring indicating that the person held a senior role, such as that of government official. On subsequent visits, some years later as rules relaxed, I also began to notice colour creeping in. Women started to wear blouses under their suits with just the hint of a collar or scarf at the neckline, and the men would bravely sport coloured socks.

2. China has three national oil companies: China National Petroleum Corporation (CNPC), the parent company of PetroChina; the China Petroleum and Chemical Corporation (Sinopec); and the China National Offshore Oil Corporation (CNOOC).

3. Chinese people between the ages of 15 and 25, during the period of the Cultural Revolution, are often referred to as the "lost generation", as they missed out on a proper education. The Cultural Revolution took place from 1965, and lasted for some ten years, when Chairman Mao attempted to impose his authority on the communist party and the country with the force of the Red Guards. The basic thrust was to reinforce a classless society, and the educated – writers, economists and teachers – were persecuted. Millions were sent to forced labour camps and tens of thousands were executed. Schools and universities were closed and much economic activity was halted. This led to an almost entire generation of under-educated individuals. Roderick MacFarquhar and Michael Schoenhals, *Mao's Last Revolution* (Cambridge, US: Harvard University Press, 2006).

4. The Sassoon family had made a fortune in the Chinese opium trade, and later established cotton mills in India in the 19th century. Victor Sassoon, born in 1881, chose Shanghai as the centre for his own business empire in the late 1920s. He built many of the landmark buildings in Shanghai, including the Cathay Hotel on Shanghai's Bund waterfront, and was one of the leading figures among the many British who dominated the city's society at the time.

5. The Gang of Four were the leading radical figures who played a dominant political role during the later years of the Cultural Revolution: Jiang Qing (Mao Zedong's fourth wife), Zhang Chunqiao, Yao Wenyuan, and Wang Hongwen. After Mao Zedong's death in September 1976, it looked as though they would seize power. But they went into hiding and were then arrested and blamed for the excesses of the Cultural Revolution. Sentences for their "anti-party" deeds ranged from death (later commuted to life in prison) to 20 years in prison.

6. Formal discussions had begun in 1982 and, after 22 rounds of talks, the Joint Declaration was signed by the Prime Minister, Margaret Thatcher, and her Chinese

counterpart, Zhao Ziyang.

7. Hong Kong Island had been ceded in perpetuity to the UK by the Treaty of Nanking (1842) and Kowloon also by the Treaty of Beijing (1860). But the control of the New Territories was on a 99-year lease, signed in 1898. By 1997 the three territories were economically interdependent and it would have been impractical to separate them, so all three were handed back to the Chinese.

8. BP's corporate policies precluded it from operating in countries such as Sudan where there are economic sanctions in place. PetroChina had no investment in Sudan at the time; its parent company CNPC had a shareholding in an oil project in Sudan. BP press release: "BP and PetroChina", 15 February 2000. www.bp.com

9. Madeleine Albright, *Madam Secretary* (New York: Hyperion, 2003).

10. "Sinopec's corrupt ex-chief gets death sentence", *Financial Times*, 16 July 2009.

11. "Corrupt Sinopec ex-chairman convicted", *China Daily*, 16 July 2009.

12. Since the 1980s China has grown at almost twice the global average at more than 9 per cent on average, year on year, reaching 13 per cent in 2007. World Economic Outlook Database, April 2009. In 2008, with the world economic decline, China's growth slowed, but it was still 9 per cent and there are signs that its growth will rise again in subsequent years. "Bamboo shoots of recovery", *Financial Times*, 16 April 2009.

13. "The Future Population of China: Prospects to 2045", Asian Metacenter for population and sustainable development analysis. www.populationasia.org

14. Philip Andrews-Speed, *Energy Policy and Regulation in the People's Republic of China* (The Hague: Kluwer Law International, 2004).

15. The World Bank reports that 13 of the 20 most polluted cities in the world are in China. "Mid-term evaluation of China's 11th five-year plan", December 2008. www.worldbank.org

16. "China's green opportunity", *McKinsey Quarterly*, May 2009.

17. Fareed Zakaria, *The Post-American World* (New York: W. W. Norton, 2008).

18. New poverty estimates published by the World Bank (26 August 2008) reveal that 1.4 billion people in the developing world (one in four) were living on less than $1.25 a day in 2005. www.worldbank.org

19. Ibid.

20. The seven largest oil companies by production and reserves in the world are now state-owned: Saudi Aramco, Russia's Gazprom, CNPC of China, NIOC of Iran, Venezuela's PDVSA, Brazil's Petrobras and Petronas of Malaysia. The *FT* ranked the "New Seven Sisters" on the basis of resource base, level of output, company's ambition, scale of their domestic market, and influence in the industry. They are shown here in order of prominence. "The new Seven Sisters: oil and gas giants dwarf western rivals", *Financial Times*, 11 March 2007.

11. UK

1. Most Admired Leader Award is presented by *Management Today* magazine. I won Most Admired Leader in 1999, 2000, 2001 and 2002; and BP won Most Admired

Company in 2002. www.managementtoday.co.uk

2. When the company had redesigned its trademark shield in 1958 it was said to be "less heraldic in a medieval way, more firm-shouldered, modern and definite" but the internal co-ordinator for the project was disappointed with the outcome and stated that it was not "sufficiently forceful with the present competition". Some years later in 1971, in a presentation to the board, an external consultant had stated that the BP shield was "defiantly ethnocentric" yet it remained for another 29 years. J. H. Bamberg, *The History of the British Petroleum Company, Vol 3: British Petroleum and Global Oil, 1950–1975: The Challenge of Nationalism* (Cambridge, UK: Cambridge University Press, 2000).

3. In effect Intel worked out how to brand an ingredient and how to market to the end-user in order to create demand for their microprocessors. The programme started as joint advertising and, as Intel Inside® began to develop, the brand began to appear on the hardware and as part of the start-up screen show. Television advertisements were quirky but memorable, the pink, green and yellow BunnyPeople™ being unforgettable. The Intel Inside® programme required the co-operation of computer manufacturers (OEMs – original equipment manufacturers), who were enthusiastic because it differentiated their machines, implying the computer had something special at its core. Intel has recently been fined by the European Commission for breaking competition law in connection with offering computer manufacturers huge discounts. Intel Inside® is a registered trademark of Intel Corporation. www.intel.com

4. Steven Prokesch, "Unleashing the power of learning", *Harvard Business Review,* Sept–Oct 1997.

5. BP speech at Cambridge Energy Research Associates (CERA) conference 1996.

6. BunnyPeople™ is a trademark of Intel Corporation. www.intel.com

7. "BP: colouring public opinion?" *Adweek*, 14 January 2008. www.adweek.com

8. We wanted to encourage discussion. Ogilvy & Mather created campaigns to engage people in understanding broader environmental issues, such as the BP "On the Street" campaign in the US which used simple vox pop consumer interviews.

9. Advertising awards included the 2007 gold Effie Award from the American Marketing Association. The head of marketing for BP at the time, Anna Catalano, now based in the US, tells me that she stills get requests to talk at marketing forums on the implementation of BP's new identity.

10. Actually very few companies follow the model of the same name for all products. Unilever, for example, has a large number of different brands – from Ben & Jerry's ice cream to Dove beauty products – and only recently started identifying them as being from the same stable with the small "U" logo. When BP had many different interests in the 1980s everything was not branded BP, which is just as well. BP sausages would not have sold too well.

11. "Exxon to stop giving benefits to partners of gay workers", *New York Times*, 7 December 1999.

12. BP speech: "The Strategic Logic of Diversity", 19 June 2002. www.bp.com

13. "Diversity drive at BP targets gay staff", *Guardian*, 20 June 2002.

14. BP press release: "BP and E.ON Go Ahead with Veba Deal and Sell Upstream Assets to Petro-Canada for $2 billion", 30 January 2002. www.bp.com

15. In January 2004, Shell admitted that it had overstated its proven oil and gas reserves by more than 20 per cent. When news of this scandal broke, Shell's share price dropped and confidence in the company and its executive team was damaged.

16. "BP should consider the 'mother of all mergers' with Shell", *Guardian*, 15 July 2004.

12. US

1. Tobias Buck and David Buchan: "Sun King of the oil industry", *Financial Times*, July 2002. www.ft.com

2. Between 1999 and 2004, BP's safety record on fatalities, days away from work case frequency, and recordable injury frequency had all improved. During that time, BP's recordable injury frequency decreased threefold to reach 0.53 in 2004. This was below the benchmark set by the American Petroleum Institute (1.09) and the Association of Oil and Gas Producers (0.79). BP annual reports 1999–2004 and BP website. www.bp.com

3. BP had won numerous awards for safety, including an award for safety management for the North Everest Platform in the North Sea from the British Safety Council in 2001, and, more recently, in 2004, BP was awarded the Frank Lees Medal by the Institute of Chemical Engineering for its "Process Safety Series", a publication on safety and loss prevention.

4. "BP suffers blow to reputation as Baker criticises safety culture", *The Times*, 17 January 2007: "Duane Wilson, a panel member, said conditions in the 1990s were very tough for oil companies. 'BP was concerned about profits, but we found no evidence that it shorted the funding for process safety' he said."

5. BP press release: "BP Assessing Damage to Thunder Horse platform in Gulf of Mexico", 12 July 2005. www.bp.com

6. BP estimated that the spill was 5,050 barrels, approximately 200,000 gallons. www.bp.com

7. Diana Vaughan quoted Maurice Mandelbaum who termed "retrospective fallacy" for the way we tend to use modern knowledge to analyse historical events. Diana Vaughan, *The Challenger Launch Decision: Risky technology, culture and deviance at NASA* (Chicago: Chicago University Press, 1996).

8. BP speech: "Beyond Retirement". www.bp.com

9. The five candidates were quoted in an article: "Browne backed Shell tie-up", *Daily Telegraph*, 22 January 2007. www.telegraph.co.uk

13. LONDON

1. The Wolfenden Report was commissioned by the British government, following the high-profile trial and incarceration of gay journalist Peter Wildeblood in 1954. The remit of the 14-member committee – chaired by Sir John Wolfenden, Vice-

Chancellor of Reading University – was to examine the laws on homosexuality and prostitution. The three-year-long inquiry concluded that outlawing homosexuality impinged upon civil liberties and that private morality or immorality was "not the law's business". The Report was published in September 1957 and recommended that homosexual behaviour between consenting adults should no longer be a criminal offence. But the government rejected the proposal. It would be a further ten years before the law permitted sexual relations between homosexual men over the age of 21 "in private" and not at all among members of the Merchant Navy or Armed Forces. The law was not applied in Scotland until 1980, and in Northern Ireland until 1982. It was only in 2000 that British laws governing permissible sexual relations were finally made equal between heterosexual and homosexual couples.

2. Auschwitz was divided into three major camps: Auschwitz I, the main camp or 'Stammlager'; Auschwitz II, or Birkenau, established in October 1941 as a 'Vernichtungslager' (extermination camp); Auschwitz III or Monowitz, established in May 1942 as an 'Arbeitslager' (work camp). My mother was selected for Auschwitz III which provided slave labourers for different factories nearby, including a major industrial plant for producing synthetic rubber. She worked with chemicals in a munitions factory. More than 40,000 prisoners are thought to have worked as slave labourers at any one time at Auschwitz or nearby and when they became too sick or weak they were then sent to the gas chambers. The estimated number of deaths at Auschwitz is 1.1 million killed in gas chambers and 330,000 from other causes. The real number of deaths is unknown but may be as high as 4 million. In total more than 6 million Jews died across Europe during the Holocaust. www. jewishvirtuallibrary.org and http://en.auschwitz.org

3. The lecture series on sustainable development in the name of Professor Amartya Sen, Nobel Laureate in Economic Sciences 1998, was organised by The European Institute for Asian Studies (EIAS), in close association with the Cambridge and Oxford Societies of Belgium, and the Harvard Club of Belgium. Sir Nicholas Stern gave the first lecture in March 2006.

4. Based on market capitalisation.

5. Confirmed in *The Times* on 29 July 2009: "When all else is cut, is BP's dividend next?"

6. The expression is originally thought to have come from an Eastern proverb.

14. VENICE

1. John Julius Norwich, *A History of Venice* (London: Penguin Books, 1983).

2. This is based on an old Venetian document which links the foundation of the city with a consular visit from Padua to establish a trading post on the islands of the Rialto. It is mixed with a legend about the founding of the church of *San Giacomo di Rialto* which claims to be the oldest in Venice, although the current building is said to date back to no more than the 11th century. Ibid.

3. Ibid.

4. William Shakespeare, *Merchant of Venice*, Act 3, Scene I.

5. Jan Morris, *Venice* (London: Faber & Faber, 1993).

6. Venice's financial systems were developed to facilitate its commerce. As early as the 13th century, Venetian bankers were located near the city's wooden Rialto Bridge. Each banker sat on a bench (*banche*) and merchants who did not want to use coins from their treasure chests to buy or sell would instruct the bankers to write the transfer details in a large journal. These bankers were called *banche del giro* as their main function was to rotate (*girare*) credits from one account to another at the command of the merchants. From this we have taken the name "bank" and the concept of the giro-bank, which was widely imitated elsewhere in the 17th century, for example in Amsterdam and Hamburg. Venice was the first place to introduce tradeable bills of exchange to allow people to borrow money to carry on their trade. Frederick C. Lane, *Venice – A Maritime Republic* (Baltimore & London: Johns Hopkins University Press, 1973).

7. Venice's rules spanned not just trade but also how people lived. These extended from sumptuary laws, which forbade extravagant displays of wealth in dress and on gondolas, to a law preventing any person from owning more than one kiln so they could not influence the price of tiles and building materials. Ibid.

8. John Maynard Keynes, "Alfred Marshall, 1842–1924" in A. C. Pigou (ed), *Memorials of Alfred Marshall* (London: Macmillan, 1925).

9. Ibid.

10. Economist Milton Friedman argued that the social responsibility of business is merely to increase its profits. Friedman believed that by business even talking about social responsibility it damaged the foundations of free society. He said it made business people appear "schizophrenic", making profits on the one hand but appeasing their social consciences on the other. Milton Friedman, "The Social Responsibility of Business is to Increase its Profits", *New York Times*, 13 September 1970.

11. Jack Welch, ex chairman and CEO of GE, often claims ownership of the concept of shareholder value but I was interested to read that he recently stated: "Shareholder value is an outcome, not a strategy". *Financial Times*, 12 March 2009.

12. Venice had no natural resources but its purpose became trade. In the Middle Ages its trade helped Venetian society to prosper and grow and also provided the goods and services needed by its citizens. Venice, for example, always had an adequate supply of food; it avoided the famines that affected many cities. Frederick C. Lane, *Venice – A Maritime Republic* (Baltimore & London: Johns Hopkins University Press, 1973).

   That purpose first began to slip in the 15th century when the East sea route was discovered by Vasco da Gama, although trading with the Levant and the Balkans survived right up until the end of the 16th century. In my view, Venice lost its way when the native-born Venetians began to focus merely on landowning. When long-distance trade finally broke down in the early 17th century, the city had no purpose. Its economy went from being outward focused and turned in on itself as the Venetian nobility lived off rental income and became *popolo grasso* (fat people).

13. ICI was a great source of ideas and management technology and was much admired

under its chairman John Harvey-Jones in the 1980s. In the 1990s the company lost its sense of purpose. The pharmaceutical arm, Zeneca, was demerged and went on to merge with Astra AB to form AstraZeneca plc, the largest pharmaceutical group in the world; other parts were hived off until the company was absorbed into Akzo Nobel. ICI plc shares were delisted in January 2008.

14. J. G. Links, *Venice for Pleasure* (London: Pallas Athene, 2008).

Epilogue, BRAZIL

1. James Lovelock, *Revenge of Gaia* (London: Allen Lane, 2006) and *The Vanishing Face of Gaia: A Final Warning* (London: Allen Lane, 2009).

2. James Lovelock, "The Earth is about to catch a morbid fever that may last as long as 100,000 years", *Independent*, 16 January 2006.

3. There have been proposals to freeze or dismantle biofuel consumption targets due to fears that biofuels are causing negative knock-on changes in land use. While clearly an important concern in some cases, the science is immature and many uncertainties remain. Biofuels remain the only material option to diversify transport fuels in the short term and a period of proper scientific analysis is required before making sweeping policy changes.

4. Daniel Sperling, and Deborah Gordon, *Two Billion Cars: Driving Toward Sustainability* (New York: Oxford University Press, 2009), pages 95–96. "Brazilian Cane Ethanol: A Policy Model." The authors consider that ethanol production in Brazil is a unique situation and it is not replicable; they think there is no other country where it makes sense to convert sugar or starch crops to ethanol, particularly the US.

5. Using energy to cook food is the evolutionary change which underpins all subsequent changes that have made humans such unusual animals, according to Dr Richard Wrangham, Harvard University. "What's cooking?", *The Economist*, 21 February 2009.

6. Daniel Yergin, *The Prize: The Epic Quest for Oil, Money & Power* (New York: Free Press, 2008).

7. As far back as 3000 BC seepages of bitumen in Mesopotamia were tapped and used as building mortar. Bitumen was traded in the Middle East and Daniel Yergin suggests that even Noah's Ark and Moses' basket were probably caulked with bitumen to make them waterproof. Ibid.

8. BP Statistical Review 2009. www.bp.com

9. Ibid.

10. International Energy Agency (IEA), World Energy Outlook 2008. www.iea.org

11. Matthew R. Simmons, *Twilight in the Desert: The Coming Saudi Oil Shock and the World Economy* (New York: John Wiley & Sons, 2005).

12. BP Statistical Review 2009. www.bp.com

13. BP quotes a figure of 42 years, using the reserves-to-production in the BP Statistical Review 2009. But, rather than use past rates of production, my calculation uses a 1 per cent per annum oil demand growth from the IEA, World Energy Outlook 2008 reference scenario to get a more realistic figure of 30 years for reserves-to-

demand. Similar calculations apply to gas and coal.

14. My calculation based on data from IEA, World Energy Outlook 2008.

15. European Commission.

16. BP Statistical Review 2009. www.bp.com

17. At the time of writing, however, renewable energy projects are struggling. A worldwide lack of debt finance has significantly raised project costs for renewable energy. In 2008 clean energy investment stalled, after growing at an average rate of 65 per cent in each of the three previous years. The underlying technology costs for renewables have continued to fall. In the case of solar photovoltaic cells, input prices fell by as much as 40 per cent year on year in 2008, more than offsetting other rising costs. New Energy Finance, www.newenergymatters.com

18. BP Statistical Review 2009. www.bp.com

19. Ibid.

20. President Carter thought the US could drill its way to oil independence, but the US simply does not have the reserves. In President Bush's 2006 State of the Union speech, he expressed these concerns by saying America was addicted to oil, pledging to cut US oil imports from the Middle East by half by 2020. Influential *New York Times* columnist Thomas Friedman, in *Hot, Flat and Crowded* (New York: Farrar, Straus & Giroux, 2008), argues that by buying oil from countries hostile to America, the US is funding both sides of the war on terror and advocates an increase in car efficiency standards and a large tax on gasoline to curb demand. President Obama was vocal on energy security even before his presidential campaign ("Energy Security is National Security", 28 February 2006) and is now developing a comprehensive strategy to tackle energy and climate security.

21. Oak Ridge was originally called Clinton Laboratories and was established in 1943 to carry out a single, well-defined mission: the pilot-scale production and separation of plutonium for the World War II Manhattan Project. The Americans started their programme after they had learned that two German scientists had discovered the splitting of uranium's nucleus. Albert Einstein understood the implications and wrote to President Franklin D. Roosevelt urging a US research programme. Einstein recognised that the discovery of uranium fission could unleash energy of unprecedented might which could be used to make a bomb. When a uranium-fuelled atomic bomb devastated Hiroshima on 6 August 1945, it was powered by the output of Oak Ridge's Y-12 and K-25 plants. http://www.ornl.gov

22. Ibid.

23. The total budget is 1 trillion tonnes of carbon – Dr Myles Allen et al, "Warming caused by cumulative carbon emissions: towards the trillionth tonne", printed in *Nature*, 30 April 2009.

24. John Maynard Keynes, *The General Theory of Employment, Interest and Money* (Cambridge, UK: Macmillan Cambridge University Press, 1936).

25. IPCC, 2007: B. Metz, O. R. Davidson, P. R. Bosch, R. Dave, L. A. Meyer (eds), *Climate Change 2007: Mitigation of Climate Change. Contribution of Working Group III to the Fourth Assessment Report of the Intergovernmental Panel on Climate Change* (Cambridge & New York: Cambridge University Press).

26. *McKinsey Quarterly*, May 2009. www.mckinseyquarterly.com

27. Electric trains are up to a 40 per cent improvement on diesel trains (source: The Railway Forum, www.railwayforum.com/electrification.php). Electric cars are 100 per cent improvement on gasoline-powered cars – source: Tesla Motors.

28. Another criticism of electric vehicles is that they will create greater surges in energy demand, making extra back-up plants necessary and adding to the costs of power supply. This is an important consideration but its impact may not be as great as some make out. Research in America suggest that if the current US light vehicle fleet were converted to electricity overnight the off-peak (overnight) production capacity would be sufficient to fuel over three-quarters of them without the need for extra capacity. "Impact Assessment of Plug-in Hybrid Vehicles on Electric Utilities and Regional US Power Grids" (US Department Of Energy, Pacific Northwest National Laboratory, December 2006).

29. In the 1970s Brazil, then under military dictatorship, made a choice to be less reliant on oil from OPEC countries after the oil crisis. They began to invest in growing sugarcane and developing ethanol products. The market did not make the choice for them, it simply catalysed the moment. Despite changes in regime, the government has stood by that decision and forged ahead with innovation to see the sugarcane ethanol industry today become a natural and important part of their economy. In 2008 Brazil supplied, for the first time, more than half of its domestic transport fuel needs using ethanol produced from its sugarcane.

30. This book went to press in October 2009 and, therefore, no account has been taken of the outcome of the UN Climate Change Conference in Copenhagen in December 2009.

31. The Waxman–Markey bill seeks to reduce US emissions by 17 per cent by 2020 (based on a 2005 baseline).

32. The net economy-wide cost per household of reducing greenhouse gas emissions to 17 per cent by 2020 is estimated to be $175, which works out at a little under 50 cents per day. Congressional Budget Office, 19 June 2009. www.cbo.gov

33. The "Human Impact Report: Climate Change – The Anatomy of a Silent Crisis" was the first ever comprehensive report looking at the human impact of climate change. The report estimated that climate change accounts for over 300,000 deaths throughout the world each year. By 2030, the annual death toll from climate change will reach half a million people a year. It also indicated that climate change today seriously impacts on the lives of 325 million people. In 20 years that number will more than double to an estimated 660 million, making it the biggest emerging humanitarian challenge in the world, impacting on the lives of 10 per cent of the world's population. Economic losses due to climate change already amount to over $125 billion per year. This is more than the individual GDP of 73 per cent of the world's countries, and is greater than the total amount of aid that currently flows from industrialised countries to developing nations each year. By 2030, the report estimated that economic losses due to climate change will have almost trebled to $340 billion annually. http://ghfgeneva.org

34. Lewis Simon, "Increasing carbon storage in intact African tropical forests", *Nature*,

19 February 2009. www.nature.com

35. The Eliasch Review, "Climate Change: Financing Global Forests", completed in October 2008, was an independent report commissioned by the UK Prime Minister, Gordon Brown, and led by Johan Eliasch, special representative on deforestation. It provides a comprehensive analysis of the financing and mechanisms needed to support sustainable management of forests and reduce emissions associated with deforestation. http://nds.coi.gov.uk

36. Ibid.

37. The Amazon rainforest is the largest in the world. It covers an area equivalent to almost one third of the US. This includes parts of Brazil and several other countries.

38. Cost Curve for greenhouse gas reduction v.2. *McKinsey Quarterly*. www. mckinseyquarterly.com

39. "Is the Boardroom Heating Up?" Whitehead Mann Partnership, www.wmpllp.com

40. Gallup's 2009 Environment survey. Full survey results at: www.gallup.com/poll/116590/increased-number-think-global-warming-exaggerated

41. "Few Americans See Solid Evidence of Global Warming", 22 October 2009, Pew Research Center. http://pewresearch.org/pubs/1386/cap-and-trade-global-warming-opinion

42. Ipsos Mori Issues Index, January–August 2009. www.ipsos-mori.com-most-important- issues-facing-britain-today

43. Anthony Giddens talks of the paradox that abstract and future risks do not motivate people to act until the effects are felt and by then it is too late. Anthony Giddens, *The Politics of Climate Change* (London: Polity, 2009). This is much the same as Charles Handy's much earlier view on people's inability to respond to gradual change. "If you put a frog in water and slowly heat it, the frog will eventually let itself be boiled to death. We, too, will not survive if we don't respond to the radical way in which the world is changing." Charles Handy, *The Age of Unreason* (London: Century Hutchinson, 1989).

ACKNOWLEDGEMENTS

A book such as this one is built on experiences with a whole range of people, good and bad. Here I simply want to acknowledge the enormous number of acts of kindness, support and loyalty.

I have already thanked the legions of people at BP, past and present, who gave me the opportunity to do the things I have talked about in this book. My father lived to see only the first 32 years of my life; my mother was with me until I was 52 years old. They gave me the foundation and my mother was my most trusted guide and counsellor. There are many others who have made and continue to make my journey both exciting and worthwhile. I thank them all.

As to this book, many people have helped in its writing. Drafts have been reviewed by: David Allen, my colleague of long standing on the BP Board; Dick Balzer, for 18 years my mentor and adviser, who taught me much about the human condition; Nick Butler, my trusted adviser on politics and strategy in BP for 17 years; Donna Leon, the writer of great Venetian mysteries; Simon Maine, my research assistant; John Millen, a columnist for the *South China Morning Post/Young Post*; Jacob Nell, formerly one of my assistants and who helped conceive the earlier version of this book which never saw the light of day; John Roberts, a great economist and adviser from the Graduate School of Business at Stanford University; and professional colleagues Ben Moxham, Malcolm Gooderham and Henry Goodwin. Sarah Paynter, my personal assistant, kept all of the drafts, communications and me in order; Roddy Kennedy of BP helped enormously with the illustrations; and John Grundon, a former BP colleague, helped remind me of BP's early time in China. I would like to thank them all.

Daniel Yergin, whom I have known since we were at Cambridge University together, has provided invaluable commentary and support. He is the master of the history of the oil industry.

Philippa Anderson was the person who, at the suggestion of my publisher Alan Samson and my agent Ed Victor, arrived to help me write this book. It would never have been written without her energy, persistence and good humour.

And finally, my thanks go to my partner, Nghi Nguyen, whose insight and patience contributed to every page.

John Browne, London and Venice, October 2009

INDEX